INSIDERS' GUIDE®

W9-BRP-304

FUN WITH THE FAMILY™ SERIES

fun WITH the Family™

MASSACHUSETTS

HUNDREDS OF IDEAS FOR DAY TRIPS WITH THE KIDS

MARCIA GLASSMAN-JAFFE

FIFTH EDITION

BEEBE LIBRARY
345 Main Street
Wakefield, MA 01880

INSIDERS' GUIDE®

GUILFORD, CONNECTICUT
AN IMPRINT OF THE GLOBE PEQUOT PRESS

The prices, rates, and hours listed in this guidebook
were confirmed at press time. We recommend, however, that you
call establishments to obtain current information before traveling.

To buy books in quantity for corporate use
or incentives, call **(800) 962–0973, ext. 4551,**
or e-mail **premiums@GlobePequot.com.**

INSIDERS' GUIDE®

Insiders' Guide is a registered trademark of The Globe Pequot Press.
Fun with the Family is a trademark of The Globe Pequot Press.

Text design by Nancy Freeborn and Linda Loiewski
Maps by Rusty Nelson © The Globe Pequot Press
Spot photography throughout © Photodisc and © RubberBall Productions

ISSN 1537-291X
ISBN 0-7627-3492-2

Manufactured in the United States of America
Fifth Edition/First Printing

To Mark, Marisa, Mallory, and Morgan.
Thank you for helping me see the wonders around us
as we travel life's many paths. I am truly blessed
with a wonderful and loving family. Thank you for your
understanding and support; I always sensed
your pride in me for my determined perseverance.
This book is dedicated to the beloved memories
of my late mother, Natalie Glassman,
and my late aunt, Frances Glassman,
who inspired my love of travel, discovery, and nature.

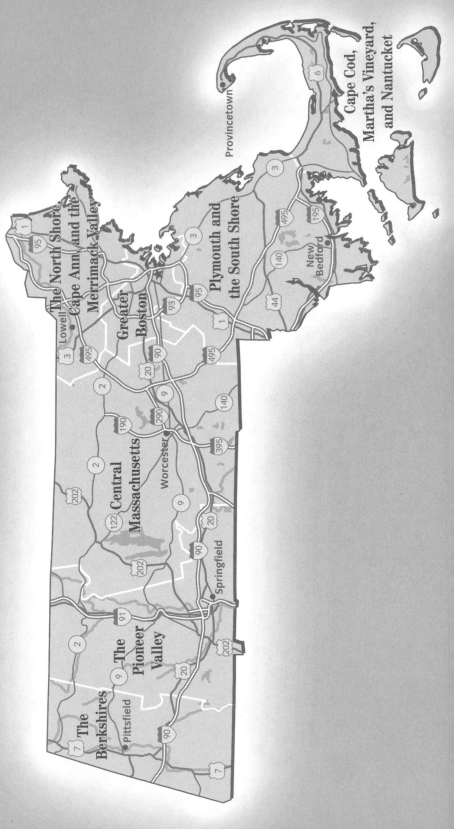

MASSACHUSETTS

The Berkshires

Pittsfield

The Pioneer Valley

Central Massachusetts

Worcester

Springfield

The North Shore, Cape Ann, and the Merrimack Valley

Lowell

Greater Boston

Plymouth and the South Shore

New Bedford

Provincetown

Cape Cod, Martha's Vineyard, and Nantucket

Contents

Acknowledgments

The author thanks the members of the Massachusetts Office of Travel and Tourism, the regional travel offices throughout the state, the National Park Service visitor centers, and the sites and attractions contained in this book for their time and cooperation in making this book as accurate and informative as possible. The author would further like to thank Mallory and Marisa Jaffe for their technological assistance, Mark Jaffe and Cyril Glassman for their navigation skills, and Morgan Jaffe for her enthusiasm for exploration.

A special thanks goes to my late mother, Natalie Glassman, who covered for me to allow me free time to do my research. My gratitude, too, to my many friends who put friendship on hold so I could follow my writing dream.

To my dear friend Diane Bair, this project wouldn't have happened without you—many thanks.

Lastly I would like to thank Erin Joyce, my editor, for her encouragement, guidance, and wonderful conversations. Erin, you've been lovely to work with.

Introduction

Massachusetts was settled in 1620 by a brave band of 101 men, women, and children. From that initial Plimoth outpost in the "wilds of Massachusetts" grew the state that has garnered a worldwide reputation for its educational institutions, medical facilities, unique sites and culture, rich history, and physical beauty. Boston, the state capital, is considered the gateway to New England and is popular with both domestic and international tourists because of the breadth of its attractions—performing and visual arts, sports facilities, and cultural institutions.

Using This Book

The book is arranged from the western part of the state toward the eastern end, then proceeds down the Massachusetts coast. Each entry includes address, telephone number, Web site (if available), and description. Where possible, hours, prices, and directions have been added to the entry. The suggested age ranges for a particular site are just that, suggested guidelines. Parents or caregivers must use their own judgment and experience based on the maturity of the child to determine whether a particular site is appropriate. The maps in the beginning of each chapter are designed to orient you to a particular area, but they are in no way intended to be a substitute for a detailed state road system map.

Rates

The following key indicates pricing by dollar sign instead of a numerical rate for lodging and restaurants. Lodging prices fluctuate depending upon location and time of year. Please be aware that lunch is usually a better value at an establishment than dinner. Be sure to inquire about family rates or discounts where indicated in this text.

Rates for Lodging

$	up to $75
$$	$76 to $150
$$$	$151 to $225
$$$$	more than $225

Rates for Restaurants

$	most entrees under $10
$$	most $11 to $18
$$$	most $19 to $26
$$$$	most over $27

Special Notes of Interest

The Massachusetts Office of Travel and Tourism is eager to send information packages to prospective tourists. The Office of Travel and Tourism can be contacted at the State Transportation Building, 10 Park Plaza, Suite 4510, Boston, Massachusetts 02115; (617) 973–8500 or (800) 227–MASS; www.mass-vacation.com. To reserve a stay at any one of the Massachusetts state campgrounds, contact Reserve America toll-free at (877) 422–6762 or online at www.reserveamerica.com. Individual state parks will no longer make reservations. The entire state park system consists of state reservations, parks, and forests, which for the most part charge an entry fee. It may be more economical to buy a season pass for $35 if you're a Massachusetts resident ($45 for out-of-staters). The national parks, refuges, monuments, and sanctuaries offer the Golden Eagle Pass, a season pass that allows entry to multiple sights.

Attractions Key

The following is a key to the icons found throughout the text.

SWIMMING		DINING	
BOATING / BOAT TOUR		LODGING	
HISTORIC SITE		CAMPING	
HIKING / WALKING		MUSEUMS	
FISHING		PERFORMING ARTS	
BIKING		SPORTS/ATHLETICS	
AMUSEMENT PARK		PICNICKING	
HORSEBACK RIDING		PLAYGROUND	
SKIING / WINTER SPORTS		SHOPPING	
PARK		PLANTS / GARDENS / NATURE TRAILS	
ANIMAL VIEWING		FARMS	

The Berkshires

C overing the western end of Massachusetts, Berkshire County changes dramatically, from the high mountains and isolated valleys in the north to the hilly forests and farmland of the area along the Connecticut border. Tell the kids to keep an eye out for the carved wooden Indians that "guard" the tourist shops along the Mohawk Trail. Williamstown, known for Williams College and its world-class art museums, is a classic New England village of white churches and clapboard houses along the edges of the town green. To the southeast is Mt. Greylock, the state's highest mountain, part of a huge park full of hiking trails of varying difficulties, as well as waterfalls, fishing areas, and campgrounds.

The southern Berkshire area is gentler in topography and more cultural in nature. The region abounds with museums, theaters, and outdoor classical music venues, the most famous of which is Tanglewood, summer home of the Boston Symphony Orchestra. Kids will marvel at the round stone barn at Hancock Shaker Village outside Pittsfield. Farther south, in Stockbridge, take the time to walk along the long porch and through the enormous lobby area of the rambling old Red Lion Inn. During the winter Berkshire County is a mecca for skiing families.

Marcia's
Top Picks in the Berkshires

1. Hancock Shaker Village, Pittsfield

2. Mt. Greylock State Reservation, Lanesborough

3. Mohawk Trail

4. Sterling and Francine Clark Art Institute, Williamstown

5. Tanglewood Music Festival, Lenox

THE BERKSHIRES

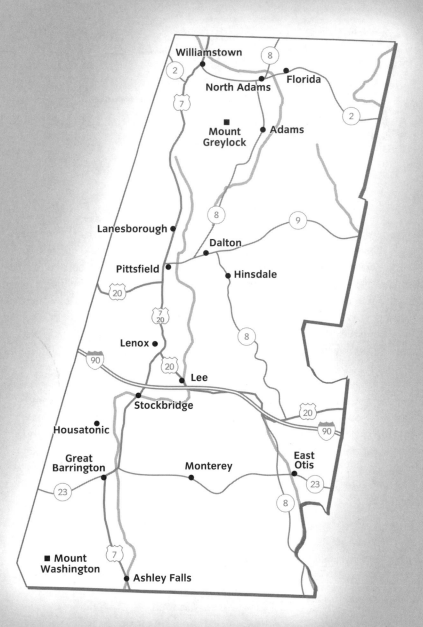

Williamstown

8

2

North Adams

Florida

7

2

Mount
Greylock

Adams

8

Lanesborough

9

Dalton

Pittsfield

Hinsdale

20

7
20

8

90

Lenox

20

Lee

Stockbridge

20

90

Housatonic

Great
Barrington

Monterey

East
Otis

23

23

8

Mount
Washington

7

Ashley Falls

The **Berkshire Visitor Bureau,** Berkshire Common, Plaza Level, Pittsfield 01201, can be contacted at (413) 443–9186 or www.Berkshires.org. They are extremely helpful if you wish information or hot tips on Berkshire County. They also have links on their Web site to the various chambers of commerce throughout the country.

Mohawk Trail

The Mohawk Trail, Route 2, is the highway version of the path that Native Americans used to travel from the Connecticut River valley to the Hudson River valley. Sixty-seven miles long, the road is only partially in the Berkshires, since it begins in the Connecticut River valley. Near the town of Florida, the trail passes by the entrance to the Hoosac Tunnel, which was the longest railway tunnel in the country when it was completed in 1875. An engineering marvel in its time, the Hoosac Tunnel was the first construction to use nitroglycerin. Stop at the Western Summit Gift Shop—not for the shop, but for the telescope (25 cents for about three minutes) on the edge of the steep hill that overlooks the northern Berkshires. The highest point on the trail is the Whitcomb Summit, at 2,240 feet (if the kids are into ascending an observation tower, it's 50 cents per person). The trail makes several hairpin turns on its way into North Adams. For more information on the Mohawk Trail contact the Mohawk Trail Association at (413) 743–8127 or www.mohawktrail.com.

North Adams

The City of Spires, as residents like to call it, is a bit run-down nowadays; the beautiful old brick factories and warehouses that produced paper, textiles, and leather goods are mostly empty now. Several of these buildings are the home of the Massachusetts Museum of Contemporary Art, which everyone already calls Mass MoCA.

Massachusetts Museum of Contemporary Art (all ages)
87 Marshall Street, North Adams; (413) 662–2111; www.massmoca.org. Open July 1 through September 6 10:00 A.M. to 6:00 P.M., September 7 through June 30, Wednesday through Monday 11:00 A.M. to 5:00 P.M. Admission: $10.00 for adults, $4.00 for children 6 to 16; free for children under 6.

Opened in May 1999, Mass MoCA is a contemporary international cultural center focusing on visual, media, and performing arts. A special kidspace has been created as a resource for schools and the public. Kidspace serves two functions: as a gallery for contemporary artists as well as an incubator for children to create their own artwork. Call for public hours, programs, and family activity schedule. Try the lobby cafe for a snack. A hotel with easy access to Mass MoCA is the Porches.

Western Gateway Heritage State Park and Tourism Information Center (all ages)

Route 8, North Adams; (413) 663–6312; www.massparks.org. Open daily year-round 10:00 A.M. to 5:00 P.M., closed Thanksgiving, Christmas, and New Year's Day. Free; donations accepted.

If your family includes a railroad buff or two, visit the Western Gateway Heritage State Park. An introductory thirty-minute video sets the tone; along with interesting tidbits about North Adams's history (changing historical exhibits) as a bustling railroad town, you'll learn about the construction of the Hoosac Tunnel. There are family programs throughout the year, a Kids Korner year-round with arts-and-crafts activities, and free weekly concerts in the park during the summer. Kids seem to like a working model railroad to scale depicting North Adams in the 1950s.

North Adams Museum of History and Science (all ages)

Route 8, Western Gateway Heritage State Park, Building 2, North Adams; (413) 664–4700; www.NorthAdams.com/history. Open Thursday through Saturday May 1 through December 31 from 10:00 A.M. to 4:00 P.M. and Sunday from 1:00 to 4:00 P.M. Limited hours during January through April: Saturday 10:00 A.M. to 4:00 P.M. and Sunday 1:00 to 4:00 P.M. Free; donations accepted.

With more than twenty-five exhibits within a 6,000-square-foot space, the museum details the history and natural environment of North Adams and the region on three amazing floors! Kids will be attracted to the two discovery rooms—one zeroing in on the history of North Adams, the other focusing on science and the outdoors.

Where to Eat

The Applachian Bean Cafe, 67 Main Street, North Adams; (413) 663–7543. Breakfast, lunch, and a wide variety of vegetarian specials. Create your own sandwich. Seating indoors and outside (weather permitting). $

Freight Yard Restaurant, 1 Furnace Park, Western Gateway Heritage State Park, North Adams; (413) 663–6547. Open year-round for lunch and dinner. Serving burgers, pasta, steak, and seafood. $–$$

Golden Eagle Restaurant, Route 2 (at the hairpin turn), North Adams; (413) 663–9834. Open Memorial Day through mid-November and winter weekends. Good old-fashioned American cooking, fabulous sunsets. Reasonably priced. $–$$

Grammercy Bistro, 24 Marshall Street, North Adams; (413) 663–5300. Bountiful weekend brunches popular with families. $$–$$$

Where to Stay

Blackinton Manor, 1391 Massachusetts Avenue, North Adams; (413) 663–5795; www.manor.com. Lovely antique home tastefully furnished. Close to Mass MoCA and Williams College. Children 7 and up. $$$

The Porches Inn, 231 River Street, North Adams; (413) 664–0400; www.porches .com. Fifty rooms and suites in six connecting Victorian-era row houses that have been renovated. Outdoor heated pool, many rooms with Jacuzzi-style tubs. Room includes continental breakfast. Condé Nast award winner. $$–$$$$

Williamstown

Williamstown hasn't changed much since the late nineteenth century—it's a quintessential New England town. It's home to one of New England's best small liberal arts colleges, Williams College, and to two exceptional art museums: the Sterling and Francine Clark Art Institute and the Williams College Museum of Art. For more information on Williamstown, contact the **Williamstown Chamber of Commerce,** P.O. Box 357, Williamstown 01267; (413) 458–9077 or (800) 214–3799; www.williamstown chamber.com.

Sterling and Francine Clark Art Institute (all ages)
225 South Street, Williamstown; (413) 458–2303; www.clarkart.edu. Open year-round, Tuesday through Sunday 10:00 A.M. to 5:00 P.M. and Monday 10:00 A.M. to 5:00 P.M. in July and August. In July and August a gallery talk takes place every day at 3:00 P.M. Admission: $10 June through October; the rest of the year it is free for adults, children under age 18 free year-round.

The Clark Art Institute has a world-class collection of late-nineteenth-century paintings by Renoir, Monet, Corot, Pissaro, and Degas, among others. Also interesting is a room with paintings by the American artists Sargent, Remington, and Homer. They were contemporaries, and all were celebrated in their time for very different styles and subject matter: Sargent for his exquisite portraits of high-society figures; Remington for his depiction of cowboys and western life; and Homer for his haunting New England sea and mountain scenes. The beautiful grounds are a great spot for a picnic and the band concerts every Tuesday in July. Call for the schedule of children's special events.

Williams College Museum of Art (all ages)
Main Street, Williamstown; (413) 597–2429; www.wcma.org. Open Tuesday through Saturday 10:00 A.M. to 5:00 P.M., Sunday 1:00 to 5:00 P.M., and major holidays that fall on Monday. Closed Thanksgiving, Christmas, and New Year's Day. Free.

The Williams College Museum of Art is one of the best college art museums in the country, in terms of the breadth of its collection from the late eighteenth century to

Play Time

From late June through August, the **Williamstown Theatre Festival,** Box 517, Williamstown 01267; (413) 597–3399 (schedules and information) or (413) 597–3400 (box office); www.wtfestival.org, one of the country's pre-eminent theater groups, presents musicals, dramas, children's theater, and special events. Most performances are at Williams College's Adams Memorial Theater.

the present including contemporary, modern American, and non-Western art. The museum's ARTWORKS program, a series of one-person exhibitions of contemporary art, has been particularly well received. Good traveling exhibitions stop here, too. Special family days and activities; call ahead.

Other Things to See and Do

Natural Bridge State Park, off Route 8, North Adams; (413) 663–6392; www.mass parks.org. Open late May to early October. White marble natural bridge that was formed 500 million years ago by glacial retreat. Summer interpretive programs. Admission is $2.00 per car.

Water Street Books, 26 Water Street, Williamstown; (413) 458–8071; www.waterstreet.bkstr.com. Children's section and Saturday morning children's programs.

Where to Eat

Hobson's Choice, 159 Water Street, Williamstown; (413) 458–9101. Homemade soups and abundant salad bar. Kids can order a half plate. $$–$$$$

Store at Five Corners, corner of Routes 7 and 43, Williamstown; (413) 458–3176; www.thestoreatfivecorners.com. Open year-round. Great sandwiches and dessert goodies, all packed to go. $

Water Street Grill, 123 Water Street, Williamstown; (413) 458–2175. Open for lunch (burgers, sandwiches, seafood) and dinner (pasta, steaks, seafood) in the comfortable dining room or the tavern. Kids' menu. $–$$

Where to Stay

Berkshire Bed-and-Breakfast, (413) 731–8785 or (800) 762–2751; www.berk shirebnbhomes.com. Reservation service.

House on Main Street B&B, 1120 Main Street, Williamstown; (413) 458–3031; www.houseonmainstreet.com. Three rooms with private baths; three others share one full and one half bath. The big screened-in porch is a nice spot to relax. $$–$$$.

The Orchards, 222 Adams Road, Williamstown; (413) 458–9611 or (800) 225–1517; www.orchardshotel.com. Antiques, four-poster beds, fireplaces, pond; outdoor pool, Jacuzzi, exercise room. Complimentary cookies and beverages every day. Great restaurant serving elegant specialties. $$–$$$$

Adams and Lanesborough

Adams is the birthplace of Susan B. Anthony, the suffragist who led the struggle to gain the vote for women and is still remembered with an annual summer festival in July called Susan B. Anthony Days. Adams is set peacefully along the banks of the Hoosic River and shadowed by Mt. Greylock. The southern entrance to Mt. Greylock is in Lanesborough.

Ashuwillticook Rail Trail Bike Path (all ages)

Current access at Cheshire Lake in Cheshire and the Berkshire Mall in Lanesborough; two future additional trailhead accesses will be in Adams; (413) 442–8928 (DEM Region 5 Headquarters); www.massparks.org. Open all year. Free.

A 10-mile trail (once a former rail bed) that is fairly flat for an easy ride. The Massachusetts State Park System is now in the process of extending the trail from Cheshire to Adams. There are beautiful vistas (a good leg of the trail is on Cheshire Lake) with potentially great views of fall foliage and mountainscapes. Obviously, all the rail trails can be used for jogging, walking, snowshoeing, and cross-country skiing.

Mt. Greylock State Reservation (all ages)

Visitor center, Rockwell Road, Lanesborough; (413) 499–4263 or (413) 499–4262; www.massparks.org. Park is open from sunrise until a half hour before sunset. Visitor center open daily year-round, 9:00 A.M. to 4:00 P.M. There are several ways to approach the mountain; one is from North Adams (1 mile west of North Adams on Route 2, take Notch Road through a residential area that turns into woody hills; signs will direct you from there); the other is via Route 7 in Lanesborough (follow the signs). The auto road is open twenty-four hours a day except during winter. Free.

Mt. Greylock State Reservation is an enormous park (more than 12,000 acres), with 45 miles of hiking trails of varying difficulties, as well as camping (contact Reserve America at 877–422–6762 or www.reserveamerica.com for one of the thirty-four sites), fishing, cross-country skiing, and snowmobiling. The visitor center in Lanesborough is an excellent first stop; be sure to get a map. A large tabletop relief map shows the park's layout and topography. Even if your family hasn't done a lot of hiking, don't be discouraged. Many of the park's trails leave from the parking area on top of the mountain (this is one of the reasons it's such a terrific family place; you can

Amazing
Massachusetts Fact

Mt. Greylock, at 3,491 feet, is the highest point in the state. Incorporated in 1898, it was the first state park in Massachusetts.

drive right to the best part). One of the best routes is a 4-mile round-trip hike from the summit down Overlook Trail to Hopper Trail, then on to March Cataract Falls.

NOTE: The weather can change quickly and unexpectedly on Mt. Greylock. Every year a few experienced hikers find themselves stranded. Get a map and talk to rangers in the visitor center before you begin your hike.

Whether or not you hike, don't end your visit to Mt. Greylock without climbing the War Memorial Tower. On a clear day you'll be able to see Mt. Monadnock in New Hampshire, 115 miles away, as well as the full Berkshire range, the Taconics in New York, southern Vermont, Connecticut, Mount Wachusetts in Central Massachusetts, and the southern part of the Appalachians for a five-state view. The tower is open 9:00 A.M. to 5:00 P.M. daily, mid-May through mid-October weather-permitting.

Each Columbus Day, the town of Adams sponsors the Mt. Greylock Ramble, an annual trek to the mountain summit from the Cheshire Harbor Trailhead on West Mountain Road.

Other Things to See and Do

Par 4-Family Fun Center, 20 Williamstown Road, Lanesborough; (413) 499–0051. Minigolf, batting cages, bumper boats, and go-karts; ice cream; and more.

Where to Eat

Greylock's Bascom Lodge, Summit Road, Lanesborough; (413) 743–1591. Open mid-May through mid-October. The lodge, built in the 1930s, sits atop Mt. Greylock. Run by the nonprofit Nature's Classroom.

Where to Stay

Greylock's Bascom Lodge, Summit Road, Lanesborough; (413) 743–1591. Open mid-May through mid-October. The eight rooms are rustic but comfortable, and vary in size from dormitory-style rooms that sleep eight people to private doubles. All rooms share baths and are provided with linens.

Take Me Out **to the Fair!**

The only major agricultural fair in the Berkshires, the **Adams Fair** takes place the last days of July/first days of August at Bowe Field off Route 8 (Old Columbia Street). Call (413) 663–3977 for more information.

Florida, Dalton, and Hinsdale

It's rumored that the small village of Florida is the most frigid spot in the state because of its location, not quite the tropical picture its name would suggest. Savoy State Park in Florida is a hidden gem. Dalton is home to the Crane Paper Company, with bragging rights to fine quality paper (Crane is the only supplier of paper for U.S. paper currency). Hinsdale takes great pride in native son Israel Bissell, who gave Paul Revere a run for his money.

Savoy Mountain State Forest (all ages)

260 Central Shaft Road, Florida; (413) 663–8469; www.massparks.org. From Route 2 in Florida, turn onto Central Shaft Road. Open year-round dawn to dusk. Day use fee of $5.00.

Savoy Mountain State Forest on 11,000 acres is a less crowded version of Mt. Greylock State Reservation. The park is especially appealing to children because of the good swimming in North Pond (there isn't much legal swimming on Greylock). Hiking is less challenging, too, and the pleasant hike to Tannery Falls brings you to one of the nicest falls in the Berkshires. There are four cabins (rentable year-round) on the banks of South Pond and forty-five campsites available Memorial Day to Columbus Day; call Reserve America at (877) 422–6762.

Crane Museum (all ages)

Housatonic Street, off Route 8, Dalton; (413) 684–2600; www.berkshireweb.com /themap/dalton/museum.html. Open June through mid-October, Monday through Friday 2:00 to 5:00 P.M. Free.

Crane Paper Company makes the paper on which all U.S. currency is printed. Tour the museum to learn how paper is made and see a display about the history of paper money.

The Midnight Ride of **Israel Bissell?**

A few miles southeast of Dalton is the small town of Hinsdale, whose claim to fame is Israel Bissell. Bissell is the man who outdid Paul Revere: In five days he rode from Hinsdale through Connecticut to New York and on to Philadelphia to carry the news of the colonists' confrontation with the British in 1775. Bissell is buried in the Maple Street Cemetery (take Route 143 east; the cemetery is at the top of the first small hill after Route 8).

Berkshire **Skiing Meccas**

During the winter Berkshire County is a mecca for skiing families. Some of New England's best small-scale, family-oriented downhill and cross-country ski areas are here. All can boast of excellent ski schools, family packages, and reasonably priced accommodations either at the base of the mountain or within a few miles:

- **Brodie Mountain,** Route 7, New Ashford; (413) 443–4752; www.ski brodie.com. Known for its tube park and snowshoeing. Open on weekends and holiday periods only. Brodie and Jiminy Peak are owned by the same parent company.

- **Bucksteep Manor,** 885 Washington Mountain Road, Washington; (413) 623–5535 or (800) 645–BUCK; www.bucksteepmanor.com. Offers 15 miles of groomed trails. The cross-country center is open December through March, and rentals are available. A twenty-two-room inn is on site, as well as one hundred campsites, a pool, tennis courts, and an outdoor hot tub for summertime use.

- **Butternut Basin,** Route 23, Great Barrington; (413) 528–2000 or (800) 438–SNOW; www.skibutternut.com. Cross-country and downhill skiing (1,000-foot vertical drop), eight lifts, two terrain parks with jumps and moguls, two lodges, camping, and rentals. Fifth-graders ski free weekdays with an accompanying adult skier ticket purchase (nonholiday weeks only). The cross-country center is open Thursday through Sunday and holidays.

- **Catamount,** Route 23, South Egremont; (413) 528–1262; www.catamountski.com. One 1,000 vertical drop; longest run is 2 miles. Ski school, nursery, rentals, night skiing, and snowboard megaplex consisting of two parks and a half-pipe with its own lift.

- **Cranwell Resort,** Route 20, 55 Lee Road, Lenox; (413) 637–1364 or (800) CRANWELL; www.cranwell.com. Cross-country skiing (must be age six or older), rentals, and lessons; 107 deluxe rooms in a rambling Tudor mansion; gourmet dining in a historic setting. Amenities include an eighteen-hole PGA golf course and an indoor and an outdoor heated pool.

- **Jiminy Peak,** Route 43 to Brodie Mountain Road, Hancock; (413) 738–5500, (800) 882–8859 (lodging); www.jiminypeak.com. Self-contained resort with nice condominiums and two slopeside inns.

The state's first six-passenger lift is here, along with six other lifts. Challenging steep intermediate runs and black-diamond slopes deserve their rating. There's a kids-only area for SKIwee lessons, and the day-care center takes kids from 6 months. A snowboard park and night skiing are other fun options. During the summer the Alpine Slide is a popular attraction as well as the scenic Berkshire Express lift.

- **Notchview Reservation,** 83 Old Route 9, Windsor; (413) 684–0148 or (413) 298–3239; www.notchview.org. Trustees of Reservations property with more than 3,000 acres for cross-country skiing and hiking.

- **Otis Ridge,** Route 23W, Otis; (413) 269–4444; www.otisridge.com. A small downhill ski area oriented to families. The vertical drop is only 400 feet, and there are just ten runs. Come here if you want your kids to learn to ski in an intimate setting; experienced skiers will be bored.

Where to Stay

Dalton House, 955 Main Street, Dalton; (413) 684–3854; www.thedaltonhouse .com. Eleven rooms (all with private bath, some with fireplace) in two buildings. The rooms in the carriage house are larger and quieter, with period furniture and exposed beams. The Dalton House includes breakfast; Sundays are blueberry pancake day! $$–$$$

Pittsfield

The residents of Pittsfield are extremely dedicated to preserving the contributions of the Shakers to the American lifestyle at Hancock Shaker Village. Pittsfield offers many recreational and cultural opportunities, with its many lakes, museums, and parks. A great source of information is the Berkshire Chamber of Commerce, 75 North Street, Suite 360, Pittsfield 01201; (413) 499–4000; www.berkshirechamber.com.

Berkshire Museum (all ages)

Route 7, 39 South Street, downtown Pittsfield; (413) 443–7171; www.berkshire museum.org. Open Monday through Saturday 10:00 A.M. to 5:00 P.M., Sunday noon to 5:00 P.M. Admission: $7.50 for adults, $6.00 for seniors and students with ID, $4.50 for ages 3 to 18, free for under 3.

An eclectic museum that is a little bit of everything. Somehow the museum combines a hands-on aquarium with science and history exhibits, paintings, sculpture, and decorative arts. A cinema runs a selection of first-rate films (call for a schedule). Children's programs crowd the museum; the museum specializes in blockbuster interactive family exhibitions year-round. A popular Refrigerator Art Gallery features guest artists (local children who create artwork), which are hung on a series of thirteen refurbished refrigerator doors.

Hancock Shaker Village (all ages)

Route 20 just west of the Route 41 Junction, Pittsfield; (413) 443–0188; www.hancock shakervillage.org. Guided tour November through May, 10:00 A.M. to 3:00 P.M. Admission: $12 for adults, kids under 18 free during guided-tour period. Self-guided tour June through October 9:30 A.M. to 5:00 P.M. Admission: $15 adults, kids under 18 are free.

Our culture reveres the Shakers for their simple, beautiful furniture and building designs. What most people don't know is that their crafting skill was a direct expression of their religious devotion to express their reverence to God by making their environment a "heaven on earth." Hancock Shaker Village was the third of eighteen Shaker communities established in the United States. Its heyday was in 1830, just after the round stone barn was completed, when 300 Shakers lived, worked, and worshiped here. They farmed, sold seeds and herbs, manufactured medicines, and made and sold all types of goods, from boxes to textiles. Eventually their population dwindled, and in 1960 the Shaker ministry in Canterbury, New Hampshire, sold the

Fish Tales or **Fantastic Fishing Spots?**

Grab your fishing license and bring the kids to one of these tried-and-true fishing holes:

- **Ashmere Lake,** Hinsdale
- **Benedict Pond,** Monterey
- **Benton Pond,** East Otis Reservoir, Otis
- **Center Pond and Yokum Pond,** Becket
- **Cheshire Reservoir,** Cheshire
- **Goose Pond and Laurel Lake,** Lee
- **Onota and Pontoosuc Lakes,** Pittsfield
- **Prospect Lake,** Egremont
- **Stockbridge Pond,** Stockbridge
- **Windsor Pond,** Windsor

Hancock property to a group of Pittsfield residents. The following year they opened Hancock Shaker Village as a museum. It's best to come at self-guided season, when the entire property consisting of twenty restored buildings is open to the public. Kids learn how the Shakers spun wool, made furniture, cooked, and did such crafts as basket making. The staff is knowledgeable, dedicated, and enthusiastic; tour guides welcome and encourage questions. A cafe is open during the season. A recent addition is a reenactment of a Shaker classroom with a costumed staff person acting as the Shaker schoolteacher and Shaker suppers during winter weekends.

Wahconah Park (all ages)

105 Wahconah Street, Pittsfield; (413) 448–2255; www.berkshireblackbears.com. Games are usually at 7:05 P.M. Monday through Saturday and 2:05 P.M. on Sunday. For a schedule, write to Box 646, Pittsfield 01202.

From June through early September, the Berkshire Black Bears, a team in the competitive Northeast League (an independent minor league), play at Wahconah Park three or four times a week. This is old-time baseball in a park that's so small, every seat is a good seat, and the players are happy to sign autographs.

Other Things to See and Do

Arrowhead, 780 Holmes Road, Pittsfield; (413) 442–1793; www.mobydick.org. Open Memorial Day through Columbus Day. Home of Herman Melville, author of *Moby-Dick.*

Bousquet Ski Area, Dan Fox Drive, Pittsfield; (413) 442–8316; www.bousquets .com. Downhill skiing and snowboarding. Rentals are available.

Pittsfield State Forest, Cascade Street, Pittsfield; (413) 442–8992; www.massparks .org. Hiking, cross-country skiing, swimming, snowmobiling, camping, canoeing, and fishing on more than 10,000 acres. $5.00 day use fee.

Where to Eat

Bagels Too, 160 North Street, Pittsfield; (413) 499–0119. Specializing in bagels and sandwiches, eat in or take out. Breakfast and lunch only. $

Dakota, Route 7, 1035 South Street, Pittsfield; (413) 499–7900; www.steakseafood .com. Steaks, seafood, salad bar, fabulous Sunday brunch; children's menu. $–$$$

Misty Moonlight Diner, 505 East Street, Pittsfield; (413) 499–2483. Classic diner. Great prices. $–$$

Where to Stay

Country Hearts Bed n' Breakfast, 52 Broad Street, Pittsfield; (413) 499–7671; www.countryheartsbnb.com. Voted one of the top fifteen country inns in 2002. Central location to all area attractions. $–$$$

The Chanticleer, 318 Williams Street, Pittsfield; (413) 443–5917; www.chanticleerbb.com. This quaint, gracious bed-and-breakfast is decorated in a French country theme and is located near Lenox and Tanglewood. The expansive wraparound porch is furnished with rocking chairs and swings. Lovely gardens and homemade breakfasts complete the experience. $$–$$$

Southern Berkshires

The southern Berkshires have been a haven for the wealthy for well over a century, and the cultural life in the towns of Lenox and Stockbridge reflects their passions: music and theater. During the high season of July and August, kids can see more live performances here than they could in many large cities—and much of it goes on outdoors. There are several excellent museums; gracious historic inns for families with well-behaved children; and parks, wildlife sanctuaries, and good skiing.

Lenox

The summer home of the Boston Symphony Orchestra, Lenox has become a tourism mecca for lovers of fine music, theater, and dance. Home to wealthy New York aristocrats at the turn of the twentieth century, many Lenox mansions are experiencing a rebirth as some of the finest hostelries in the area.

A potpourri of information on Lenox is found at www.lenox.org or at the **Lenox Chamber of Commerce** on Curtison Walker Street. Call (413) 637–3646.

Tanglewood Music Festival (all ages) 🎵
West Street, Lenox; (413) 637–5165, toll free (888) 266–1200 (box office), or (617) 266–1492 (off-season); www.bso.org. Shed and Hall tickets range from $18 to $92. Lawn tickets (purchased on site only) are $16 to $22, depending on the event; lawn tickets for children under 12 are free (four per family). Children under 5 are not allowed in the Shed or the Hall during concerts. Write ahead for a full summer schedule: Symphony Hall, 301 Massachusetts Avenue, Boston 02115.

Tanglewood is the summer home of the Boston Symphony Orchestra, whose members, on summer weekends, perform concerts from the afternoon into the evening, often with the assistance of internationally known musicians and conductors. Most people who come to hear them sit outside on the lawn, arriving early with elaborate picnics and making a day of it. Some devotees choose to sit "inside," which means under the roof of one of the two buildings: the Shed (which is anything but), with seating for more than 5,000, and Seiji Ozawa Hall, with seating for 1,180. If your kids are lucky enough to have music lovers for parents, your entire family will enjoy an outing to Tanglewood, especially on a warm summer evening when the BSO plays the *1812 Overture,* complete with fireworks under the stars.

Tanglewood on Parade

Tanglewood on Parade is a daylong outdoor celebration in midsummer featuring both the BSO and the Boston Pops, finishing with a gala evening performance topped off with fireworks.

Other Things to See and Do

Berkshire Horseback Adventures, 293 Main Street, Route 7A, Lenox; (413) 637–9090; www.berkshirehorseback.net. Open mid-May through October. All ability levels, ages 7 and up. Can arrange one-hour, half-day, or overnight trips.

The Berkshire Scenic Railway and the Railway Museum, off Routes 7 and 20, Willow Creek Road, Lenox; (413) 637–2210; www.berkshirescenicrailroad.org. A restored 1902 Lenox railway station and the Railway Museum.

Edith Wharton's Estate and Gardens, The Mount, Plunkett Street, Routes 7 and 7A, Lenox; (413) 637–1899; www.edith wharton.org. House and gardens open daily May through early November. Look closely, things aren't what they seem. Extensive renovations to the house and gardens.

Flyin' High Ballooning Adventures, 594 Loop Road, Savoy; (413) 743–7633. Up, up, and away for a beautiful bird's-eye view.

Pleasant Valley Wildlife Sanctuary, 472 West Mountain Road, Lenox; (413) 637–0320; www.massaudubon.org. Seven miles of walking trails.

Ventfort Hall, Museum of the Gilded Age, 104 Walker Street, Lenox; (413) 637–3206; www.gildedage.org. Open May through October. Magnificent mansion undergoing restoration; built by the Morgan family. Set location for the movie *The Cider House Rules.*

Wild n' Wet Snow & Water and Bike Rentals, summer location—Pontoosuc Lake; winter location—Mt. Greylock, P.O. Box 2284, Lenox 01240; (413) 445–5211. Jet Ski, canoe, bike, and paddleboat rentals for summer fun. Snowmobile tours of the Berkshires during winter wonderland season.

Where to Eat

Candlelight Inn, 35 Walker Street, Lenox; (413) 637–1555 or (800) 428–0580; www .candlelightinn-lenox.com. Rack of lamb, confit duck, pecan chicken—gourmet food in a casual upper-end setting. $$–$$$

Church Street Cafe, 65 Church Street, Lenox; (413) 637–2745; www.churchstreet cafe.biz. Pasta and grilled fish specialties. Dine under the stars in season. $$$–$$$$

Firefly Restaurant, 71 Church Street, Lenox; (413) 637–2700. Call for hours. Recommended by those in the know as fun and family friendly, serving comfort food. Owner studied under James Beard, author of many highly regarded cookbooks. $–$$$

Napa, 30 Church Street, Lenox; (413) 637–3204. Homestyle cooking featuring full turkey dinners, briskets, homemade soups and desserts, and Napa California cuisine. $–$$$

Perfect **Picnics**

Sit on the lawn listening to the fortissimo crescendo of a Tchaikovsky piece while having a gourmet experience to the max courtesy of **Perfect Picnics,** 67 Church Street, Lenox; (413–637–3015; www.tanglewood picnics.com). All the fixin's are included. Just order ahead and bring to your favorite performance. Bravo! Magnifico!

Where to Stay

Apple Tree Inn and Restaurant, 10 Richmond Mt. Road, Lenox; (413) 637–1477; www.appletree-inn.com. Open year-round. Thirty-five rooms on lovely twenty-two-acre estate. Family friendly, heated pool, tennis, complimentary continental breakfast. Near Tanglewood. $–$$$$

Rookwood Inn, P.O. Box 1717, 11 Old Stockbridge Road, Lenox 01240; (413) 637–9750; www.rookwoodinn.com. Charming and comfortable Victorian-style

inn, ½ block from Lenox center and 1 mile from Tanglewood. Afternoon tea (in summer iced tea and lemonade) and a sweet. Children welcome for an additional fee. $$–$$$$

Yankee Inn, 461 Pittsfield Road, Routes 7 and 20, Lenox; (413) 499–3700 or (800) 835–2364; www.berkshireinns.com. Cross between a country inn and a full-service hotel. Indoor swimming pool and Jacuzzi. Some bedrooms with fireplaces in the new addition (ninety-six rooms). Complimentary continental breakfast. $$–$$$$

Stockbridge and Lee

Authentic New England charm permeates this town that was home to Norman Rockwell and where he drew his inspiration for his scenes of Americana. The Red Lion Inn's long wraparound porch is a town fixture for a welcoming cool summer drink. Lee has early-twentieth-century charm, and its downtown is listed in the National Registry of Historic Areas.

Berkshire Botanical Garden (all ages)

Junction of Routes 102 and 183, Stockbridge; (413) 298–3926; www.berkshirebotanical .org. Open daily May through October 10:00 A.M. to 5:00 P.M. Admission: $7.00 for adults, $5.00 for students; free for children under 12.

Berkshire Botanical Garden offers fifteen acres of gardens that vary from herbs to lilies to vegetables of all kinds. This is a different kind of green space that young children will enjoy: It's accessible to them because the plants are just their size. Picnicking is encouraged here. Children's summer programs are held midweek.

"Sedgewick **Pie**"

Route 102 in Stockbridge is the village cemetery, where, among other local notables, the Sedgewick family is buried. In 1781 Thomas Sedgewick, a lawyer, successfully defended Elizabeth "Mumbet" Freeman, who became the first slave freed by law in the United States. The trial also rendered slavery illegal in Massachusetts. Mumbet is buried with the Sedgewick family in the "Sedgewick Pie," the family grave plot, so called because family members are buried in a circle with their feet in the center. Why? They hoped that when they sit up on Judgment Day, they will see each other before they see anything else. The Sedgewick plot is toward the rear of the cemetery, surrounded by trees and shrubs.

Norman Rockwell Museum (all ages)

Route 183, Stockbridge; (413) 298–4100; www.nrm.org. Open daily, 10:00 A.M. to 5:00 P.M. May through October. Open November through April 10:00 A.M. to 4:00 P.M. weekdays and 10:00 A.M. to 5:00 P.M. weekends and holidays. Extended hours during school vacation periods; closed Thanksgiving, Christmas, and New Year's Day. The studio building is open from May through October. Admission: $12 for adults, **free** for children under 18, admitted with an adult (up to four per adult).

Rockwell, chronicler of life in America for seven decades, lived in Stockbridge for the last twenty-five years of his life. The Norman Rockwell Museum holds the largest collection of original Rockwells. Changing exhibits feature works of other illustrators. The museum has special family days, programs, and art activities. The grounds are a pleasant spot for a walk or a picnic. Outdoor sculptures are by Rockwell's son Peter.

October Mountain State Forest (all ages)

Woodland Road, Lee; (413) 243–1778; www.massparks.org. Open year-round dawn to dusk. **Free** except for campsites. Call Reserve America (877) 422–6762 or www.reserveamerica.com.

Covering more than 16,127 acres, October Mountain is the largest of the state forests. Most people come here to hike, fish, or boat, but in the winter cross-country skiing and snowshoeing trails have a following as well. There are forty-five campsites, flush toilets, and showers. No swimming.

Other Things to See and Do

Berkshire Mountain Llama Treks, 322 Landers Road, Lee; (413) 243–2224; www.bcn.net/llamahike. Llama treks at Hawk Meadow Farm.

Chesterwood, off Route 183 on Williamsville Road, Stockbridge; (413) 298–3579; www.chesterwood.org. Estate of sculptor Daniel Chester French.

Naumkeag, Prospect Hill Road, Stockbridge; (413) 298–3239; www.thetrustees.org. Joseph Hodges Choate's summer home designed by Stanford White in the Shingle style. Gardens by Fletcher Steele, famous landscape architect.

Prime Outlet Village, 50 Water Street, Lee; (413) 243–8186 or (877) GO OUTLETS; www.primeoutlets.com. Savings on designer brands.

Santarella, 75 Tyringham Road (3½ miles from Route 102 in Lee), Tyringham; (413) 243–3260. Gingerbread house, museum, and gardens of sculptor Sir Henry Hudson Kitson.

Where to Eat

Elm Street Market, Elm Street (off Main Street), Stockbridge; (413) 298–3634; www.elmstreetmarket.com. Breakfast and lunch only. An old-fashioned general store with a lunch counter serving plain food—eggs, bacon, pancakes, sub sandwiches—and lots of local gossip. $

Joe's Diner, 63 Center Street, Lee; (413) 243–9756. Open from noon to midnight daily, year-round. Serving classic diner food—open-faced sandwiches, fries and gravy, and the like. *The Runaway,* Norman Rockwell's painting of a boy seated next to a policeman on a diner stool, was rendered with Joe's Diner as the backdrop. $

Red Lion Inn Dining Room and Tavern, 30 Main Street, Stockbridge; (413) 298–5545; www.redlion.com. Open for breakfast, lunch, and dinner. Traditional decor, lots of antiques. Food is contemporary regional cuisine. $–$$$$

Where to Stay

Hawk Meadow Guest Farm, 322 Landers Road, Lee; (413) 243–2224; www.bcn.net/llamahike. Three rooms, country-style decor. Breakfast ingredients from their organic fruit and vegetable garden. $$

Historic Merrell Inn, 1565 Pleasant Street, South Lee; (413) 243–1794 or (800) 243–1794; www.merrell-inn.com. Original wide-plank floors, fireplaces, and antiques. Breakfasts are delicious and filling. Not appropriate for young children. $$–$$$$

Red Lion Inn, 30 Main Street, Stockbridge; (413) 298–5545; www.redlioninn.com. Open year-round (very crowded in July and August). Treat yourselves to a stay at this quintessential rambling New England inn that many others try to emulate. Rooms vary in size, from quite small to almost palatial. Families will be happiest in the suites with connecting bathroom. The annex buildings tend to be quieter than the main inn building. $$–$$$$

Hidden Berkshires

Picturesque towns and villages near the corner of the state bordering Connecticut and New York are a bit off the beaten path but not to be overlooked. Butternut Basin and Catamount are nice beginner downhill ski areas for families (see sidebar on Ski Meccas in this chapter). Many properties managed by the Trustees of Reservations are found here, as well as many wilderness areas.

Mt. Washington State Forest and Bash Bish Falls (all ages)

East Street, Mt. Washington; (413) 528–0330; www.massparks.org. Directions: Take the Mass Pike to exit 2, go Route 102 West, then Route 7 South to Route 23 West, take Route 41 South, then follow the signs for Bash Bish Falls and the Mt. Washington State Forest. Turn into the second parking area. Open daily, dawn to dusk. Free.

Bash Bish Falls is a great name for a great place. From the second parking area you can hike 1 mile, then clamber, climb, or walk down a stone stairway to see the 60-foot waterfall that plunges into a churning pool. Unfortunately, you can't swim here—too dangerous—but the boulders that border the falls are still a cool spot to relax on a hot day.

Great Barrington, Monterey, Housatonic, and East Otis

Imagine an area that is mall free, that is clean and quaint—a Norman Rockwell snippet of New England charm. A great source of information on such a place is the **Southern Berkshire Chamber of Commerce,** 362 Main Street, Great Barrington 01230; (413) 528–1510; www.greatbarrington.org.

Beartown State Forest (all ages)

Blue Hill Road, Monterey; (413) 528–0904; www.massparks.org. Open year-round. Parking is $5.00 for day use.

Crossed by the Appalachian Trail, the park has good hiking and cross-country skiing, but its highlight is Benedict Pond, one of the region's best swimming holes.

Monument Mountain Reservation (all ages)

Route 7, Great Barrington; www.thetrustees.org. Open dawn to dusk. Free.

Noted for its easy hiking trails and outcrops of quartzite rock, Monument Mountain has a colorful history. Squaw Peak at the summit got its name from an Indian maiden, who wasn't allowed to marry her lover, plunging to her death from this spot. A cluster of rocks mark where she landed, put there as a tribute to her by members of her

Marcia's
TopAnnualEvents
in the Berkshires

- **Butternut Basin Family Fun Day,** March, Great Barrington; (413) 528–2000; www.skibutternut.com

- **Family Week at Williams College Museum of Art,** April, Williamstown; (413) 597–2429

- **Winter Week at Hancock Shaker Village,** February, Pittsfield; (413) 443–0188; www.hancockshakervillage.org

- **Chesterwood Antique Car Show,** May, Stockbridge; (413) 298–3579; www.chesterwood.org

- **Sheep Shearing Days at Hancock Shaker Village,** June, Pittsfield; (413) 443–0188; www.hancockshakervillage.org

- **Berkshire Summer Arts Festival,** Butternut Basin, July, Great Barrington; (800) 834–9437; www.berkshiresartsfestival.com.

- **Celebrate Pittsfield Street Festival,** June, Pittsfield; (413) 443–6501; www.downtownpittsfield.com

- **Berkshire Theatre Festival,** June through August, Stockbridge; (413) 298–5576; www.berkshiretheatre.org

- **La Festa,** June, North Adams; (413) 66–FESTA

- **Robbins-Zust Family Marionettes,** summer, Lenox; (413) 698–2591; www.berkshireweb.com/zust

- **Jacob's Pillow Dance Festival,** June through August, George Carter Road, Becket; (413) 243–0745; www.jacobspillow.org

- **Shakespeare and Company,** summer, Old Berkshire Performing Arts Center, The Founders Theater, Lenox; (413) 637–3353 or (413) 637–1199; www.shakespeare.org

- **Tanglewood Music Festival,** June through August, Lenox; (413) 637–5165 or (617) 266–1492 or (888) 266–1200; www.BSO.org

- **Williamstown Theatre Festival,** June through August, Williamstown; (413) 597–3400 (box office), (413) 597–3399 (info line); www.wt festival.org

- **Sterling and Francine Clark Art Institute Outdoor Festival,** midsummer, Williamstown; (413) 458–9545; www.clarkart.edu

- **Annual Monument Mountain Climb,** August, Great Barrington; (413) 442–1793; www.mobydick.org

- **Autumn Farm Weekend,** September, Hancock Shaker Village, Pittsfield; (413) 443–0188; www.hancockshakervillage.org

- **Apple Squeeze,** September, Lenox; (413) 637–3646; www.lenox.org

- **Great Josh Billings Runaground,** triathalon, mid-September, Great Barrington to Lenox; (413) 637–6913; www.joshbillings.com

- **Taste of the Berkshires,** late summer, Great Barrington; (413) 528–1947

- **Fall Foliage Festival,** October, North Adams; (413) 663–3735; www.berkshirechamber.com

- **Tub Parade,** September, Lenox; (413) 637–3646; www.lenox.org

- **Berkshire Museum Festival of Trees,** November through December, 39 South Street, Pittsfield; (413) 443–7171; www.berkshiremuseum.org

- **Main Street at Christmas,** Main Street, first weekend in December, Stockbridge; (413) 298–5200; www.stockbridgechamber.org

- **Community Christmas at Hancock Shaker Village,** early December, Pittsfield; (413) 443–0188; www.hancockshakervillage.org

tribe. It is also the meeting place of famous writers Herman Melville and Nathaniel Hawthorne, arranged by a group of friends. They enjoyed a picnic, drank champagne, and became lifelong friends. Owned by the Trustees of Reservations.

Other Things to See and Do

Berkshire Carriage Company, Great Barrington; (413) 528–0202; www.berkshirecarriage.com. Horse-drawn carriages, wagons, and sleighs for rent.

Tolland State Forest, 410 Tolland Road, East Otis; (413) 269–6002; www.massparks.com. Highly regarded for its great fishing, Tolland State Forest has a multitude of water-based activities including swimming and boating. Other popular recreational opportunities are hiking, mountain biking, cross-country skiing, and snowshoeing.

Where to Eat

Four Brothers, Route 7, Great Barrington; (413) 528–9684. Part of a chain of Greek pizza places that covers upstate New York and the Berkshires, serving delicious pizza and eggplant dishes. $–$$

Jack's Grill, 1063 Main Street, Housatonic Village; (413) 274–1000; www.jacksgrill .com. Seasonal. Family-friendly place with fun menu, funky decor. Affiliated with the Red Lion Inn. $–$$

Martin's, 49 Railroad Street, Great Barrington; (413) 528–5455. Serves breakfast all day, along with lunch specials. Try the omelet made with Monterey chèvre, the strawberry-banana pancakes, or the lentil stew. $

Where to Stay

The Egremont Inn, 10 Old Sheffield Road, South Egremont; (413) 528–2111; www.egremontinn.com. Inn and restaurant. Old-fashioned pleasures await. Gourmet restaurant. Pool and tennis court. Listed in National Register of Historic Places. $–$$$

Windflower, 684 South Egremont Road, Great Barrington; (413) 528–2720 or (800) 992–1993; www.windflowerinn.com. Thirteen rooms, fireplaces, gardens, pool. Children welcome, extra charge for cribs and cots. Full breakfast. $$–$$$

Ashley Falls

This tiny town near the Connecticut border is the site of two interesting attractions owned by the Trustees of Reservations: the oldest dwelling in Berkshire County, the Colonel John Ashley House; and Bartholomew's Cobble, a national natural landmark.

Bartholomew's Cobble (all ages)

Off Route 7A to Rannapo Road to Weatogue Road, Ashley Falls; (413) 229–8600 or (413) 298–3239; www.thetrustees.org. Museum and information center open daily, 9:00 A.M. to 4:30 P.M. Closed Sunday and Monday December through March. Admission: $4.00 for adults, $1.00 for children 6 to 12, free for kids under age 6.

Bartholomew's Cobble is an unusual natural hilly rock garden, studded with limestone outcroppings (the cobbles) and featuring distinctive flora, such as forty species of ferns and many wildflowers. Bird-watching is excellent here due to the abundant plant life. There are 6 miles of hiking trails (the easygoing Ledges Trail is particularly pleasant for families with younger kids), picnic facilities, and a small natural history museum.

Colonel John Ashley House (all ages)

Cooper Hill Road, Ashley Falls; (413) 229–8600 or (413) 298–3239; www.thetrustees .org. Open Memorial Day weekend through Columbus Day weekend and Monday 10:00 A.M. to 5:00 P.M. Admission: $5.00 for adults, $3.00 for children.

Colonel John Ashley House is named for one of the first citizens of the town of Sheffield, which was purchased in 1722 from Native Americans for 460 pounds sterling, three barrels of cider, and thirty quarts of rum. Ashley, a surveyor and lawyer, built his house in 1735. In 1773 the Ashley house was the site of the signing of the Sheffield Declaration, now considered the first "declaration of independence" from Britain. The house features a collection of colonial-era tools and tableware. The herb gardens are particularly interesting. Learn how seventeenth-century Americans used herbs for cooking meals, healing the sick, and freshening their homes.

The Pioneer Valley

The Pioneer Valley borders the Connecticut River, which stretches north to south through the state. The river valley is broad and fertile, making it excellent farming country. Many crops are raised here, including corn, tobacco, and sod for golf courses. The area was one of the first regions of inland New England to be secured by English settlers during the turbulent late seventeenth and early eighteenth centuries, when they battled Native American tribes and French militia. The town of Deerfield is one of the best sources of information about this early period of colonial history. At Turners Falls there's an interesting underwater view of a fish ladder, where salmon and shad swim during the spring. In Agawam, Six Flags is New England's largest amusement park. It features all the essentials—roller coasters, bumper cars, water rides, and lots of sticky fried food. Finally, for twelve days every September, the Big E (the Eastern States Exposition), in Springfield, is the biggest annual fair on the East Coast. It's family fare all the way—livestock shows, crafts contests, musical entertainment, rides, and midways. For information on where to stay, contact **Berkshire/Folkstone Bed and Breakfast Homes,** 101 Mulberry Street, Springfield 01105; (413) 731–8785 or (800) 762–2751; www.berkshirebnbhomes .com. **The Greater Springfield Convention and Visitors Bureau,** 1441 Main

Marcia's
TopPicks in the Pioneer Valley

1. Historic Deerfield and Yankee Candle Company, Deerfield

2. Six Flags, Agawam

3. Basketball Hall of Fame, Springfield

4. Northfield Mountain Power Station and Entertainment Center and its associated properties

THE PIONEER VALLEY

Northfield

5
10

Bernardston

2 Charlemont

Turners
Falls
2

Shelburne
Greenfield

Deerfield
5

9

91

Amherst
9

Northampton
Hadley

South
Hadley
202

90
20
10

23
32

Holyoke
202
391
90

20
291
20

20

5 Springfield
Agawam
91
202

Street, Box 15589, Springfield 01103 (413–787–1548 or 800–723–1548; www.valley
visitor.com/visit), has information on the entire Pioneer Valley. For information on
Franklin County contact the **Franklin County Chamber of Commerce,** P.O. Box
898, Greenfield 01302; (413) 773–9393 (visitor center) or (413) 773–5463;
www.co.franklin.ma.us.

Mohawk Trail Region

The Mohawk Trail (Route 2) was the first road designated a Scenic Byway. The route is
much more dramatic when you drive it from east to west. The trail starts in central
Massachusetts and ends on the New York/Massachusetts border. As the road begins
climbing into the foothills, look back over the Connecticut River Valley. To contact the
Mohawk Trail Association, call (413) 743–8127; www.mohawktrail.com.

Northfield and Bernardston

The historic village of Bernardston boasts several buildings on the National Register
of Historic Places, including the library, the Unitarian Church, the town halls, and the
old high school, all of which are on Main Street. The quaint New England town of
Northfield on the banks of the Connecticut River is home to the prestigious private
secondary school Northfield/Mt. Hermon.

Northfield Mountain Power Station and Environmental Center
(all ages) 🎎 🎿 🏕
99 Millers Falls Road, off Route 63, Northfield; (413) 659–3714 or (800) 859–2960;
www.nu.com/northfield/. Cross-country skiing mid-December through March. Call for
hours and fees. Hiking in the off-season is free.

Inside Northfield Mountain is Northfield Mountain Power Station and Environmental
Center, an enormous power-generating facility that's owned by Northeast Utilities.
Atop the mountain is a water reservoir that's used to generate power when con-
sumer demand exceeds supply from other power sources. The property is open to
the public for cross-country skiing, hiking, picnicking, mountain biking, snowshoeing,
and wildlife viewing. The altitude makes for fairly consistent snow on the 25 miles of
cross-country skiing trails (that are groomed regularly), which in warm weather are
used for hiking. The lodge offers ski and snowshoe rentals and lessons, a heated
lounge, and outdoor picnic tables with a fire pit. Northfield Mountain also maintains a
Web camera focusing on the nesting habits of bald eagles; images are updated four
to twelve times an hour.

Tap into **This!**

Many of the maple sugaring houses in the Pioneer Valley offer tours and eating facilities. For a copy of the *Massachusetts Maple Producers Directory*, contact the **Massachusetts Maple Producers Association**, Watson-Spruce Corner Road, Ashfield 01330; (413) 628–3912; www.massmaple.org.

Quinnetukut II (all ages)
Route 63, Northfield; (413) 659–3714 or (800) 859–2960; www.nu.com/northfield/. Operates Wednesday through Sunday, mid-June to mid-October (call for a schedule). Admission: $9.00 for adults, $5.00 for children under 14.

The *Quinnetukut II* takes up to sixty passengers on a ninety-minute, 12-mile round-trip cruise on the Connecticut River between Northfield and Gill. Knowledgeable guides comment on the flora, fauna, and history of the areas. The highlight of the trip is through the French King Gorge, a spectacular sight. Boats leave from the River View area, across from the entrance to Northfield Mountain. Reservations required.

Barton Cove and Barton Cove Campground (all ages)
Route 2, Gill; (413) 863–9300 or (800) 859–2960; www.nu.com/northfield/. Open Memorial Day to Labor Day. Kayak and canoe rentals are $10 per hour, $25 for the day, or $50 per three-day rental. Camping costs $15 per night.

You can rent canoes at Barton Cove (operated by the Northfield Mountain Recreation and Environmental Center) on the Connecticut River. There's a campground with showers (call for reservations and fees).

There is also a weekend canoe shuttle service that drops you off at 5-, 13-, or 20-mile intervals. It allows you to paddle back to your car parked at Barton Cove. A fun destination for a camp-over is Munn's Ferry, reachable by canoe, with primitive facilities and a rustic atmosphere. Barton Cove is home to nesting bald eagles, which can be observed year-round by going to the Northfield Web site.

Other Things to See and Do

Wendell State Forest, Montague Road, Wendell; (413) 659–3797; www.massparks.org. State park with crystal-clear ten-acre Ruggles pond, a great place for fishing, swimming, and boating. Activities at Wendell State Park also include cross-country skiing, mountain biking, hiking, and field sports.

Where to Eat

Bella Notte Ristorante, 199 Huckle Hill, Bernardston; (413) 648–9107. Great views; serving Italian and American dishes for lunch and dinner. $–$$

Four Leaf Clover, Route 5, Bernardston; (413) 648–9514. Family-oriented restaurant open for lunch and dinner year-round. $–$$

Where to Stay

Centennial House, Routes 10 and 6, 94 Main Street, Northfield; (413) 498–5921; www.thecentennialhouse.com. Estate setting, five bedrooms with fireplaces and brass or sleigh beds; complimentary breakfast. $$–$$$$

Cross-Country **Skiing Meccas**

- **Hickory Hill Ski Touring Center,** Buffington Hill Road, Worthington; (413) 238–5813; www.xcskimass.com. A 500-acre farm with 15 miles of carefully groomed trails and a funky old lodge. During snow season it's open Friday through Monday. The trails are groomed for both classical and freestyle skiing.

- **Maple Corner Farm,** 794 Beech Hill Road, Granville; (413) 357–8829 or (413) 357–6697 (snow conditions); www.xcskimass.com/ MapleCorner. Open Monday through Friday 10:00 A.M. to 5:00 P.M., weekends and holidays 9:00 A.M. to 5:00 P.M. A working farm since the mid-1800s; 500 acres of varied terrain with more than 12 groomed miles of trail for all levels of skiers and snowshoers. Snowshoe and ski rentals, lessons, snack bar in fireplaced lodge.

- **Northfield Mountain Cross-country Ski Area,** off Route 63, Northfield; (413) 659–3713 or (800) 859–2960 (ski conditions); www.xcski mass.com. Offers 26 miles of trails. Rentals available. See Northfield Mountain Power Station and Environmental Center.

- **Stump Sprouts Ski Touring Center,** 64 West Hill Road, West Hawley; (413) 339–4265; www.stumpsprouts.com. Twelve miles of groomed trails on 450 acres. Instruction, rentals, and guided tours available. Simple rooms accommodating two to six people can be reserved, but bring your own linens.

- **The Worthington Inn,** Old North Road/Route 143, Worthington; (413) 238–4441. A three-bedroom bed and breakfast ($$–$$$) located near an excellent cross-country ski center. Child friendly.

The Covered Bridges
of Franklin County!

Scenic covered bridges of interest:

- Colrain—**Arthur Smith Covered Bridge** over the North River

- Charlemont—**Bissel Covered Bridge** on Route 8A

- Conway—**Burkeville Covered Bridge** over the South River off Route 116

- Greenfield—**Greenfield Covered Bridge** over the Green River on Leydon Road

Greenfield and Turners Falls

Longview Tower in Greenfield has observation decks that offer views of Massachusetts, Vermont, and New York. A wonderful full-service information center is located in Greenfield at the intersection of Interstate 91 and Route 2. The center is open daily year-round from 8:30 A.M. to 6:00 P.M. From Greenfield, drive through the town of Montague to reach Turners Falls, the site of the first dam on the Connecticut River.

Turners Falls Fishway Ladder (all ages)

First Street (off Avenue A), Turners Falls; (413) 659–3714 or (800) 859–2960; www.nu .com/northfield/. Open mid-May through mid-June, Wednesday through Sunday 9:00 A.M. to 5:00 P.M. Interpreter on site. Free.

Owned and maintained by Northeast Utilities, the draw here is the underground/under-river viewing facility that allows kids to watch sea lamprey, shad, and other anadromous fish (those that migrate upriver from the sea to breed in freshwater) pass by a window on their way to their favorite spawning grounds upstream. The facility is on the south side of the dam, just before the bridge; look for the sign. Just below the dam, Unity Park is a nice spot for a picnic; there's a playground here, too.

Amazing
Massachusetts Fact

Longview Tower is the highest steel observation tower in Massachusetts.

Other Things to See and Do

Great Falls Discovery Center, 38 Avenue A, Turners Falls; (413) 863–3676. The Discovery Center focuses on the history of the Connecticut River and contains a bicycle museum.

Old Greenfield Village, Mohawk Trail, Route 2, P.O. Box 1124, Greenfield 01302; (413) 774–7138. Open mid-May through mid-October 10:00 A.M. to 4:00 P.M. on Saturday and holidays and from noon to 4:00 P.M. Sunday. Admission: Adults $5.00, kids ages 6 to 16 $3.00. Wayne Morse's thirty-five-year-old collection of memorabilia and antiques re-creates a New England Village of 1895.

Poets Seat Tower, Mountain Road and Maple Street, Greenfield; (413) 773–5463. Hiking, birding, and views.

Where to Eat

Famous Bill's, 30 Federal Street/Route 5, Greenfield; (413) 773–9230; www.bills restaurant.com. Serves down-home food—chicken potpie, burgers, and such—in a friendly atmosphere. Children's menu. $–$$$

Taylor's Tavern Restaurant, 238 Main Street, Greenfield; (413) 773–8313. Lunch and dinner daily; breakfast served on weekends. Voted best restaurant in Greenfield by the local paper; children's menu. $–$$

Where to Stay

Brandt House Country Inn, 29 Highland Avenue, Greenfield; (413) 774–3329; www.brandthouse.com. Estate with eight guest rooms (some with fireplaces), clay tennis courts, billiards, and a wraparound porch. Well-behaved dogs are allowed with prior notice. Rates include breakfast. $$–$$$

West Winds Bed and Breakfast, 151 Smead Hill Road, Greenfield; (413) 774–4025; www.westwindsinn.com. Nine rooms, all attractively decorated in contemporary New Age decor with delightful views (especially during foliage season) and extensive grounds. $$–$$$$

Cruising Down the River

The **Connecticut River Greenway State Park** extends from the border with Connecticut (Chicopee) to the New Hampshire/Vermont border. The park encompasses six public boat accesses to the Connecticut River, the Mount Sugarloaf Observation Area, the Norwottuck Rail Trail, and public lands acquired to create a public greenway along the Connecticut River. The gentlest portion of the river for kayaking and canoeing is from Turners Falls in Montague south for 15 miles to Hatfield. The Connecticut River was designated one of fourteen American Heritage Rivers in 1998. For further information, call (413) 586–8706; www.massparks.org.

Shelburne and Charlemont

At Shelburne's Bridge of Flowers, more than 500 varieties of flowers are planted and cultivated. Shelburne Falls is considered to be one of the hundred best small art towns in America; see artists at work creating quilts, glass objects, pottery, and weaving. Make sure to be on the lookout for Josh Simpson, a nationally known glass artist and the owner of the Salmon Falls Art Gallery. One of Josh's signature themes is paperweights that seem to have a planetary influence, with smaller globes floating inside the larger glass that is encasing them. Maybe his creativity is influenced by his wife, astronaut Cady Coleman, whom he thinks is out of this world! The Shelburne Falls village information center can be reached at (413) 625–2544; www.shelburnefalls.com. The Mohawk Trail State Forest (Route 2, Charlemont; 413–339–5504) has camping, hiking, cabin rentals, fishing, nature programs, swimming, and a good picnic area.

The Bridge of Flowers (all ages)

16–22 Water Street (in the center of town), Shelburne Falls; (413) 625–2544; www .shelburnefalls.com. The bridge is in full bloom from May to October. Free parking.

In the riverside village of Shelburne Falls, a quick detour off Route 2, see the Bridge of Flowers. It's a 400-foot retired trolley bridge that has been planted with flower beds. The best time for viewing the bridge is in July and August. Don't miss the nearby Salmon Falls, with the country's most numerous glacial potholes formed by retreating ice from the glaciation period.

Berkshire East (all ages)

P.O. Box 727, South River Road, Charlemont 01339; (413) 339–6617; www.berkshire east.com. Call for schedule and prices. Open mid-December through mid-March. Night skiing is Wednesday through Saturday.

Day and night skiing opportunities abound here. Berkshire East is where a lot of skiers learn the ropes (no pun intended). I first discovered this gem while in college. Berkshire East has a 1,180-foot vertical drop, a base lodge to warm up in, five lifts, and forty trails ranging from beginner to double black diamond. For the snowboard enthusiast in your family, try the half-pipe and terrain park. Lessons and rentals are available. There is a cafeteria on the premises.

Shelburne Falls Trolley Museum (all ages)

14 Depot Street, Shelburne Falls; (413) 625–9443; www.SFTM.org. Open late May to early November, weekends and holidays 11:00 A.M. to 5:00 P.M. Open 1:00 to 5:00 P.M. Mondays and Wednesdays in July and August. Weekday operations may be added.

The museum is dedicated to preserving the Shelburne Falls and Colrain Railway Combine No. 10, which served the valley for thirty years; over the years other cars have

Climbing Up a Wall

Kids ages two to fifteen who love outdoor challenges will love the vertical challenge of rock climbing with **Zoar Outdoor,** Mohawk Trail, Route 2, Charlemont; (413) 339–4010 or (800) 532–7483; www.zoaroutdoor.com.

been added to the collection. The route crossed the Deerfield River over the trolley bridge, which has since been converted to the present-day Bridge of Flowers, and delivered passengers, freight, and mail. Still in operation, the combine makes a short journey around its new home in the freight yard.

Where to Eat

Gould's SugarHouse, 587 Mohawk Trail, Route 2, Shelburne; (413) 625–6170. Open daily March and April and September and October, 8:00 A.M. to 2:00 P.M. Good breakfast or lunch stop along the Mohawk Trail, especially if you're into pancakes and syrup. $

McCusker's Market and Deli Cafe, 5 State Street, Shelburne Falls ; (413) 625–9411; www.mccuskersmarket.com. Open Monday through Friday 6:00 A.M. to 7:00 P.M. and Saturday and Sunday from 7:00 A.M. to 6:00 P.M. Extended hours during the summer. Natural gourmet food, including baked goods and ice cream, and extensive health food store. Tables are in the rear. $

Tusk'n Rattle Cafe, 10 Bridge Street, Shelburne Falls; (413) 625–0200. Open for dinner nightly 5:00 to 11:00 P.M. Owned by two caterers, this forty-seat dining room with an exposed stone wall is very attractive. After 9:00 P.M. tapas are served. $–$$

The Warfield House, 200 Warfield Road, off Route 2, Charlemont; (413) 339–6600 or (888) 339–VIEW; www.warfieldhouse inn.com. Located on 530 mountaintop acres of farmland, featuring llama treks, emus, a sugar house, snowshoeing, hayrides, sleigh rides, and a gourmet restaurant. $$–$$$

Where to Stay

The Charlemont Inn, Route 2, 107 Main Street, Mohawk Trail, Charlemont; (413) 339–5796; www.charlemontinn.com. Interesting guest list including Benedict Arnold, Mark Twain, Calvin Coolidge, and the sighting of a ghost named Elizabeth. Great location and pricing. $–$$

Hail to **the Sunrise**

Just beyond Charlemont on Route 2 is a 900-pound bronze statue of an Indian chief figure with his arms and face lifted to the east. The piece is called *Hail to the Sunrise*. It's one of many statues that you'll see along the Mohawk Trail.

Deerfield

Deerfield has survived more than just 300 years of farming in New England's unpredictable climate. In 1675 the Bloody Brook Massacre battle of King Philip's War resulted in the deaths of sixty-seven Deerfield residents. In 1704 a band of French and Indian soldiers attacked, killing forty-nine of the inhabitants and carrying off 111 more to Quebec. Miraculously, a few of these people survived and were able to make their way back to Deerfield. Historic Deerfield has an interesting story to reveal of the history and lifestyles of a struggling inland settlement. Today, the Yankee Candle Company of Deerfield is the second largest tourist destination in Massachusetts with more than 2.5 million visitors annually.

Magic Wings Butterfly Conservatory and Gardens (all ages)

281 Greenfield Road, Routes 5 and 10, Deerfield; (413) 665–2805; www.magicwings .net. Open daily from 9:00 A.M. to 5:00 P.M.; until 6:00 P.M. from Memorial Day to Labor Day. Admission is $7.50 per adult, $4.50 per child ages 3 through 17. Free for kids under age 3. Admission packages are available.

The newly expanded 8,000-square-foot Magic Wings conservatory is planted with exotic vegetation and holds within it butterflies that are both native and tropical.

Set the **Mood**

Set the mood before going to Deerfield with these books geared to older children in grades five through seven:

- *The Boy Captive in Canada* by Mary Wells Smith
- *The Boy Captive in Old Deerfield* by Mary Wells Smith
- *The Ransom of Mary Carter* by Caroline Cooney

For younger children, pick up a copy of the *Cobblestone* magazine on Deerfield for $4.95 in the gift shop at Historic Deerfield.

Imagine if you will, hundreds of butterflies (more than 2,500) silently fluttering by, unaware of their grace and beauty and the delight that they bring to all ages. Do not be surprised if a butterfly alights upon you; a truly magical moment. The grounds have one and a half acres of gardens with native trees and flowers along with quiet little resting places to view nature's bounty.

Historic Deerfield (ages 6 and up)
Route 5/The Street, Deerfield; (413) 774–5581; www.historic-deerfield.org. Open daily April through December 9:30 A.M. to 4:30 P.M.; closed Thanksgiving and Christmas. Admission (good for two consecutive days): $14.00 for adults, $5.00 for children 6 to 21. Special ticket pricing for a partial taste of Historic Deerfield.

Twelve of the restored houses along The Street form an association called Historic Deerfield. These spectacular examples of eighteenth- and nineteenth-century architecture, design, furnishings, and lifestyles will probably be most interesting to older kids, who can appreciate the work that has gone into these houses, as well as the rich history of the town and its inhabitants. Don't try to see more than three houses in one day; they're all worth visiting, but more than three would be too much for any but the most ardent historic preservationist, let alone a family with children. A popular outdoor family education program offered by Historic Deerfield is a child pack that is rented for use along the Channing Blake Trail (a child-friendly ½-mile meadow walk). The pack comes equipped with a mini-microscope, a workbook, pencils, pens, and various measurement devices to explore nature and the outdoors. *TIP:* Watch for special family days geared toward children with special pricing and family-fun activities.

Up the Creek without a Paddle

Contact these tour companies for whitewater adventures and calmer river trips on the Deerfield, West, and Millers Rivers. All tours provide lunch, offer instruction and equipment, and have a variety of trips suited for the neophyte and the old hand.

- Crab Apple Whitewater, Mohawk Trail, Route 2, Charlemont; (800) 553–7238; www.crabappleinc.com

- Moxie Outdoor Adventures, Mohawk Trail, Route 2, HC 63 Box 60, The Forks, ME 04985; (800) 866–6943; www.moxierafting.com

- Zoar Outdoor, Mohawk Trail, Route 2, 7 Main Street, P.O. Box 245, Charlemont 01339; (800) 532–7483; www.zaroutdoor.com

The Yankee Candle Company (all ages)

Route 5, South Deerfield; (413) 665–2929 or (877) 636–7707 (special event hotline); www.yankeecandle.com. Open daily 9:30 A.M. to 6:00 P.M.; closed Thanksgiving and Christmas. Admission to all is free.

The Yankee Candle Company began in 1969 in a kitchen here, and the rest is history—at least, the company thinks so. At this complex that seems to sprout new buildings every season, you can dip your own candles, visit a Bavarian Christmas village (a toy factory with Santa and Mrs. Claus), and a museum that demonstrates candle making through history. Of course, selling candles is the main focus of the Yankee Candle Company, and there's a huge variety. Chandler's Restaurant is on site if you get hungry. Call for a schedule of special events.

Where to Eat

Chandler's at Yankee Candle, Routes 5 and 10, South Deerfield; (413) 665–1277; www.yankeecandle.com. Open for lunch and candlelit dinner. Traditional yet with a wide range to suit any palate. No dress code. Kids' menu. $–$$$

Deerfield Inn, 81 Old Main Street, Deerfield; (413) 774–5587 or (800) 926–3865; www.deerfieldinn.com. Historic setting for delicious regional dishes. $$–$$$$

Wolfie's, 52 South Main Street, South Deerfield; (413) 665–7068. Open for lunch and dinner year-round, Monday through Saturday, 11:00 A.M. to 10:00 P.M. Great sandwiches and a calm atmosphere. Good food for a reasonable price. $–$$

Where to Stay

Deerfield Inn, 81 Old Main Street, Deerfield; (413) 774–5587 or (800) 926–3865; www.DeerfieldInn.com. With only twenty-three rooms in this historic setting, make your reservation early (Deerfield Academy parent weekends tend to sell out the inn). Room rates include breakfast. $$$–$$$$

The Five College Area

Families with near-college-age children will find lots to do here, especially if the kids are interested in visiting any of the five colleges—the University of Massachusetts (which everyone calls UMass), Amherst College, Hampshire College, Smith College, and Mount Holyoke College. Campus tours are given several times a week at most colleges, and each has a lovely campus with a different flavor.

Amherst

This quintessential college town is home to Amherst College, Hampshire College, and the University of Massachusetts. Two well-known Amherst poets are the beloved Robert Frost, who taught poetry at Amherst College, and Emily Dickinson.

Emily Dickinson Homestead and the Evergreens (all ages)

280 Main Street, Amherst; (413) 542–8161; www.dickinsonhomestead.org. Open March to mid-December. Call for the schedule and to reserve your spot ahead of time. Admission: $8.00 for adults, $5.00 for children 6 to 18; free for children under 6.

If you have a poetry fan in the family, be sure to walk by the Emily Dickinson Homestead near the campus of Amherst College. Dickinson was born and spent most of her life in this house. Her gravesite is not far from the house at West Cemetery on Triangle Street. Ask for directions, and recite one of her poems over her grave, as do the U. Mass American poetry students. Don't forget to go next door to visit the Evergreens, home of Emily's brother, Austin, and sister-in-law, Susan, that remains as it once was, untouched by time!

The Eric Carle Museum of Picture Book Art (ages 2 to 10)

125 West Bay Road, Amherst; (413) 658–1100; www.picturebookart.org. Open Tuesday through Saturday 10:00 A.M. to 4:00 P.M. and Sunday noon to 4:00 P.M. Adults are $4.00; children and students are $2.00; children younger than 1 year are free. Ask about the special $10.00 family rate.

This museum contains more than 40,000 square feet and features picture book art from around the world. Founded by Eric Carle, author and illustrator of the popular and beloved children's books *The Very Hungry Caterpillar* and *The Tiny Seed,* the museum will fascinate your children. Guest picture book artist exhibits are on display; see if you recognize any of your favorite books! Book signings, lectures, creative crafts, and storytelling all bring the process of illustration and the art of the story to life. There are a nice cafe, library, and museum shop on-site.

Museums of the Five Colleges
of the Pioneer Valley

- **Hampshire College Art Gallery,** Amherst; (413) 549–4600; www.library.hampshire.edu/gallery.html

- **Mead Art Museum and Pratt Museum of Natural History,** Amherst College, Amherst; (413) 542–2335 for the Mead (www.amherst.edu/~mead) and (413) 542–2165 for the Pratt (www.amherst.edu/~pratt)

- **Mount Holyoke College Art Museum and the Arboretum,** South Hadley; (413) 538–2245; www.mtholyoke.edu/offices/artmuseum

- **Smith College Museum of Art,** Northampton; (413) 585–2760; www.smith.edu/artmuseum/

- **University Gallery,** University of Massachusetts, Amherst; (413) 545–3670; www.umass.edu/fac

Jones Library (all ages)

43 Amity Street, Amherst; (413) 256–4090; www.joneslibrary.org. Free; call for a schedule.

The library's special collections rooms hold a precious store of handwritten works by Dickinson, as well as a comprehensive collection of papers and other articles owned by Robert Frost, another native of Amherst.

The Belle of Amherst

Beautifully illustrated and riveting children's bedtime storybooks on Emily Dickinson are *Emily* (Bantam/ Doubleday) by Michael Bedard, illustrated by Barbara Cooney, and *The Mouse of Amherst* by Elizabeth Spires. These sweet tales would be a great read prior to a tour of the Emily Dickinson Homestead. For older children, we recommend a selection of Emily Dickinson poetry entitled *Final Harvest* by Thomas Johnson.

Other Things to See and Do

Mullins Center, University of Massachusetts, Amherst; (413) 545–0505; www .mullinscenter.com. Athletic and entertainment complex.

Stone House Museum, 20 Maple Street, Belchertown; (413) 323–6573. Sculpture, antique carriages and sleighs, and late 1700s furnishings.

Where to Eat

Judie's, 51 North Pleasant Street, Amherst; (413) 253–3491; www.judies restaurant.com. Lunch and dinner. Creative continental food with a flair; expect a sampling of foods from France, Mexico, and Spain. Home of the popover with apple butter and vegetarian specials. Setting has art hanging on the walls and hand-painted tables with Matisse or Georgia O'Keeffe motifs. Kids' menu. $–$$$

La Cucina de Pinocchio's, 30 Boltwood Walk, Amherst; (413) 256–4110; www .pinocchiosamherst.com. Fine dining with Tuscan decor. Italian food is the focus. Family friendly, nonsmoking. $$–$$$

La Veracruzana, 63 South Pleasant Street, Amherst; (413) 253–6900. Mouthwatering Mexican food; great art collection. $–$$

Where to Stay

The Lord Jeffery Inn, 30 Boltwood Avenue, Amherst; (413) 253–2576 or (800) 742–0358; www.lordjefferyinn.com. Forty-eight-room inn loaded with charm, facing Amherst Common. Highly regarded pub fare and dining room. $$–$$$$

Hadley

Don't be surprised if you drive by tobacco drying in the tobacco barns at harvesttime. This is a sleepy agricultural community bordered by its sophisticated sister communities of Amherst and Northampton.

Skinner State Park (all ages)

Route 47, Hadley; (413) 586–0350 or (413) 253–2883 (visitor center); www.massparks .org. Open May through October; seasonal hours. $2.00 parking fee.

A road and several hiking trails lead to the summit of Mt. Holyoke and extend to the Holyoke Range State Park. The summit is a great picnic spot, with tables, a few grills, and a superb view of the Connecticut River Valley. The Summit House at Skinner State Park (413–586–0350; open weekends May through October) is a recently restored old mountain inn that's now the site of summer concerts.

Norwottuck Rail Trail **Bike Path**

The Norwottuck is an 8½-mile bike path on the former Boston and Maine Railroad railway bed. The path is a paved 8-foot-wide trail connecting Northampton, Hadley, Amherst, and Belchertown. Run by the Department of Environmental Management (DEM; www.massparks.org) and part of the Connecticut River Greenway State Park, the path meanders through forest, pastureland, and residential areas. A highlight of the route is Beaver Pond in South Amherst. To access the path, enter at Elwell State Park in Damon in Northampton and Station Road in South Amherst. (Caution: Public restrooms are at Elwell State Park only!) Bikes can be rented at the Valley Bicycle Trailside Store, 8 Railroad Street, Hadley; (413) 584–4466 or (800) 831–5437. For an off-trail bite, try the Ice Cream Pedaler, 8 Railroad Street, Hadley; (413) 584–2223, for sandwiches and desserts. For a trail map, write DEM, 136 Damon Street, Northampton 01060, Attention: Conn. River Greenway State Park, or contact them at (413) 586–8706 or www.hadleyonline.com/railtrail. **Free.**

Other Things to See and Do

Hadley Farm Museum, 147 Russell Street (Route 9), Hadley; (413) 584–3120; www.hadleyonline.com/farmmuseum/main .htm. Open mid-May through mid-October. Donations accepted. Colonial farm tools in a restored barn.

Where to Stay

Howard Johnson, 401 Russell Street, Hadley; (413) 586–0114 or (800) 654–2000; www.hojo.com. One hundred rooms in central location on Route 9; outdoor pool. $–$$$

Norwottuck Inn, Route 9, Hadley; (413) 587–9866 or (877) 667–9688; www.norwot tuckinn.com. Great location near the Five College Area of the Pioneer Valley and next to the Norwottuck Rail Trail. Amenities include outdoor pool, bike rentals, and complimentary breakfast. $–$$

Northampton

Northampton, an artsy town, is a cultural mecca for this region, influenced by Smith College.

Smith College Museum of Art, the Lyman Plant House, and the Botanic Gardens (all ages)

The Museum of Art is located on Elm Street, Northampton; (413) 585–2760; www .smith.edu/artmuseum. Open September through May, Tuesday through Saturday 10:00 A.M. to 4:00 P.M., and Sunday noon to 4:00 P.M. Closed Monday and major holidays. Call for summer schedule. The Lyman Plant House is located within the campus arboretum and The Botanic Gardens are campuswide, Smith College Campus, Northampton; (413) 585–2740; www.smith.edu/garden. Open every day 8:30 A.M. to 4:00 P.M. year-round except for Thanksgiving and Christmas. All are free.

Art lovers will enjoy a visit to the Smith College Museum of Art, reopened in April 2003 after an almost three-year renovation, whose fine collection of more than 25,000 works of art are displayed in an outstanding building. The Botanic Gardens have systematic beds where plants are classified according to families, and the rock and knot gardens are quite beautiful. The greenhouses have annual flower spectaculars in March (spring bulbs) and November (chrysanthemums).

The Frank Newhall Look Memorial Park (all ages)

300 North Main Street, Route 9, Northampton; (413) 584–5457; www.lookpark.org. Open dawn to dusk. Parking is $2.00 on weekdays, $3.00 on weekends. Seasonal hours and activities; call for a schedule. Separate fees for pedalboats, tennis courts, picnic sites, train rides, minigolf, and bumper boats.

Look Memorial Park is a 150-acre conservation area with many water activities available—swimming (there is a 5,000-square-foot waterspray park), bumper boats, and pedal boats—as well as a miniature railroad, an outdoor theater, where summer concerts are held on most weekends, a small zoo, minigolf, tennis courts, playgrounds, walking paths, and lots of picnic tables and grills. Other activities include cross-country skiing, snowshoeing, biking, and hiking.

Other Things to See and Do

Beyond Words Bookstore, 189 Main Street, Northampton; (413) 586–6304; www.beyondwordsbookshop.com. Excellent children's section.

Pioneer Valley Balloons, Old Ferry Road, Northampton Airport, Northampton; (413) 584–7980; www.pioneervalley balloons.com. Open all year. Sunrise or sunset rides, with complimentary champagne for adults. Serving pastries in the morning and European-style picnics in the afternoon.

Where to Eat

Ben and Bill's Chocolate Emporium, 141 Main Street, Northampton; (413) 584–5695. Indulge in handmade chocolate treats made right on the premises, ice cream, and hot drinks. $

Spoleto, 50 Main Street, Northampton; (413) 586–6313; www.fundining.com. Open for dinner and Sunday brunch. Voted Best in the Valley, specializing in Italian cuisine. Will do half portions or pastas for kids. $$–$$$

Who's Next?! Deli, 159 Main Street, Northampton; (413) 584–4458. New York–style deli featuring homemade desserts and soups, sandwiches, salads, and some hot entrees, too. $

Where to Stay

Hotel Northampton and Historic Wiggins Tavern, 36 King Street, Northampton; (413) 584–3100 or (800) 547–3529; www.hotelnorthampton.com. Lovely ninety-nine-room hotel, great cafe and dining room, centrally located. $$–$$$$

South Hadley

A charming, quieter college town very proud of the Mount Holyoke campus, South Hadley is between Northampton and Springfield.

Other Things to See and Do

Nash Dinosaur Tracks, off Route 116, South Hadley; (413) 467–9566. Open April through Thanksgiving. Admission: $2.00 for adults, $1.00 for kids. Dinosaur tracks.

Joseph Skinner Museum, 35 Woodbridge Street, South Hadley; (413) 538–7127 or (413) 538–2085. Musical instruments, minerals, glassware, and regional furnishings. Open May through October.

Holyoke

Like Lowell, Holyoke is a mill city, planned around the canals built in the mid-nineteenth century as the power source for the Holyoke Water Power Company. The 150-year-old system still generates hydroelectric power and supplies process water to manufacturing companies that occupy the old mill buildings.

Holyoke Heritage State Park (all ages)

21 Appleton Street, Holyoke; (413) 534–1723; www.massparks.org. The visitor center can be contacted at (413) 534–1723. Open Tuesday through Sunday 10:00 A.M. to 4:00 P.M. The visitor center features historical exhibits on the history of Holyoke and revolving contemporary exhibits showcasing local artists. There are loads of children's programming throughout the year focusing on environmental education and activities.

Holyoke Heritage State Park is an eight-acre complex of enormous mill buildings and outdoor spaces, with exhibits about the city's growth. There are two main attractions for families here: the Holyoke Merry-Go-Round and the Children's Museum.

- **Children's Museum (age 8 and under);** 444 Dwight Street, Holyoke; (413) 536–KIDS. Open Tuesday through Saturday 9:30 A.M. to 4:30 P.M., Sunday noon to 5:00 P.M. Admission: $4.00 per person. The Children's Museum emphasizes family participation in educational games and interactive exhibits. Make your own paper or try your hand at one of the mock-ups of local businesses, including a "working" TV station.

- **Holyoke Merry-Go-Round;** (413) 538–9838. Open weekends noon to 4:00 P.M. from September through May and daily from 11:00 A.M. to 4:30 P.M. in summer and during Holyoke School vacations. Price: $1.00 per ride. The antique merry-go-round was built in 1929 in Philadelphia. Housed in a colorful new building near the entrance to the park, the large carousel has forty-eight horses and two chariots, all carved by hand, plus a loud, cheerful band organ.

The Holyoke **Dam**

Located on Route 116, left at the fishway sign just before the South Hadley Falls Bridge, the Holyoke Dam has a viewing window and observation platform for watching more than a million migrating shad and salmon in early May and June. Call (413) 659–3714 or (413) 659–4462 for more information.

Other Things to See and Do

Mt. Tom State Reservation, off Route 5, Holyoke; (413) 534–1186; www.mass parks.org. Hiking, natural history museum, wildlife watchtower, snowshoeing and cross-country skiing trails.

Volleyball Hall of Fame, 444 Dwight Street (at Heritage State Park), Holyoke; (413) 536–0926; www.volleyhall.org. A look at this sport's history.

Wistariahurst Museum, 238 Cabot Street, Holyoke; (413) 322–5660; www.holyoke.org/wistariahurst.htm.

Mansion of silk manufacturer William Skinner. *TIP:* Abuts questionable section of town.

Where to Eat and Stay

Yankee Pedlar Inn, 1866 Northampton Street (Route 5), Holyoke; (413) 532–9494; www.yankeepedlarinn.com. Twenty-eight-room Victorian-style inn known for its fine food and decor. $–$$

Greater Springfield

Dr. James Naismith invented basketball here when he made a game of throwing a soccer ball into a peach basket at Springfield College in 1891. Homeboy Theodor Seuss Geisel (alias Dr. Seuss) has a national memorial in tribute to his work at the Quadrangle. The Naismith Basketball Hall of Fame is a family favorite, as well as the museums of the Quadrangle. Springfield is the largest city in the Greater Springfield region, as well as in the entire Pioneer Valley. It is also considered the gateway to western Massachusetts and Connecticut. Six Flags in Agawam is an enormous amusement park, New England's largest.

Naismith Basketball Hall of Fame (all ages)

1000 West Columbus Avenue, Springfield; (413) 781–6500 or (877) 4–HOOPLA; www .hoophall.com. Open daily, 10:00 A.M. to 6:00 P.M. with extended hours on Friday and Saturday. Closed Thanksgiving, Christmas, and Easter Sunday. Admission: $15.99 for adults, $10.99 for children 5 to 15; free for children under 5 accompanied by a parent. Directions: Exit 4 off the Massachusetts Turnpike to Route 91S. Take exit 7, then follow the signs.

The Naismith Basketball Hall of Fame is an entertainment center/museum that will be interesting to any visitor who's ever had even a remote connection to the game. A state-of-the-art museum doubling its size opened in September 2002. The exterior architecture of the museum is a sphere with a tower beside it. On top of the tower is a perpetually lit orange ball that serves as a beacon to beckon and attract those traveling down Interstate 91 to visit. The main showpiece of the new museum is the

Center Court, which features a full-size basketball court and scoreboard visible from balconies on each of the museum's three levels. All of your favorite Hall of Famers are on display, timelined with world history and great moments in basketball. The second floor features a coach's gallery honoring high school, college, national, and international teams. The Game Gallery is very interactive and showcases the game and the evolution of the equipment from its earliest humble beginnings to the present. The Media Gallery will allow you to relive broadcasts, have a photo of you e-mailed, or act out an interview and be taped. Challenge your basketball knowledge. Shoot hoops of various shapes, sizes, and heights. Play Jason Kidd or Cheryl Swoopes in the Virtual Reality game. Or compare your height and arm span to those of the game's biggest players. Legends of the game will be brought in to lecture and conduct clinics. The basketball theme carries over to the McDonald's and the gift shops. Enshrinement into the Basketball Hall of Fame in October.

The Springfield Museums at the Quadrangle and the Dr. Seuss National Memorial Sculpture Garden

220 State Street, corner of State and Chestnut Streets, Springfield; (413) 263–6800; www.catinthehat.org or www.quadrangle.org. Open year-round, Wednesday through Friday noon to 4:00 P.M., Saturday and Sunday 11:00 A.M. to 4:00 P.M. Admission (includes entry to all four museums): $7.00 for adults, $3.00 for children 6 to 19; free for children under 6. Museum cafe, three museum shops, and Sunday family programs.

Winner of the Commonwealth Award in 1999, the Springfield Museums at the Quadrangle, a complex that incorporates four museums and the main branch of the Springfield City Library, is a nice place to spend time. Parking is free at the museums' and library's lots on State Street and Edwards Street. The Dr. Seuss National Memorial Sculpture Garden includes five bronze sculptures, which are a tribute to Theodor Geisel, author of the Dr. Seuss books. Museums at the Quadrangle include:

- Connecticut Valley Historical Museum—more than 365 years of Pioneer Valley and Springfield history

- George Walter Vincent Smith Art Museum—Middle Eastern rugs, largest collection of Chinese cloisonné in the West, Shinto shrine, and nineteenth-century American paintings

- Springfield Museum of Fine Arts—European and American paintings, sculpture, and paper mediums

- Springfield Science Museum—The African Hall focuses on the diverse wildlife of the African continent, and Dinosaur Hall (the kids' favorite) includes a full-size replica of a towering tyrannosaur. Other attractions include a hands-on Exploration Center, an aquarium, an observatory, an antique airplane, and a planetarium

Marcia's
TopAnnualEvents
in the Pioneer Valley

- **Basketball Hall of Fame High School Invitational,** January, Springfield College, Springfield; (413) 781–6500; www.hoophall.com

- **Dr. Seuss Birthday,** early March, the Quadrangle, Springfield; (413) 263–6800; www.quadrangle.org

- **Holyoke St. Patrick's Day Parade,** mid-March, downtown Holyoke; (413) 533–1700

- **Spring Bulb Show,** March, Smith College Lyman Conservatory, Northampton; (413) 585–2740; www.smith.edu/artmuseum

- **Massachusetts International Festival of the Arts,** late April, Amherst, Northampton, Holyoke, and Springfield; (800) 224–MIFA; www.mifafestival.org

- **Tour De Sol,** mid-May, Pittsfield and Greenfield; (413) 774–6051; www.nesea.org

- **Spawning migrations,** May/June, Holyoke Dam and Turners Falls; (413) 659–3714; www.nu.com/northfield/

- **Shelburne Falls Riverfest,** early June, Shelburne Falls; (413) 625–2544; www.shelburnefalls.com

- **Taste of Springfield,** mid-June, Court Street, Springfield; (413) 733–3800; www.thespiritofspringfield.org

- **Kidsfest,** late June, Six Flags of New England, Agawam; (413) 786–9300; www.sixflags.com/newengland

- **Green River Music and Up-Country Hot-Air Balloon Fair,** July, Greenfield; (413) 773–5463; www.greenriverfestival.com

- **Turn-of-the-Century Ice Cream Social,** July, Deerfield; (413) 774–7476; www.old-deerfield.org

- **Annual Glasgow Lands Scottish Festival,** mid-July, Look Park, Northampton; (413) 862–8095

- **Teddy Bear Rally,** August, Amherst Town Common; (413) 256–8983

- **The Big E (Eastern States Exposition),** September, West Springfield; (413) 737–2443; www.thebige.com

- **Old Deerfield Craft Fair,** mid-September, Deerfield; (413) 774–7476; www.deerfield-craft.org

- **Volleyball Hall of Fame Enshrinement,** October, Springfield; (413) 536–0926 or (413) 787–1540; www.volleyhall.org

- **Annual Flashlight Safari,** mid-October, The Zoo in Forest Park; (413) 733–2251; www.forestparkzoo.com

- **Boo at the Zoo,** end of October, The Zoo in Forest Park; Springfield; (413) 733–2251; www.forestparkzoo.com

- **Basketball Hall of Fame Enshrinement,** fall, Springfield; (413) 781–6500; www.hoophall.com

- **Chrysanthemum Show,** early November, Smith College, Lyman Conservatory, Northampton; (413) 585–2740; www.smith.edu/artmuseum

- **November Peace Week,** mid-November, Holyoke Heritage Visitor Center, Holyoke; (413) 534–1723

- **Spirit of the Holiday,** late November to beginning of January, Look Park, Northampton; (413) 584–5457; www.lookpark.org

- **Bright Nights,** December, Forest Park, Springfield; (413) 733–2251; www.springfieldparks.com

Forest Park (all ages)

Route 83, off Route 21/Sumner Street, Springfield; (413) 733–2251 (zoo) or (413) 787–6440 (park); www.forestparkzoo.com. Open daily April 15 to November 14. Open weekends, holidays, and school vacations November 15 through April 14. Closed Thanksgiving, Christmas, and January. Admission: $4.50 for adults, $3.50 ages 5 to 12, $2.00 up to age 4, train rides $2.50. $1.00 for the animal food.

Forest Park is a large city park with a small zoo, nature trails, picnic spots, swimming pools, and other recreational activities. During the December holidays the park has several drive-through lighting displays with various themes, such as the North Pole and Barney's Victorian Village (admission is $10 per car).

Six Flags New England (all ages)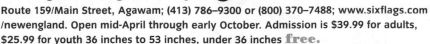

Route 159/Main Street, Agawam; (413) 786–9300 or (800) 370–7488; www.sixflags.com /newengland. Open mid-April through early October. Admission is $39.99 for adults, $25.99 for youth 36 inches to 53 inches, under 36 inches free.

Six Flags of New England has spared no expense ($150 million in renovations) to give you a "high." Additions include a new children's area, the Looney Tune Movietown, a new DC Comic area, a children's interactive area, and the Batman Thrill Spectacular. Home to the number-one roller coaster on the planet, Superman, Ride of Steel (a distinction bestowed by *Park World Magazine*), Six Flags is also home to the largest water park in New England (in 2003 the water park doubled in size). With a hundred rides, shows, and attractions spread over 235 acres, Six Flags can be crowded on summer weekends, but the tumult can add to the experience. There are three water rides in the theme park, eight roller coasters (three are inverted), a Ferris wheel, two Kiddieland areas, and a nice old merry-go-round on the grounds. Favorite rides for those with nerve and verve are the Scream (three Scream towers; starts on bottom, shoots you up prior to your twenty-story free-fall drop) and Shipwreck Falls (a twenty-passenger boat climbing a gradual 100-foot grade, with a steep plunge from the top). There are daily performances. The Hurricane Harbor Waterpark has seven complexes with water slides, two lazy rivers, and two wave pools. Note that one price admits you to both Six Flags of New England and Hurricane Harbor Waterpark (the water park is within the theme park). Check the Web site for concerts, special events, and festivals.

Other Things to See and Do

Amelia Park and Ice Arena, 21 South Broad Street, Westfield; (413) 568–2503; www.ameliapark.org. Indoor ice arena, outdoor in-line skating. Garden with summertime concerts and outdoor movies.

Indian Motorcycle Museum and Hall of Fame, 33 Hendee Street, Springfield; (413) 737–2624. Open seven days a week. Collection of toys, motorcycles, and related memorabilia.

Riverfront Park and Tinkerbell Cruises, foot of State Street, Springfield; (413) 787–6440 (park) and (413) 781–3320 (cruise line); www.peterpanbus.com/river bus/. Cruises May through October. Seven-acre park with playground.

Springfield Armory National Historic Site, 1 Armory Square, Springfield; (413) 734–8551; www.nps.gov/spar. First National Armory, site chosen by General Washington. Museum features huge firearm collection, interactive exhibits, introductory film, and bookstore.

Springfield Civic Center, 1277 Main Street, Springfield; (413) 787–6600 or (800) 639–8602; www.mccahome.com. Sports and entertainment venue.

Springfield Falcons, Springfield Civic Center, 1277 Main Street, Springfield; (413) 739–3344 or (413) 787–6600 for tickets; www.falconsahl.com. Price: $14.00 for adults, $9.00 for children 18 and under. American Hockey League team, an affiliate of the NHL Phoenix Coyotes.

Storrowton Village Museum, Eastern States Exposition, 1305 Memorial Avenue, West Springfield; (413) 205–5051 or www.thebige.com. Re-created nineteenth-century New England village.

***Titanic* Historical Society,** 208 Main Street, Indian Orchard; (413) 543 4770; www.titanichistoricalsociety.org. Artifacts and displays from the *Titanic* and its survivors. Fee for nonmembers $4.00; under 6 **free.**

Whip City Speedway, Airport Industrial Park Road, Westfield; (413) 562–8092; www.whipcityspeedway.com. Fast car racing.

Where to Eat

Gus and Paul's, Tower Square, 1500 Main Street, Springfield; (413) 781–2253; www.gusandpauls.com. Deli and bakery in a family setting. $

Where to Stay

Springfield Marriott Hotel, Boland Way and Columbus Avenue, Springfield; (413) 781–7111 or (800) 228–9290. Indoor pool and health club, 265 rooms, downtown location. $$–$$$

Major Agricultural Fairs in the
Pioneer Valley (www.mafa.org)

- **Blandford Fair,** early September, North Street, Blandford; (413) 848–2888; www.theblandfordfair.com
- **Cummington Fair,** late August, Fairgrounds Road, Cummington; (413) 238–7724
- **Eastern States Exposition,** mid-September, 1305 Memorial Avenue, West Springfield; (413) 737–2443; www.thebige.com
- **Franklin County Fair,** early September, Wisdom Way, Greenfield; (413) 774–4282; www.fcas.com
- **Heath Fair,** mid-August, Heath; (413) 337–4733 or (413) 337–5716
- **Littleville Fair,** early August, Kinne Brook Road, Chester; (413) 789–1243
- **Middlefield Fair,** mid-August, 7 Bell Road, Middlefield; (413) 623–6423
- **Three-County Fair,** late August, Fair Street, Northampton; (413) 584–2237; www.3countyfair.com
- **Westfield Fair,** mid-August, Russellville Road, Westfield; (413) 562–4640

Oh What a **Fun Thing to Do!**

For me—and for you—
to read all of Dr. Seuss's stories
at the Springfield Quadrangle in all their glory
while looking at bronze sculptures of Theodor Geisel.
It's more fun—believe me—than riding on a carousel!
Green Eggs and Ham, The Cat in the Hat, can only be beat
by *And to Think That I Saw It on Mulberry Street.*

Central Massachusetts

Rolling hills run through most of this peaceful area, a region that Boston families treasure as a nearby source of seasonal rural activities. In spring, pastures are full of young animals kicking up their heels. Clear lakes and large parks welcome picnickers on summer afternoons. The city of Worcester has several good family-oriented museums. Orchards provide hours of fun for enthusiastic apple-pickers from late August through late October. Quiet country roads lead to the hiking and cross-country skiing trails that crisscross the region. The **Central Massachusetts Tourism Council,** 306 Main Street, Worcester 01608 (800–231–7557; www .worcester.org), is a helpful resource. South of Worcester, Old Sturbridge Village is an early-nineteenth-century "village" that was constructed in 1946. Unpaved roads, costumed interpreters, and working artisans give kids a flavor of what it might have been like to visit a typical New England village during the first fifty years of the republic.

Marcia's
TopPicks in Central Massachusetts

1. Old Sturbridge Village, Sturbridge

2. Quabbin Reservoir and Park, Ware

3. Museum of the New England Landscape, Harvard

4. Worcester museums (Worcester Art Museum, Ecotarium, and Higgins Armory)

5. Farm fun on the Johnny Appleseed Trail

6. Southwick's Animal Farm, Mendon

CENTRAL MASSACHUSETTS

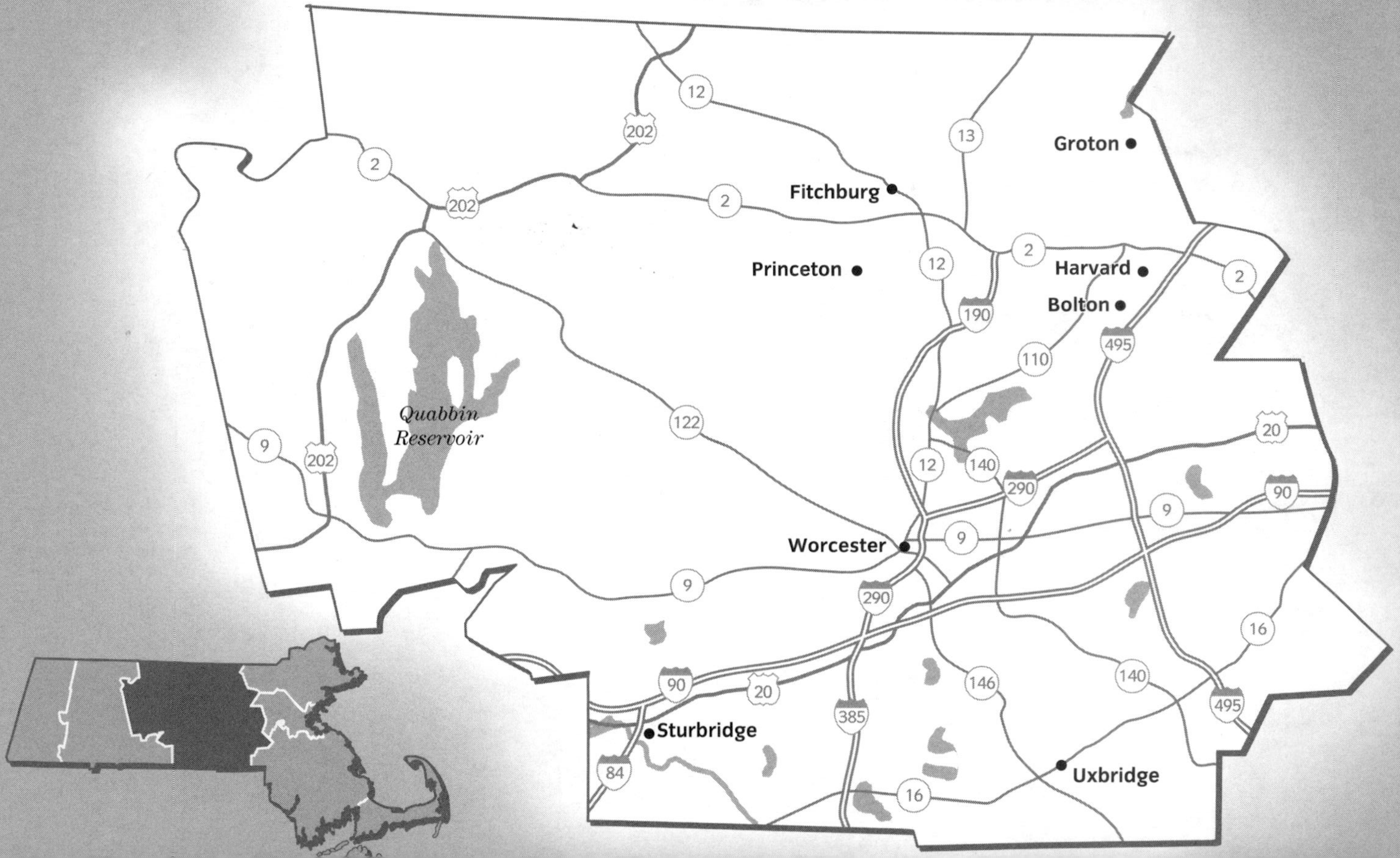

Groton
Fitchburg
Princeton
Harvard
Bolton
Quabbin Reservoir
Worcester
Sturbridge
Uxbridge
2
12
13
202
9
122
190
110
495
20
140
290
90
16
146
385
84

The Nashoba Valley and the Johnny Appleseed Trail

A hilly region that's served Bostonians as an easy escape for well over a century, the Nashoba Valley hasn't changed much since the Alcott family set up a commune in Harvard with other transcendentalists in 1843. The **Johnny Appleseed Visitor Center,** Route 2 West, Lancaster 01523 (978–534–2302; www.appleseed.org), and the **North Central Massachusetts Chamber of Commerce,** 110 Erdman Way, Leominster 01453 (978–840–4300; www.northcentralmass.com), offer maps and brochures on area sights and attractions.

Harvard, Bolton, and Fitchburg

Nashoba Valley Winery and Orchards (all ages)

100 Wattaquadoc Hill Road, Bolton; (978) 779–5521; www.NashobaWinery.com. Open year-round 10:00 A.M. to 5:00 P.M.; twenty-minute tours are given Saturday and Sunday, 11:00 A.M. to 5:00 P.M. (last tour at 4:00 P.M.). Tours are $3.00 for adults, **free** for children under 21. Great gift shop full of gourmet specialties and premium Nashoba wine!

Pick berries during the summer and early fall, apples throughout the fall (named the best place to pick apples by the *Boston Parents' Paper*), and be sure to bring a picnic. In the winter it's a nice place to cross-country ski. Regardless of the season, you can take a tour of the winery, winner of national and international wine competitions. A restaurant on the premises is open Tuesday through Saturday for lunch, Wednesday through Saturday evening for dinner, and Sunday for brunch. An annual Harvest Festival is held the second Saturday in September. Other festivals are held throughout the year. Call for the schedule.

Museum of the New England Landscape (all ages)

102 Prospect Hill Road, Harvard; (978) 456–3924; www.fruitlands.org. Open daily from mid-May through October 31, 11:00 A.M. to 4:00 P.M. Monday through Friday, 11:00 A.M. to 5:00 P.M. weekends and holidays. Guided tours are at 3:15 P.M. daily. Admission: $10.00 for adults, $2.00 for children age 4 through 17. The grounds are open to museum ticket holders for picnics.

Formerly the Fruitlands Museum and Farmhouse, the 200-acre property surrounding the four museums provides stunning views of the Nashua River Valley and, in the far distance, of mountains in southern New Hampshire. The Fruitlands Farmhouse Museum is dedicated to the memory of the transcendentalists, many of whom spent seven months of 1843 in the farmhouse at the bottom of the hill. The transcendentalists believed that God exists in humans and nature alike. Their beliefs led them to a distinct "back-to-nature" lifestyle, very unusual during their time. They tried living in a communal building on a farm where they could be as self-sufficient as possible.

Among them were the Alcott family (Louisa, her three sisters, and her parents). The group gave its communal home the hopeful name of Fruitlands in the expectation that its orchards would produce an abundance of fruit. Unfortunately, the site wasn't optimal, and the trees didn't provide as much sustenance as the group had hoped. For this reason and others, its members left Harvard and went back to Concord.

In 1910 Clara Endicott Sears purchased the property, which had become run-down. She restored the farmhouse and opened it as a museum in honor of the Alcotts and their friends Emerson, Thoreau, and Margaret Fuller. The building houses mementos of the group.

Also on the property are the Shaker Museum, the Picture Gallery, and the Indian Museum. The Shaker Museum is dedicated to the Shaker towns of Harvard (which donated journals and an original Shaker office building) and Shirley. Exhibits depict the many industries of the Shaker communities (look for the Sisters' Work Room full of looms and spinning wheels) and illustrate how business was conducted between the Shakers and the outside world. The Picture Gallery houses portraits by primitive folk artists and landscape paintings, with a sizable collection of paintings from the Hudson River School of painters. The Indian Museum holds Thoreau's rock and mineral collection and interesting artifacts of the Native Americans who once lived in the area.

Nature trails (used for cross-country skiing in the winter), two archaeological sites depicting different periods of New England history, the Museum Store, and the Tea Room round out your day at the museum. Watch for the summer concert series and the Harvest Festival in September.

TIP: A shuttle bus is available upon request for help up the hill. The terrain can be uneven, so wear walking shoes. Hats are recommended for protection from the elements.

Nashua River Rail Trail (all ages)

Parking areas to access the trail can be found in Ayer (sixty spaces, access to the Boston and Fitchburg commuter rail, and nonflush public toilets), Groton (twelve spaces), or Dunstable (ten spaces). For more information visit www.state.ma.us/dem /parks/nash.htm on the Web or call (978) 597–8802. Free.

The 10-foot-wide trail travels 11 miles through four towns (Ayer, Groton, Pepperell, and Dunstable) along a defunct railroad bed (thus the name rail trail!). It's very picturesque for bikers and hikers, and a slice of the real New England can be found here, particularly on a sunny crisp autumn day. Directions to the trailheads:

Ayer: Take Route 2 to exit 38B, then take Route 111 north to the Ayer Rotary. Take Route 2A off the rotary and follow to Ayer Center. Turn right after Ayer Center, and take the first right onto Groton Street to the parking area on the right.

Groton: Take 495 to exit 31, then Route 119 west for 7 miles to Groton Center. Take a left at Station Avenue to the parking lot beside the trail.

Dunstable: Take Route 3 to exit 35, then Route 113 west through Dunstable Center. Take a right onto Hollis Street to the New Hampshire line. Parking is on the left.

Tour de Fitchburg

Fitchburg's **Longsjo Classic Bicycle Race**—a tribute to former Olympian cyclist Arthur Longsjo—is a four-day race held in late June. It's one of the premier amateur bicycle races, attracting competitors from around the world. For more information, call (978) 534–9966, check out the Web site at www.longsjo.com, or call (978) 840–4300.

Drawbridge Puppet Theater (ages 10 and under)
181 Main Street, Fitchburg; (978) 342–2552 or (800) 401–3694; www.drawbridge puppets.com.

Each marionette show has original songs, skits, and special effects and ends with a demonstration of the art of "mastering the strings." Special performances and traveling puppet and marionette shows for any occasion.

Fitchburg Art Museum (ages 8 and up)
185 Elm Street, Fitchburg; (978) 345–4207; www.fitchburgartmuseum.org. Open Tuesday through Sunday noon to 4:00 P.M., closed Monday and major holidays. Admission: $5.00 for adults, $3.00 for seniors; **free** for children and students.

The focus is on American and European art and local contemporary New England artists. There's also a minor collection of classical art and antiquities from Greece, Rome, Asia, Africa, and South America. Big hits are the permanent Egyptian exhibit and the twelve galleries of decorative arts.

The Rat Pack

The **River Rat Race** (mid-April) from Athol to Orange started as a bet in 1963 among friends as to whether or not the Millers River was navigable for canoeists (dams and rapids were problems). The bet escalated into a 6-mile race, and today the best canoeists in North America take the challenge to be crowned the King River Rat. The affair starts with a pancake breakfast, River Rat Parade, and Duck Race, leading to the River Rat Race, with a field of more than 280 canoeists. For more information contact the **North Quabbin/Athol/Orange Chamber of Commerce,** 521 Main Street, Athol 01331; (978) 249–3849; www.northquabbinchamber.com.

Farm Fun (www.mass.gov/massgrown)

Information on every farm in the state, fruit and vegetable seasons, and farmers market locations and dates.

- **Alta Vista Bison Farm,** 80 Hillside Road, Rutland; (508) 886–4365. Bison herd, tours, picnicking.

- **Arrowhead Acres,** 92 Aldrich Street, Uxbridge; (508) 278–5017; www.arrowheadacres.com. Petting farm, pumpkins, hayrides, and swimming pool.

- **Berlin Orchards,** 200 Central Street, Berlin; (978) 838–2400; www .berlinorchards.com. Apples, hayrides, farm animals, ice cream, picnicking, cider press, farm tours, beehive observation window, and Family Festivals. Restaurant serving breakfast and lunch. Open year-round.

- **Bolton Spring Farm,** 149 Main Street, Bolton; (978) 779–2898; www .boltonorchards.com. Apples and pumpkins, hayrides, and helicopter rides.

- **Breezy Gardens,** 1872 West Main Street, Leicester; (508) 892–3374. Springtime through autumn tours of vegetable and berry fields, greenhouses, and gardens. Llama hayrides in the fall.

- **Brookfield Orchards,** 12 Lincoln Road, North Brookfield; (508) 867–6858; www.farmstands.com. Apples, cross-country skiing, farm tours, harvest festivals, country store, playground.

- **A Clear View Farm,** 4 Kendall Road, Sterling; (978) 422–6442; www .clearviewfarmstand.com. Home of the true story of "Mary Had a Little Lamb." Pick-your-own apples, hayrides, and school groups.

- **Clover Hill,** 1839 Lower Road, Hardwick; (413) 477–0316. Petting farm, hayrides, sleigh rides, llamas, emus. Locally produced meat, bacon, and lamb plus pick-your-own pumpkins, old-fashioned country store, and ice-cream stand.

- **The Country Apple at Marshall Farm,** 340 Marshall Road, Fitchburg; (978) 343–6255; www.marshallfarm.com. Pick your own apples and pumpkins. Fire engines and hayrides and weekly events.

- **Davis Farmland and Megamaze,** 145 Redstone Hill, Sterling; (978) 422–6666; www.davisfarmland.com. Children's farm and museum, petting farm, play park, largest collection of endangered livestock in United States. The latest attraction is a huge corn maze (megamaze hot line: 978–422–8888). Fun for all!

- **Fay Mountain Farm,** 12 Cemetery Road, Charlton; (508) 248–0241. Apples, peaches, pears, blueberries, raspberries, cider mill tours, hayrides, picnic area, and pond.

- **George Hill Orchard,** George Hill Road, Lancaster; (978) 365–4331 or (800) 699–4331; www.yourfavoritefarm.com. Pick-your-own farm, home of Apple Tree Theatre. Seasonal hay- and pony rides, farm animal petting area.

- **Great Brook Trout Farm,** 120 Meadow Road, Bolton; (978) 779–0077 or (978) 779–6899. Fee fishing for trout, bass, perch, and sunfish.

- **Nourse Farm,** 70 Norse Street, Westboro; (508) 366–2644. Tours, pony rides, hayrides, farm animals, pies, ice cream, jams and jellies, two-acre maze.

- **Overlook Farm,** 216 Wachusett Street, Rutland; (508) 886–2221; www.heifer.org. Heifer Project International, hay and sleigh rides, hiking, picnicking. Educates the public about world hunger and poverty and solutions through animal agriculture. Ships animals to developing nations.

- **Red Apple Farm,** 455 Highland Avenue, Phillipston; (978) 249–6763 or (800) 628–4851; www.redapplefarm.com. Scenic views and trails, apples, blueberries, raspberries, pumpkins, picnicking, farm animals, hayrides, mazes, bonfires, and barbeque and picnic area. See the apple tree with 108 varieties of apples on one tree!

- **Sleighbell Christmas Tree Farm and Gift Barn,** 130 Whittins Road, Sutton; (508) 234–6953; www.sleighbelltreefarm.com. Choose-and-cut Christmas tree farm. Holiday gifts, wreaths, centerpieces, kissing balls, and ornaments. Seasonal hayrides, picnicking, and ducks.

- **Smith Country Cheese,** 20 Otter Road, Winchendon; (978) 939–5738. Award-winning Gouda and cheddar cheese from milk produced by their own dairy herd. Children's tour of cheese factory.

- **Tougas Family Farm,** 246 Ball Street, Northboro; (508) 393–6470; www.tougasfarm.com. Pick-your-own fruits, petting zoo, hay- and wagon rides, cider pressing, farm tours, and ice-cream stand.

- **Zukas Homestead Farm and B&B,** 89 Smithville Road, Spencer; (508) 885–5320; www.zukas.com. Heifers, miniature horses, small animals, hiking, sledding, cross-country skiing, B&B.

Harnessing the Huskies—
Dog Sledding Tours

- **Mt. Lynx Outdoor Adventures,** P.O. Box 902, Ashburnham 01430; (978) 827–5971
- **Northern Illusion,** 501 Ashby West Road, Fitchburg; (978) 345–1912

Wachusett Mountain Ski Area (all ages)

499 Mountain Road, Princeton; (978) 464–2300; www.wachusett.com. Skiing from late November to early April. Open daily for day and night skiing. Call for the schedule and the rates. $$$–$$$$.

Full snowmaking coverage makes this a fun family ski mountain. Features day and night skiing, five lifts (including the only high-speed detachable quad in the state), and twenty trails. During the off-season you can hike and picnic here, or take the auto road to reach the summit, Wachusett Mountain State Reservation.

Wachusett Mountain Ski Area is open in the fall for festivals and outings. (Extremely popular is the annual Kidsfest held in late September.)

Wachusett Mountain State Reservation (all ages)

Mountain Road, Princeton; (978) 464–2987; www.state.ma.us/dem/parks/wach.htm. Open seasonally from dawn to dusk. Visitor center.

Take the auto road to the highest point in Massachusetts east of the Berkshires, with spectacular views of Boston, the Western Massachusetts Berkshires, and the New Hampshire mountains, hawk migrations, and the autumn foliage spectacle. Within the 3,000-acre reservation there are 17 miles of hiking trails used in the winter for cross-country skiing. *WARNING:* Hunting is allowed at various times during the year. Check with the mountain before you hike.

Other Things
to See and Do

Central Mass Paddle Sports, Lake Dennison Recreation Area, Route 202, Paxton; (508) 754–2393; www.cmpaddlesports .com. Discover Central Mass boatways by paddle boats, canoes, and kayaks for rent. Shuttle service from several area hotels to vaious boating points is available. Also rents pedal boats at Dunn Pond State Park, Route 101, Gardner.

Lancaster Golf Center, 438 Old Union Turnpike (exit 34 off Route 2), Lancaster; (978) 537–8922; www.lancastergolfcenter .com. Miniature golf, eighteen-hole putting course, nine batting cages, and bank shot basketball (hoopsters proceed through eighteen stations, scoring points by making bank shots off a wild assortment of angled, curved, and unconventionally configured backboards).

Nashoba Paddler Rentals, Groton; (978) 448–8699; www.nashobapaddler.com. Open May 1 through November. Hourly and daily rentals.

National Plastics Center and Hall of Fame Museum, 210 Lancaster Street, Leominster; (978) 537–9529; www.plastics museum.com. Open Wednesday through Saturday 11:00 A.M. to 4:00 P.M. Discovery Corner; medical and environmental displays.

Top Fun Aviation Toy Museum, 22 Murdock Avenue, Winchendon; (978) 297–4337; www.topfunaviation.com. Open weekends year-round. More than 1,000 toy airplanes, games, and puzzles from 1828 to the present. Fine tin toys from Germany, Japan, Hungary, and the United States. On-the-wall-airport.

Wallace Civic Center and Planetarium, 1000 John Fitch Highway, Fitchburg; (978) 345–7593. Planetarium theater, two ice rinks, and concerts.

Where to Eat

Boardwalk Restaurant, 28 Center Street, Gardner; (978) 632–4888. Eclectic menu from the old standbys to Asian stir-fry and fajitas. All-inclusive kids' menu. $–$$

Cornerstones's, 616 Central Street, Leominster; (978) 537–1991. From burgers to pasta, poultry to seafood and meat. Seven vegetarian entrees and a kids' menu. $–$$$

The 1761 Old Mill, Route 2A East, Westminster; (978) 874–5941. Former sawmill. Standard New England fare—hearty, filling, and delicious. Children's menu. $–$$$

Slattery's Restaurant, 106 Lunenburg Street, Fitchburg; (978) 342–8880; www.slatterysrestaurant.com. Charming restaurant, extensive menu with kid specialties. $–$$

Twin Oak Restaurant, 228 Leominster Road, Sterling; (978) 422–6100. Full children's menu, wide range of choices, can combine with sides and salads for an extra fee. $–$$$

Where to Stay

Bona Vista Farm Bed and Breakfast, 10 Cummings Road, Winchendon; (978) 297–0460. Relax in the hot tub, have a Reiki session, or join in with the farm chores. Organic farm, 1780s antique on eighty acres. French, Spanish, and Russian spoken. Children welcome. Complimentary full breakfast. $$

Chocksett Inn, 59 Laurel Wood Road, Sterling; (978) 422–3355; www.Chocksett Inn.com. Junction of I–90 and Route 12. Country inn, very colonial. Guest laundry, gym, pub, library with fireplace. Full continental breakfast. $$

Friendly Crossways, 247 Littleton County Road, Harvard; (978) 456–9386 or (978) 456–3649; www.friendlycrossways.com. The first youth hostel in the United States, this stayover offers family rooms, dorm rooms, or private rooms. Rent linens or bring your own; kitchen privileges. $

Wachusett Village Inn, 9 Village Inn Road, Westminster; (978) 874–2000 or (800) 342–1905; www.wachusett.com. Full recreation center with indoor pool and hot tubs; restaurant with children's menu. The Inn's Club has tennis courts, hot tub, sauna, steam room, exercise room, and a tanning booth. Outdoor pool. $$–$$$

Greater Worcester and the Blackstone Valley

The second largest city in Massachusetts as well as New England, Worcester loses a lot of tourists to Boston, but it has managed to build a busy cultural life for itself with several good museums.

The **Worcester Tourism Bureau,** 33 Waldo Street, Worcester 01608 (508–755–7400; www.worcester.org), can provide you with information and maps.

The Blackstone Valley, designated a National Heritage Corridor, has several formerly company-owned mill towns representative of the Industrial Revolution. It's a picturesque area with recreational opportunities.

Worcester

John Woodman Higgins Armory (12 and under)

100 Barber Avenue, Worcester; (508) 853–6015; www.higgins.org. Open year-round Tuesday through Saturday 10:00 A.M. to 4:00 P.M., Sunday noon to 4:00 P.M.; closed most holidays. Admission: $7.75 for adults, $6.75 for children 6 to 16; free for children under 6. Free admission on Founder's Day (second weekend in January).

Try on a helmet—or perhaps a full suit of armor, if you're big enough—at this remarkable collection, the only museum in the Western Hemisphere dedicated to arms and armor. The orientation is fun for everyone; the interpreter selects a visitor to suit up, encouraging him or her to describe how uncomfortable and restrictive the armor actually is. The Quest Gallery has costumes for everyone: princesses and princes, queens and kings, and helmets for moms and dads. The museum runs interesting workshops for kids in which they learn to make gargoyles, books, masks, pennants, and shields; call for a schedule. Chess games are always going on in the Quest Gallery. New program called Saturdays at the Higgins features scavenger hunts, films, and demonstrations.

Events at the **Higgins Armory**

- **Higgins Faire,** first Saturday in May. Medieval festival with games, food, face painting, hair wraps, and period entertainment and demonstrations.

- **Falconry Demonstrations at the Higgins Armory Museum,** November.

- **Knight before Christmas,** second weekend in December. Decorate gingerbread ornaments and castles, listen to traditional holiday songs and entertainment.

Worcester Art Museum (all ages)

55 Salisbury Street, Worcester; (508) 799–4406; www.worcesterart.org. Open year-round, Wednesday, Friday, and Sunday 11:00 A.M. to 5:00 P.M., Thursday 11:00 A.M. to 8.00 P.M., Saturday 10:00 A.M. to 5:00 P.M.; closed major holidays. Admission: $8.00 for adults, $6.00 for seniors and students; free for children under 18. Free admission on Saturday from 10:00 A.M. to noon. Sunday museum tours at 2:00 P.M.

Nearly every period of art is featured in this small, excellent city museum. Highlights include a sixth-century floor mosaic in the central court area; a twelfth-century Romanesque house that was moved here, stone by stone, from France; an eleven-headed, ninth-century Japanese sculpture; and an extensive collection of pre-Columbian sculpture in various media, including gold and ceramic. The Museum Cafe serves light snacks and lunches. A garden cafe is open during the summer.

Ecotarium (all ages)

222 Harrington Way, Worcester; (508) 791–9211; www.ecotarium.org. Open year-round, Tuesday through Saturday 10:00 A.M. to 5:00 P.M., Sunday noon to 5:00 P.M., select Monday openings. Closed New Year's Day, Easter, Thanksgiving, and Christmas. Admission: $8.00 for adults, $6.00 for children 3 to 16. Free admission the first Sunday of each month. Planetarium programs $3.00 per person, Explorers Express Train $2.50 per person.

The focus at the Ecotarium (formerly the New England Science Center) is on the environment. An $18 million expansion and renovation plan created trails, an outdoor observation walkway, and renovations to the existing building's architecture. The Nature Trail traverses the property and rounds the two existing ponds, the Water Pavilion, and the Pier, giving access to more than sixty acres of lake and woods. A Tree Canopy Walkway allows you to study and inspect the leafline of the trees. The walkway, suspended approximately 20 feet above the ground, allows you to observe the habitat of birds, insects, and wildlife. There's a zoo with larger animals, such as polar bears and big cats. Inside the three-story building are several good interactive environmental exhibits, three large aquariums, and a planetarium show (the planetarium schedule is subject to change; call for a schedule). *TIP:* Start your visit at the Fuller Orientation Theater for an overview of the museum.

Blackstone River Valley National Heritage Corridor (all ages)

The visitor center at River Bend Farm, located in the Blackstone River and Canal Heritage State Park, 287 Oak Street in Uxbridge, has information on the corridor; (508) 278–7604; www.nps.gov/blac/.

The Blackstone River Valley National Heritage Corridor covers communities from Worcester, Massachusetts, to Providence, Rhode Island. Contact the visitor center for a listing of museums and sites and a full schedule of events. The area's mills, villages, and canals help to reveal the history of the Industrial Revolution. Recreational opportunities include hiking, hayrides, canal boat rides, historic sites and natural areas, canoeing, cross-country skiing, and ice-skating. Ask for the auto route tour map.

Southwick's Wild Animal Farm (12 and under)

Follow signs off Route 16, Mendon; (508) 883–9182 or (800) 258–9182; www.southwick zoo.com. Open daily mid-April to late October (call for off-season hours). Hours: 10:00 A.M. to 5:00 P.M. Admission: $14.50 for adults, $10.50 for children 3 to 12; free for children under 3. Free parking.

If the kids are into animals, they'll love a visit to Southwick's Wild Animal Farm, where they're likely to see giraffes, peacocks, alligators, and more than a hundred other species of animals on a 300-acre farm. There's a petting zoo and a deer forest where they can approach the deer. Kids can take rides on ponies, elephants, and sometimes camels (extra fee). During the summer there's a circus every day. An education building has informative presentations by Earth Limited.

Douglas State Forest and Wallum Lake (all ages)

Wallum Lake Road, Route 15, Douglas; (508) 476–7872; www.massparks.org. Open daily dawn to dusk; building and restrooms open Memorial Day to Labor Day. Parking is $5.00 per car. (Directions: I–90, exit 10, Route 395 south, Route 16 east for 5 miles, follow signs.)

Douglas State Forest and Wallum Lake is an enormous state forest—nearly 4,640 acres—with a plethora of picnic sites and a big lake for boating and swimming. The beach has a bathhouse and lifeguards. Activities include hiking, mountain biking, horseback riding, swimming, boating, snowmobiling, cross-country skiing, fishing, hunting, and snowshoeing.

Center of **Attention!**

For those who like to be in the middle of things, the geographic center of the state of Massachusetts is the town of Rutland, 12 miles northwest of Worcester.

Purgatory Chasm State Reservation (all ages)

Purgatory Road, Sutton; (508) 234–3733; www.massparks.org. Open daily sunrise to sunset. (Directions: I–90 to exit 10A, Route 141 south to Purgatory Road, Sutton, follow signs.)

The deep chasm is a dramatic sight and a nice spot to hike any time of year, but in the summer the cool, damp air is especially pleasant. A marked path leads down the series of ravines that form the chasm. *NOTE:* This path is steep in spots and isn't appropriate for children under 10 unless they are experienced hikers. There are numerous picnic spots in the reservation, as well as a good playground area and a short marked path through the woods that's more appropriate for younger kids.

Other Things to See and Do

Broad Meadow Brook Wildlife Sanctuary, 414 Massasoit Road, Worcester; (508) 753–6087; www.massaudubon.org. Trails open daily dawn to dusk. Visitor center open Tuesday to Saturday 9:00 A.M. to 4:00 P.M., Sunday 12:30 to 4:00 P.M. Largest urban wildlife sanctuary in New England.

Mechanics Hall, 321 Main Street, Worcester; (508) 752–5608; www.mechanicshall.com. Elegant pre–Civil War concert hall with superb acoustics.

Tower Hill Botanic Garden, 11 French Drive, Boylston; (508) 869–6111; www.towerhillbg.org. Open year-round; call for schedule. Distinctive 132-acre horticultural collection featuring a lawn garden, wildlife and cottage garden, a secret garden, a systematic garden, an apple orchard, and an orangerie.

Vertical World Adventures, 45 Richmond Avenue, Worcester; (508) 757–4996; www.verticalworldadventures.com. Professionally guided, outfitted adventure company. Hiking, rock climbing, mountaineering, and ice climbing.

Willard House and Clock Museum, 11 Willard Street, North Grafton; (508) 839–3500; www.willardhouse.org. One-hour guided tour offered on the hour Tuesday through Saturday 10:00 A.M. to 4:00 P.M., Sunday 1:00 to 4:00 P.M. Admission: $6.00 for adults, $3.00 for children 12 and under.

Worcester Centrum Centre, 50 Foster Street, Worcester; (508) 755–6800; www.centrumcentre.com. Home of the AHL Ice Cats, national and international musical acts, and family shows. Buy tickets at the box office, or call Ticketmaster at (617) 931–2000.

Worcester Common Outlets, 100 Front Street, Worcester; (508) 798–2581 or (888) GET–IN–ON–IT; www.worcestercommon .com. Discount outlet shopping.

Worcester Ice Cats of the AHL, 303 Main Street, Worcester; (508) 798–5400 or (800) 830–CATS (tickets); www.worcester icecats.com. Preseason starts in September, season is October through April. Farm team for the St. Louis Blues.

Where to Eat

Flying Rhino Cafe and Watering Hole, 278 Shrewsbury Street, Worcester; (508) 757–1450; www.flyingrhinocafe.com. Follow the trail to mouthwatering food! Daily specials, kids' menu. $–$$$

Hebert Candies Mansion, 575 Hartford Turnpike (Route 20), Shrewsbury; (508) 845–8051; www.hebertcandies.com. Headquarters of Heberts Candies, **free** factory tour given at this national landmark on Tuesday through Thursday 10:30 A.M. to 2:30 P.M. (America's first roadside candy store). Great chocolates and make-your-own sundae bar. $

Maxwell Siverman's Toolhouse, 25 Union Street, Worcester; (508) 755–1200; www.maxwellmaxine.com. Restored factory building; steak and seafood specialties. $–$$$

Tatnuck Bookseller Marketplace and Restaurant, 335 Chandler Street, Worcester; (508) 756–7644; www.tatnuck.com. Book warehouse store and restaurant combo. Voted Worcester's Best by *Worcester* magazine. Diverse menu serving all three meals. $–$$$

Webster House, 1 Webster Street, Worcester; (508) 757–7208; www.webster houseweb.com. Family-friendly; Greek specialties, homemade pies. Worcester landmark. $–$$

Where to Stay

Beechwood Hotel, 363 Plantation Street, Worcester; (508) 754–5789; www.beechwoodhotel.com. Boutique hotel of seventy-three rooms (some with fireplaces or skylights). Five-star, Five-Diamond-rated restaurant called Le Harlequin. Complimentary breakfast. $$–$$$$

Crowne Plaza, 10 Lincoln Square, Worcester; (508) 791–1600; www.crowne plaza.com. Offers 243 rooms. Indoor and outdoor pool. $$–$$$$

General Quarters Bed and Breakfast, 881 Aldrich Street, Route 98, Uxbridge; (508) 278–6927. Located on a country lane. Three bedrooms, children over 8 only. $$

More Than a Mouthful

The Native American name for Webster Lake (off Routes 16 and 193, Webster) is Lake Chargoggagogmanchauggagoggchaubunagungamaugg. Not surprisingly, this is the longest geographic name in the United States. Rough translation: I fish on my side of the lake, you fish on yours, and no one fishes in between. The road atlas tends to shorten it to Lake Chaubunagunga-maug because of lack of space!

Quabbin Reservoir and the Greater Sturbridge Area

Quabbin, which means "place of many waters," lives up to its name. The Quabbin Reservoir covers more than 39 square miles, with 120,000 acres of state-owned watershed land surrounding it. Scenic hikes and trails are especially magnificent in the autumn. Another draw is Old Sturbridge Village, one of the best outdoor living history museum/villages in the country. Contact the **Sturbridge Area Tourist Association,** 380 Main Street, Sturbridge 01566; (800) 628–8379; www.sturbridge.org, for more information.

Quabbin Reservoir and Park (all ages)

485 Ware Road, entrance on Route 9 between Ware and Belchertown; (413) 323–7221; www.state.ma.us/mdc (follow links to Quabbin Reservoir). The reservation is open daily dawn to dusk. Visitor center has seasonal hours. Free, except for charge for fishing. *WARNING:* The west entrance now only accesses the visitor center and the administration building. Only foot or bike traffic is allowed to the Winsor Dam because of security restrictions.

Quabbin Reservoir and Park is a protected watershed of the Quabbin Reservoir, which supplies water to 2.4 million residents of Massachusetts (40 percent of Massachusetts residents). The man-made watershed lands also supply wilderness, wildlife, forest, research, historical, and recreational resources. The visitor center, located at Winsor Dam, provides information about the many hiking trails on the 87-square-mile reservation and a few exhibits about the reservoir's construction. The reservoir was begun in 1926; the towns of Dana, Prescott, Greenwich, and Enfield were "discontinued," which means that the state bought the land from the residents and moved them away, then flooded the land. Enfield Lookout, up a winding road after you cross the dam, overlooks a spectacular view of the reservoir and the hills that were once the town of Enfield. A good, though hilly, walk begins across the road from the lookout (pick up maps at the visitor center). Fishing and boating for fishing purposes only are at designated areas. No dogs, swimming, camping or fires, off-road vehicles, sliding on dams, or cross-country skiing. *TIP:* Go to the east or middle entrances for vehicle access to Quabbin Reservoir and Park.

Marcia's
TopAnnualEvents
in Central Massachusetts

- **Washington's Birthday Celebration,** February, Old Sturbridge Village, Sturbridge; (508) 347–3362; www.osv.org

- **Central Massachusetts Flower Show,** late February, Worcester Centrum, Worcester; (800) 533–0229; www.centralmaflowershow.com

- **Athol to Orange River Rat Race,** April, Athol; (978) 249–3849; www.riverratrace.com

- **All American River Race,** last Sunday of April, Sturbridge; (508) 347–9636

- **Eastern Sprints Regatta rowing championships,** May, Lake Quinsigamond, Quinsigamond State Park, Worcester; www.qra.org

- **Brimfield Flea Market,** May, July (Fourth of July weekend), and September (Labor Day weekend), Brimfield Common, Brimfield; (413) 283–6149 or (413) 283–2418; www.brimfieldshow.com

- **New England Aerobatics Championships,** mid-May, Orange Municipal Airport; (978) 249–3849 or (508) 429–1171; http://acro.harvard.edu

- **Yankee Engine Steam Show,** mid-June, Orange Municipal Airport, Orange; (978) 249–3849

- **Jazz at Sunset,** summer, Ecotarium, Worcester; (508) 929–2700; www.ecotarium.org. Buy tickets at (508) 929–2703

- **Independence Day Celebration,** July Fourth, Old Sturbridge Village, Sturbridge; (508) 347–3362; www.osv.org

- **Early Nineteenth Century Agricultural Fair,** September, Old Sturbridge Village, Sturbridge; (508) 347–3362; www.osv.org

- **Taste with Us,** mid-August, Nashoba Valley Winery; Bolton; (978) 779–5521; www.nashobawinery.com

- **Three Apples Storytelling Festival,** mid-autumn, Harvard; (617) 499–9529; www.threeapples.org

- **Wachusetts Mountain Annual Kidsfest,** late September, Princeton, (978) 464–2300; www.wachusett.com

- **Spooky World,** October, 100 River Road, Berlin; (978) 838–0200; www.spookyworld.com

- **Pumpkin Commission Weigh In and Festival,** October, Phillipston; (978) 249–3849

- **Thanksgiving at Olde Sturbridge Village,** November, Old Sturbridge Village, Sturbridge; (508) 347–3362; www.osv.org

- **Chain of Lights Holiday Celebration,** December, Worcester County; (508) 753–2920

- **Twin Cities First Night,** December, Leominster and Fitchburg; (978) 840–4300, ext. 233

The Salem Cross Inn Farm and Restaurant (all ages)

Route 9, West Brookfield; (508) 867–2345; www.salemcrossinn.com. Restaurant is open year-round. Seasonal schedule; call for dates and hours.

Listed in the National Register of Historic Places, the Salem Cross Inn is named for the hex mark on the front door latch that was placed there to fend off witchcraft when the building was erected in 1720. It was built by a grandson of Peregrine White, the only baby born on the *Mayflower* while in Plymouth Harbor. The 600-acre property is a working farm. In winter sleigh rides are offered. Hayrides are offered in the warmer months, and hiking is allowed. The dining room menu changes with the season. During the winter, roasts are cooked on a roasting jack (the only one remaining in the country), and breads are baked in an original beehive oven. A spring or summer evening might feature a roast cooked outdoors over a pit, served with chowder. There is a special all-inclusive children's menu for under $6.95.

Old Sturbridge Village (all ages)

1 Old Sturbridge Village Road, Sturbridge; (508) 347–3362 or (800) SEE–1830; www .osv.org. Open January 1 to Washington's Birthday, weekends only, 9:30 A.M. to 4:00 P.M.; Washington's Birthday to the last weekend in March Tuesday through Sunday 9:30 A.M. to 4:00 P.M.; April through the end of October daily, 9:30 A.M. to 5:00 P.M.; November through December daily, 9:30 A.M. to 4:00 P.M. Closed Christmas. Admission (good for two consecutive days): $20 for adults, $10 for youths 3 to 17; free for children under 3.

Worth at least one full day's visit for any family, the village re-creates the daily life of a rural early-nineteenth-century community, with its farms, fields, shops, houses, and outlying mill areas. More than forty buildings from all over New England were carefully dismantled and transported here in the mid-1940s, then painstakingly reassembled and furnished in period style. The period portrayed by the village is particularly significant because it was a time when New Englanders' lives were transformed by the rise of commerce and manufacturing, improvements in agriculture and trans-portation, emigration and growing urbanization, and the political and social changes of a prospering young country. Younger children will enjoy seeing the costumed interpreters who set the scene, as well as the animals, the unpaved streets, and the interesting simple tools and machines that the interpreters use. A new exhibit that will be added to the permanent collection is the historical construction of a small two-room house that will depict building techniques of the era. Visitors will be allowed to participate in the process.

Sampson's Children Museum opened in 1999, catering to kids age 3 to 7. This interactive area allows the children to try on the settlers' garb and Native American dress of the early 1800s, pretend to cook over a hearth stove, and reenact the life of a student or a schoolmarm in a period school room. New to Sampson's is a puppet theater with story-specific puppets. Older kids will enjoy the interaction with the interpreters, who welcome questions and participation in many activities such as sheep shearing, spinning, weaving, gardening, fireplace cooking, tinsmithing, water-color painting, and candle making. Special events occur all year; call for a schedule.

NOTE: Advance registration is required for fee-based activities. Wear comfortable shoes; the property is large. Bring a stroller for younger children, although you'll have to leave it outside many of the buildings. The village is accessible for visitors with dis-abilities (more than half of the buildings are wheelchair accessible), and sign-language interpreters are available by prior arrangement.

Other Things to See and Do

Clara Barton Birthplace, 68 Clara Barton Road, Oxford; (508) 987–5375; www.clarabartonbirthplace.org. Home of America's most famous nurse and founder of the American Red Cross.

Neewollah's Haunted Forest, 120 Northside Road, Charlton; (508) 248–7706. Haunted Happenings Friday through Sunday nights in October.

Norcross Wildlife Sanctuary, 30 Peck Road, Monson; (413) 267–9654; www.norcrossws.org. Trails open April through November. Two natural history museums and 4,000 acres of rare wildflowers and plants. Picnic area. No dogs allowed.

Rocking M Ranch, 120 Northside Road, Charlton; (508) 248–7706; www.neewollahs.com. Forty-five-acre riding stable. Trail and cross-country rides for beginners to expert.

Stageloft Repertory Theater, 450A Main Street, Sturbridge; (508) 347–9005; www.stageloft.com. Musicals and comedies. Semiprofessional.

White's Landing, Route 148, Brookfield; (508) 867–5561; www.whiteslanding.com. Open 6:00 A.M. to 6:00 P.M. Boat rentals, bait and tackle shop, indoor and outdoor music series, and snack stop.

Where to Eat

Afternoon Tea at the Evergreens, Route 148, Brookfield; (508) 867–4361. Open September through June 1:00 to 4:00 P.M., $15 per person. Old-fashioned tea parties; includes tea, scones, and pastries.

Cedar Street Restaurant, 12 Cedar Street, Sturbridge; (508) 347–5800; www.cedarstreetrestaurant.com. Gourmet food in colonial setting. Kids' menu. $$–$$$

Publick House Restaurant, Route 131, 295 Main Street (on the common), Sturbridge; (508) 347–3313; www.publickhouse.com. Six dining rooms in a traditional setting. New England cooking: thick chops, pot roast, lobster pie, and Indian pudding for dessert. Open for all three meals, kids' menu, bake shop. $$–$$$

Rom's, Route 131, 179 Main Street, Sturbridge; (508) 347–3340; www.romsrestaurant.com. Six dining rooms serving classic meals at reasonable prices. $–$$

The Tavern at Old Sturbridge Village, 1 Old Sturbridge Village Road, Sturbridge; (508) 347–0395; www.osv.org. New restaurant affiliated with Old Sturbridge Village (right at the gate). Reproduction of an early-nineteenth-century tavern—menu, furnishings, and table settings. Great way to end your day at Old Sturbridge Village. Entrance fee not required. Ongoing events include cooking demonstrations and literary character evenings. $–$$$

Where to Stay

Nathan Goodale House B&B, Warren Road, Brimfield; (413) 245–9228. Wonderful location near the center of Brimfield. Beautiful Victorian home. No small children or pets. $$

Old Sturbridge Village Lodges and Oliver Wight House, 371 Main Street, Sturbridge; (506) 347–3327; www.osv.org. Little individual colonial houses furnished in 1830s style. Outdoor swimming pool. Packages available including tickets for Sturbridge Village. $$–$$$

Publick House Properties, Route 131 (on the Common), 295 Main Street, Sturbridge; (800) 782–5425 or (508) 347–3313; www.publickhouse.com. Large complex of accommodations consisting of the 1771 **Publick House Historic Inn,** the modern **Country Motor Lodge,** and the **Chamberlain House,** with suite accommodations. A mile away is the gracious **Colonel Ebenezer Crafts Inn,** furnished with four-poster beds. All guests have access to the pool, tennis courts, and playground at the Publick House. Packages during the Yankee Winter Weekends (January–March) include admission to Old Sturbridge Village. $$–$$$

The North Shore, Cape Ann, and the Merrimack Valley

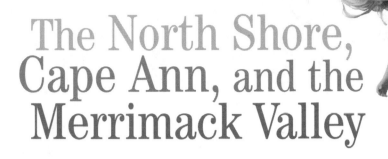

T he ragged coastline of the North Shore begins in the shipyards on Boston's north edges. As the crow flies, it stretches for 30 miles, up and around the fist of Cape Ann, in and out of Ipswich Bay, and so along to the New Hampshire border. Along the way are the historic towns of Saugus, Lynn, Marblehead, Salem, Gloucester, Rockport, Ipswich, and Newburyport. Families flock to the museums of old Salem to hear the dark tales of the country's early history, retold here on-site and in chilling detail. Enchanting Marblehead's narrow streets and dollhouselike buildings stand in stark contrast to the workaday fishing villages of Gloucester and Rockport. Beautiful beaches and state parks bring families to Ipswich, Salisbury, Topsfield, and Newburyport. Mill towns such as Lowell and Lynn, which were on the cutting edge of the Industrial Revolution, are now sites of learning and history. For further information, contact the **North of Boston Convention and Visitors Bureau,** 17 Peabody Square, Peabody 01960; (978) 977–7760 or (800) 742–5306;

Marcia's Top Picks for the North Shore, Cape Ann, and the Merrimack Valley

1. Parker River National Wildlife Refuge and Plum Island, Newburyport

2. Crane Beach, Ipswich

3. Salem Maritime National Historic Site and the Peabody and Essex Museums, Salem

4. Marblehead Harbor, especially during Race Week

5. Boott Cotton Mills and the American Textile History Museum, Lowell

6. Bearskin Neck, Rockport

THE NORTH SHORE, CAPE ANN, AND THE MERRIMACK VALLEY

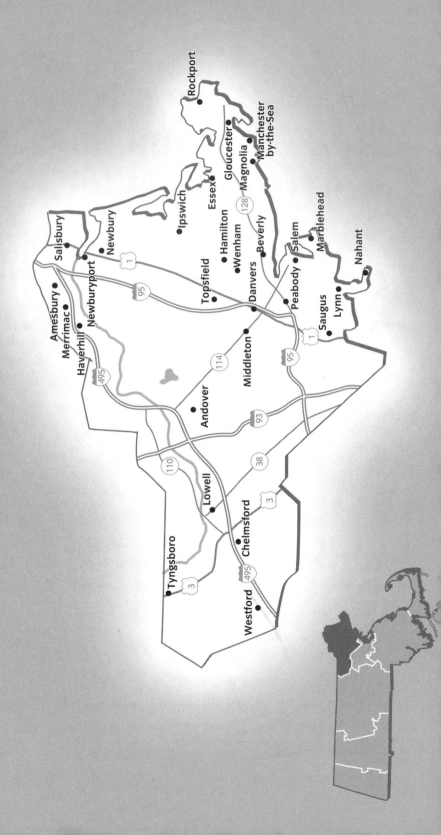

www.northofboston.org or the **Greater Merrimack Valley Convention and Visitor's Bureau,** 9 Central Street, Suite 201, Lowell 01852; (978) 459–6150 or (800) 443–3332; www.merrimackvalley.org/lowell.php.

Saugus

Saugus's main commercial street is Route 1, which divides the town into two parts. On either side of the highway are found two interesting tourism sites, the Saugus Ironworks and the Breakheart Reservation. Saugus was settled in 1630, and the first successful ironworks in the country was established here. The Breakheart Reservation is a 600-acre oasis straddling the communities of Saugus and Wakefield. For more information, contact the **Saugus Chamber of Commerce** (781–233–8407).

Saugus Ironworks National Historic Site (all ages)
244 Central Street, Saugus; (781) 233–0050; www.nps.gov/sair. Directions: From Route 1 take the Walnut Street exit and follow the National Historic Site signs. Open daily November 1 to March 31, 9:00 A.M. to 4:00 P.M., April 1 to October 31, 9:00 A.M. to 5:00 P.M.; closed Christmas Day and New Year's Day. Call for times of guided tours. **Free.**

The Saugus Ironworks is the birthplace of the ironmaking industry in the colonies. The Iron Works House, one of the last seventeenth century buildings in Saugus, was saved and restored in 1915 by Wallace Nutting, an authority on colonial American buildings and furniture and a founder of the colonial revitalist movement. Archaeological digs unearthed the remains of the ironworks, and in 1954 reconstruction of the site was completed. The ironworks has seven functioning waterwheels. There are four sets of bellows, a 500-pound water-powered hammer, and a rolling and slitting mill. Park guides run the machinery, but the waterwheels operate only from April through October. Blacksmiths demonstrate their skills year-round during tours. Educational programs for kids are offered. Don't forget to visit the interpretive museum.

Breakheart Reservation (all ages)
177 Forest Street, Saugus; (781) 233–0834; www.state.ma.us/mdc.reserv.htm. Open dawn to dusk year-round. **Free.**

Breakheart is busy year-round. The property includes forest land with a variety of hiking trails, two freshwater lakes, playgrounds, and picnicking shelters with stoves. Pearce Lake, framed by Eagle Rock, is a great spot for a cooling splash on a hot summer's day. The beach is lifeguarded in season (July 4 to Labor Day) and wheelchair accessible. Activities include hiking, mountain biking, cross-country skiing, in-line skating, swimming, fishing, bicycling, snowshoeing, and wildlife viewing. Annual events include Maple Sugarin', a First-Day Hike, and birding tours. Reservations for special events are required, and a small fee may be charged. For schools and nonprofit groups, there is Camp Nihan Environmental Education Camp and Center, with overnight facilities. For more information call (781) 662–5230 or (781) 231–1203. Adjacent to Breakheart is the Kasabuski Ice Skating Arena (781–231–4183), which can be paired with a visit to the reservation.

Where to Eat

Hilltop Steak House and Butcher Shop, Route 1 South, Saugus; (781) 233–7700; www.hilltop-steak-house.com. Local landmark (look for the huge 68-foot-high by 45-foot-wide neon cactus) famous for its large portions. Children's menu. $–$$

Kowloon, 948 Broadway, Route 1 North, Saugus; (781) 233–0077; www.kowloon restaurant.com. Specialties include Thai, Polynesian, Cantonese, and Mandarin food. House band Wednesday through Saturday in the main dining room. $–$$$

Prince Restaurant and Giggles Comedy Club, 517 Broadway, Route 1, Saugus; (781) 233–9950; www.prince restaurant.com. Pizza and pasta under the leaning tower. Kids' menu. $–$$

Lynn and Nahant

Once part of the same township, Lynn and Nahant evolved into two separate entities. Lynn is an urban center, while Nahant has retained its charm as a small seaside village. A popular seacoast haven for the wealthy in the 1800s, Nahant is connected to Lynn by a causeway. Lynn's earliest settlers were shoemakers by trade, giving birth to a city that in its heyday would earn an international reputation for shoe production.

Lynn Heritage State Park (all ages)

590 Washington Street, Lynn; (781) 598–1974; www.massparks.org. Visitor center open Wednesday, Saturday, and Sunday 12:00 to 4:00 P.M. Free.

The Lynn Heritage State Park includes a visitor center/exhibition area and Waterfront Park. Start your tour of the center with the informative eight-minute video, then wind your way through the interactive displays depicting Lynn's history, its industries, and its citizens. Once you've finished your tour, follow the yellow footsteps to Waterfront Park. The park sponsors outdoor concerts and recreational activities, such as paddle-

Halloween in August

Dress up as your favorite sea monster at the **Harbor Monster Day** festival at Waterfront Park. Prizes are given. Look for the arrival of Seamore! Contact the Lynn Heritage State Park Visitors Center for a schedule of events.

boat rentals and fishing at the marina. There are water shuttles for a fee to the Boston Harbor Islands National Recreational Area. Schedules can be picked up at the visitor center.

Lynn Woods Reservation (all ages)

Main entrance is accessed from Walnut Street, Lynn; (781) 477–7123 or (781) 477–7094 (the Lynn Woods Rangers Program Information line); www.flw.org. Open dawn to dusk. Free.

Upon entering the park, stop in at the park headquarters for a map. Lynn Woods is the second-largest municipal park in the Greater Boston area, covering 2,200 acres. A favorite hike for kids is the Jackson Path trail leading to Dungeon Rocks. There's a cave here that you can enter May 1 to October 31 from 11:00 A.M. to 4:00 P.M. For a special treat, a guide, costumed as a pirate, will take the children to the bowels of the cave the Saturday before Halloween. Other fun trails lead to the stone tower on Burrill Hill, the rose garden, and the steel tower on Mount Gilead. Other activities are mountain biking, horseback riding, and cross-country skiing. There's also a playground. Landscape architect Frederick Law Olmsted consulted here and advised that Lynn Woods be left a rugged forest environment; thus, the park is not wheelchair- or stroller-friendly. Call for a schedule of seasonal events.

Lynn Shore Reservation/Nahant Beach (all ages)

1 Causeway Street, Nahant; (617) 727–1368; www.state.ma.us/mdc/lynn_sh.htm. Main parking lot open dawn to dusk, end of June to the end of September. Side parking lots accessible year-round. Parking fee at Long Beach May through September 8:00 A.M. to 4:00 P.M.

Nahant Beach, also known as Long Beach, is a crescent of pure white sand lifeguarded until 6:00 P.M. in season. There are swings, ball fields, racquetball, tennis courts, showers and toilets, and a playground near the Lynn end of the beach. The beach promenade (aka Lynn Shore Reservation) goes from King's Beach on the Lynn/Nahant line to Swampscott. The reservation and beach are available year-round for walking, jogging, and biking. Boats can be launched at Lynn Harbor Marina.

Raiders of the **Lost Rock**

The notorious pirate Thomas Veal is said to be buried with his treasure in Dungeon Rock. As the legend goes, Veal was trapped in the cave while examining his treasure when an earthquake struck, bringing down boulders and burying him with his booty for eternity. Children dream of uncovering the treasure.

Woman **of Valor**

Mary Baker Eddy, a resident of Lynn from 1875 to 1882, was honored in the National Women's Hall of Fame as the only American woman to found a world religion. The Christian Science Church, which she founded, advocates healing through prayer.

Where to Eat

Tides Restaurant and Bar, 2B Wilson Road, Nahant Beach, Nahant; (781) 593–7500. Open year-round for lunch and dinner 11:30 A.M. to 10:00 P.M. This restaurant has great views of Nahant Beach and the Lynn/Boston skyline. Varied kid's menu; standard menu runs from sandwiches to seafood. $–$$

Marblehead

In the picturesque harbor town of Marblehead, the streets are so narrow and many of the buildings so small that the town resembles a scaled-down model, but it's a real place where real people live. Walk the twisting streets, eat seafood while you watch the boats, see a historic painting, and immerse yourselves in one of the best-preserved seaside villages in Massachusetts.

When you arrive in Marblehead, visit the **Marblehead Chamber of Commerce** at 62 Pleasant Street (781–631–2868; www.visitmarblehead.com) or go to the chamber's information booth on Route 114, corner of Pleasant and Spring Streets (781–631–8469; www.marbleheadchamber.org) to pick up a copy of the self-guided walking-tour brochure and to ask questions about the day's activities. The booth is open daily, noon to 5:30 P.M. midweek and 10:00 A.M. to 6:00 P.M. weekends from Memorial Day through Columbus Day.

Abbot Hall and the Waterfront Parks and Sights (all ages)

188 Washington Street, Marblehead; (781) 631–0528. Open Monday, Tuesday, and Thursday 8:00 A.M. to 5:00 P.M., Wednesday 7:30 A.M. to 7:30 P.M., Friday 8:00 A.M. to 1:00 P.M. year-round. Memorial Day through October 31 the hours are extended to Saturday 9:00 A.M. to 6:00 P.M. and Sunday 11:00 A.M. to 6:00 P.M. Free.

Abbot Hall, which still operates as the town hall, is the prime tourist destination in Marblehead. Walk through the lobby and then into the room on your left. You'll be confronted by an enormous painting (9 feet by 12 feet) of the original *Spirit of '76*, by Archibald Willard, given to the town in 1876 by General John Devereux, whose son was the model for the drummer boy. After you've seen the painting, follow the walking tour through Marblehead's narrow streets, ending up by the water. Watch the boats from Clark Landing (at the end of State Street) or from Crocker Park (off State Street). If you want to have a picnic lunch, there are two excellent sites to choose from: Fort Sewall, at the end of Front Street, and Chandler Hovey Park, at the end of Follett Street on the eastern end of Marblehead Neck, overlooking Marblehead Lighthouse and the harbor.

Jeremiah Lee Mansion and J. O. J. Frost Folk Art Gallery
(ages 6 and up)

170 Washington Street, Marblehead; (781) 631–1768. The Jeremiah Lee Mansion is open June 1 through October 15, Tuesday through Saturday 10:00 A.M. to 4:00 P.M. and Sunday from 1:00 to 4:00 P.M. The J. O. J. Frost Folk Art Gallery is open year-round Tuesday through Friday 10:00 A.M. to 4:00 P.M. and Saturday 10:00 A.M. to 4:00 P.M. June through September. Admission: $5.00 for adults, $4.50 for students and seniors; free for children 12 and under. Call for schedule.

Tour this outstanding example of Georgian architecture, with original handpainted wallpaper dating from 1771. There's a collection of nineteenth-century children's furniture and toys scattered throughout the mansion. Across the road from the Lee home is the J. O. J. Frost Folk Art Gallery, which has a painting and a model depicting life in Marblehead from a seafarer's point of view.

Other Things to See and Do

Crowninshield Island, also known as Brown Island, Beacon Street to Dolliber Cove, Marblehead; www.thetrustees.org. **Free.** This island off the coast of Marblehead is owned by the Trustees of Reservations. The idyllic setting is great for nature walks, birding, picnicking, swimming, and fishing. To reach the island, you can walk across during low tide or go by boat. *WARNING:* Check the tide schedule, or you'll get caught on the island.

Marblehead Model Yacht Club, Races are held every Sunday at 10:00 A.M. at Redd's Pond on Pond Street from the end of March through mid-November. When the ice freezes, the location shifts to harbor sailing at the Boston Yacht Club, 1 Front Street. There are regattas held four to five times a year. For information, contact Worth Marine at (781) 639–1835.

Hide and **Seek**

Militia weapons were stored in Marblehead Powder House in 1775, when the British occupied Boston. Today, the Powder House on Green Street stands as one of the few powder houses left in the United States.

Brace for **the Race**

The America's Cup Title was held for three consecutive years in Marblehead in the 1880s. While it may not be the America's Cup, **Race Week in Marblehead** is big doings nowadays, with competitors from around the globe. Race week is held the last week in July. Call the Boston Yacht Club at (781) 631–3100 or go to www.mheadrace.org for details.

Where to Eat

The Barnacle, 141 Front Street, Marblehead; (781) 631–4236. Lunch and dinner. Great chowder and harbor views. Outdoor dining. Casual. $–$$$

The Driftwood, 63 Front Street, Marblehead; (781) 631–1145. Serving breakfast, all day until 2:00 P.M. Lots of local color, attracting fishermen, the yachting set, families, and visitors. $

Flynnies at the Beach, Devereux Beach, Marblehead; (781) 639–3035; www.flynnies .com. Open May through November. Deck and beach dining, with ocean views of Marblehead Neck, the harbor, and the Atlantic. Inside dining on chillier days. Breakfast, lunch, and dinner. Serving sandwiches, seafood, chicken, and beef. Wheelchair accessible. $–$$

Flynnies on the Avenue, 28 Atlantic Avenue, Marblehead; (781) 639–2100; www.flynnies.com. Warm and cozy atmosphere, wide range of choices from vegetarian to seasonal specials to tried-and-true standards. $–$$

The Landing, 81 Front Street, Marblehead; (781) 631–1878 or (781) 639–1266; e-mail thenewlanding@aol.com. Lunch and dinner every day. Upscale menu, lots of fresh seafood, loads of specials. Kids' menu. Dine inside or outside on the deck. $–$$$

Where to Stay

The Bishop's B&B, 10 Harding Lane, Marblehead; (781) 631–4954. All rooms with water views; walking distance to historic Old Marblehead. Small beach. Children over 6 are welcome, but pets and smoking are banned. $$–$$$

The Marblehead Inn, 264 Pleasant Street, Marblehead; (781) 639–9999 or (800) 399–5843; www.marbleheadinn.com. Ten suites with private bath; great for non-smoking families. Rates include continental breakfast. $$–$$$

Special Times

Sandwiched around the Fourth of July holiday, the Marblehead Festival of the Arts is the big kickoff to summer. There is an arts competition for all ages, food, street performances, derbies, and competitions sponsored by area organizations. Parking for some events can be scarce, particularly in Old Town Marblehead.

Salem

Salem makes the most of its reputation as the location of the infamous Salem witch trials during the seventeenth century. But there's a lot more to it than this sad and rather gruesome period: A top-notch waterfront area, a world-class museum, and a historic house with a secret stairway are among the highlights of Salem that have nothing to do with witches or trials.

When you arrive in Salem, go to the **Chamber of Commerce** (63 Wharf Street, Suite 2C; 978–744–0004; www.salem-chamber.org) for **free** self-guided tour maps and information about the day's activities or **Destination Salem** (Office of Tourism and Events), 63 Wharf Street, Suite 2C, Salem 01970; (978) 744–3663; www.salem .org or www.salemweb.com. Another place for information on Salem and Essex County is the **National Park Service Regional Visitor Center** at the corner of New Liberty and Essex Streets (978–740–1650; www.nps.gov/sama). The Park Service has created three heritage trails through thirty-four communities based on three themes: Early Settlement, the Maritime Trail, and the Industrial Trail (www.essexheritage.org). Brochures on area attractions not included in these themes are also available.

Salem Trolley Tours (all ages)
8 Central Street, Salem; (978) 744–5469; www.salemtrolley.com. Open from April through October 10:00 A.M. to 5:00 P.M. (weekends only in March and November, weather permitting). Price: $10.00 for adults, $3.00 for children 6 to 14; free for children under 6. Be sure to ask about the $25 family pass, which covers fare for two adults and two children under 12.

If you'd rather let someone else do the driving (and that's not a bad idea in busy Salem), the trolley tours are a good deal. The trolley covers 8 miles with twelve stops that include the major sights and attractions of Salem. You can get on and off all day long. Tours start hourly at the Salem Visitor Center.

Amazing
Massachusetts Facts

- Both the town of Marblehead and the city of Beverly lay claim to being the birthplace of the American navy.

- The Wenham Tea House is the oldest teahouse in America.

- Marco the Magi's "Le Grand David and His Own Spectacular Magic Company" is the longest-running family stage attraction.

- The Myopia Polo Field is the oldest polo field in the country (created in 1888) and is the oldest polo club in America.

- The American Textile History Museum in Lowell is the world's largest textile museum.

Salem Maritime National Historic Site (all ages)

174 Derby Street, Salem; (978) 740–1660; www.nps.gov/sama. Open daily year-round, 9:00 A.M. to 5:00 P.M.; closed Thanksgiving, Christmas, and New Year's Day. Admission: $5.00 for adults; $3.00 for seniors and children 6 to 16.

Located on the waterfront, the site encompasses the Custom House (where Nathaniel Hawthorne worked), the Derby House, and the Narbonne House, among other historic buildings. Start your tour with the seventeen-minute video presentation on the early maritime history of Salem and its role in international trade. Then take the tour of the Custom House, the Elias Derby mansion, and the Narbonne House. The weights and measures at the Custom House are especially fascinating to kids. They'll also enjoy watching demonstrations of the intricate skills required in shipbuilding. The work was completed in 2002, and the ship was commissioned in 2003. You can tour the replica of the three-masted square rigged vessel *Friendship* now. Special programming and demonstrations are given by park rangers; call for a schedule.

Friendship Renewed

The Salem Maritime National Historic Site is proud of the newest addition to its collection, the *Friendship*, a replica of a 1797 ship built in Salem and owned by Waitt and Pierce. Be sure to pick up a copy of *The Friendship* newspaper; it's full of fun and games.

Peabody Essex Museum (all ages)

East India Square, Salem; (978) 745–9500 or (866) 745–1876; www.pem.org. Open daily 10:00 A.M. to 5:00 P.M. Admission: $13.00 for adults, **free** for children to 16; senior and family discounts; includes admittance to the galleries, house tours, and library. House tours only, $6.00 per person.

Described by the *New York Times* as a "cross-cultural marvel with world-class collections of art, architecture, and culture dating back to 1799," the collection of items gathered by Salem sea captains on their round-the-world voyages is varied and eclectic. The museum has already been recognized in the past for the quality of its collection in Asian export, American decorative, maritime, and oceanic art.

With the addition of 250,000 square feet of new and renovated galleries and public spaces (the new wing was designed by Moshe Safdie), the Peabody Essex Museum can now showcase the entire range of its collection, including African, Korean and Indian art, photography, architecture and design, and contemporary Native American art. One of the highlights of your visit will be a Chinese merchant's 200-year-old house from the Anhui province reassembled on the museum's campus. Try to take a **free** tour of the museum; check the schedule for times. Historic homes representing three centuries in Salem are included in the admission price. The original court documents from the Salem witchcraft trials are part of the collection at Phillips's Library. There is a new Atrium Cafe for quicker snacks in the new addition, as well as the established Museum Restaurant.

House of the Seven Gables (all ages)

54 Turner Street, Salem; (978) 744–0991; www.7gables.org. Open daily 10:00 A.M. to 5:00 P.M., and to 7:00 P.M. July through October. Closed Thanksgiving, Christmas, and the first three weeks of January. Admission: $11.00 for adults; $10.00 for seniors; $7.25 for children 5 to 12. Four and under **free.** Ask about the combination ticket to Salem 1630: Pioneer Village.

A fun place to visit, even for people who aren't familiar with Nathaniel Hawthorne's book, *The House of the Seven Gables.* Begin your visit by watching the short multimedia presentation of Hawthorne's story, then walk through the house to see the secret staircase, which winds up through a wall (this may be all that the younger kids will remember about the house), and the low-beamed attic. Hawthorne's birthplace is on the property; it's furnished with period furniture, and the guides know a lot about the family and their times. Come celebrate Hawthorne's birthday bash on July Fourth every year.

How Salem **Got Its Name**

To smooth over conflict between groups of settlers on the Naumkeag Peninsula (near present-day Pioneer Village), the area was renamed Salem, from the Hebrew word *Shalom*, or peace.

Salem Witch Museum (ages 7 and up)

19½ Washington Square, Salem; (978) 744–1692; www.salemwitchmuseum.com. Open daily, September through June, 10:00 A.M. to 5:00 P.M.; July and August, 10:00 A.M. to 7:00 P.M. Admission: $6.50 for adults; $4.50 for children 6 to 14.

Can't keep the kids away from the witch stories? Head for the thirty-minute multimedia presentation about the witchcraft hysteria that gripped seventeenth-century Salem. The show is a bit scary and gruesome, and it is definitely not appropriate for kids under 7. A new exhibit—*Witches: Evolving Perceptions*—looks at the different meanings and interpretations of the word *witch* over time, the practice of witchcraft today, and the phenomenon of witch-hunting.

Salem Wax Museum of Witches and Seafarers (ages 6 and up)

282 Derby Street, Salem; (978) 740–2929 or (800) 298–2929; www.salemwaxmuseum .com. Open daily 10:00 A.M. to 6:00 P.M.; extended hours during Haunted Happenings and summer. Admission: $6.50 for adults, $3.00 for ages 6 to 14. Free for ages 5 and under. Ask about the combination ticket for Salem Witch Village called the Hysteria Pass. In addition, if you purchase your tickets online, there is a discount.

Featuring wax figures of life-size witches, the museum puts the witch stories in the context of Salem's seventeenth-century life as a major seaport, and it's not nearly as scary as the Salem Witch Museum. Self-guided.

Salem Witch Village (ages 6 and up)

288 Derby Street, Salem; (978) 740–9229 or (800) 298–2929; www.salemwitchvillage .com. Open daily year-round 10:00 A.M. to 6:00 P.M. Extended hours during Haunted Happenings. Admission: adults $5.50; children $3.00. Free for ages 5 and under. Ask about the combination ticket for the Salem Wax Museum.

Traces the history of witchcraft from medieval Europe to modern-day America. The guides are all practicing witches. Burning incense permeates the museum and can be headache-inducing. Even though the displays can be trite at times, the guides are interesting and informative. The only way to describe the experience is "All you wanted to know about witchcraft but were afraid to ask." Call for a schedule of workshops. If you visit during Halloween (the Celtic New Year), be sure to ask for the Hysteria Pass ticket with Salem Wax Museum of Witches and Seafarers. *CAUTION:* Displays can be scary for little ones.

New England Pirate Museum (all ages)

274 Derby Street, Salem; (978) 741–2800; www.piratemuseum.com. Open May through October, 10:00 A.M. to 5:00 P.M. and weekends in November. Extended hours during Haunted Happenings. Admission: $6.00 for adults, $5.00 for seniors, $4.00 for children 4 to 13. A combination ticket with the Witch Dungeon Museum and the Witch History Museum can be purchased.

Buried treasure and pirates are actually part of the North Shore's history. This attraction has it all; it's educational, historical, and fun for kids who enjoy learning about the local looters such as Blackbeard and Captain Kidd. The museum takes about thirty minutes to view all the displays.

Friendship Carriage Tours (all ages)

(978) 745–3806. Operates year-round by appointment. Price: $35 and up for a half-hour reserved tour.

All aboard for a narrated carriage ride with commentary and gossip of the 1800s. Guides dress in period costume. Molly and Buck (the horses of Friendship Carriage Tours) are very fond of children and like to eat hay cubes and carrots provided by the guide. Specialty rides can be arranged. My family's favorite is the Chocolate Ride, which stops at Harbor Sweets. Hay wagon rides available by request only.

Haunted Footsteps Ghost Tour (ages 8 and up)

175 Essex Street, 2nd Floor, Salem; (978) 745–0666; www.hauntedfootstepsghosttour .com. Open Wednesday through Sunday April through October 31. Price: $12.50 for adults, $8.00 for children 6 to 12. Reservations suggested.

Under the cover of night, Haunted Footsteps Ghost Tour is a historically based hour-and-a-half walking tour geared to older unflappable kids and their families. Some of the topics covered are sites of documented hauntings and the witchcraft hysteria of the 1600s. The guides are costumed, adding to the spooky atmosphere.

Misery Islands (all ages)

Salem Bay, ½ mile from West Beach; (978) 526–8687; www.thetrustees.org. If arriving by private boat, the price is $3.00 for adults, $1.00 for children 12 and under.

Great Misery and Little Misery are accessible by boat. According to local lore, the islands got their moniker from a man who was shipwrecked and stranded there for three frigid December days in the 1600s.

Nowadays, they're a great spot for fishing, picnicking, swimming, hiking, and bird sightings. Great views, particularly of Manchester-by-the-Sea.

For Your **Amusement**

At the tip of land that juts into Salem Bay is Salem Willows Park, a fine destination for an afternoon of picnicking and outdoor activities. The views are good—Beverly's harbor on one side, the south coast of Cape Ann on the other. There's a small amusement park with a nice merry-go-round and a pier for fishing.

Salem 1630: Pioneer Village (all ages)

Located in Forest River Park, Salem; (978) 744–0991; www.7gables.org. Directions: Take Lafayette Street to West Street; enter Forest River Park. Open for group tours or educational programs May through October by appointment. The village is open to the general public July through August, Monday through Saturday 10:00 A.M. to 5:00 P.M., Sunday noon to 5:00 P.M. Admission: $7.00 for adults, $5.00 for children 5 to 12, **free** for children under 5. Ask about the combination ticket for House of the Seven Gables.

Want to see how the settlers lived in one of the first enclaves of the Massachusetts Bay Colony? Pioneer Village is the re-created seventeenth-century fishing village bordering Salem Harbor managed by the House of the Seven Gables. This area was originally referred to as Naumkeag, or "fishing place," by local tribes. Thatched roof cottages, a wigwam, and live barnyard animals await you. Guides dress in period costume and demonstrate culinary skills of the time using authentic recipes. Hands-on activities allow kids to test their skills at spinning, churning butter, and carding. A special event occurring in late June is the Muster, a reenactment of military operations of the 1600s.

Salem Whale Watch Tours and Cruises (all ages)

57 Wharf Street and Pickering Wharf, Salem; (800) 745–9594; salemwhales@yahoo .com. Call for schedule and pricing.

The ship heads out to both Stellwagen Bank and Jeffrey's Ledge, popular feeding grounds of a variety of whales and dolphins. Experienced naturalists give a background of the area's history and will help you spot marine creatures that are encountered along the way. Back by popular demand is a classroom at sea, with an anatomically correct scale model of a whale, a touch tank aquarium with various crustaceans, and a microscope area to examine the plankton and microscopic animals that the whales eat. This interactive experience is not limited to school groups. Full galley and bar onboard.

Salem **Historical Tours**

Salem Historical Tours (8 Central Street, Salem; 978–745–0666; www .salemhistoricaltours.com) offers historical walking tours of Salem—a History and Architecture tour or the Witch Trial Memorial and Old Burial Point tour (witch trail and cemetery tour). Each tour is one hour in length. Prices are $6.00 for ages 13 and over, $5.00 for ages 6 to 12, **free** for ages 5 and under.

Witch Dungeon Museum (ages 6 and up)

16 Lynde Street, Salem; (978) 741–3570; www.witchdungeon.com. Open April through November 30 10:00 A.M. to 5:00 P.M. Admission: $6.00 for adults, $5.00 for seniors, $4.00 for children ages 4 to 13, **free** for children under 4. Combination ticket available with the New England Pirate Museum and the Witch History Museum.

A highly acclaimed reenactment of the witch trial of Sarah Good by professional actors leads to a chilling conclusion. A tour of the dungeon completes this thought-provoking experience.

Winter Island Maritime Park (all ages)

50 Winter Island Road, Salem; (978) 745–9430; www.salemweb.com/winterisland. Open daily May through October, 6:00 A.M. to 10:00 P.M.; 7:00 A.M. to 4:00 P.M. in the winter. Closed Christmas. Admission: $10 per car for nonresidents midweek, $15 weekends and holidays. Fee for campsites and boat launch.

Owned by the city of Salem, this hidden gem features the remains of Historic Fort Pickering and a working lighthouse. Unique to most city parks, there is camping with fifty-seven RV and tent sites, with showerhouse. Other facilities include a boat launch area, a picnic area, and a camp store. If you wish to leave your vehicle, the Salem Trolley services the park in the summer. Every summer there is a Blues Festival in July and a Taste of the North Shore. Call for the schedule.

Very **Bewitching**

Laurie Cabot, "Official Witch of Salem," has been invited to the season opener of the Red Sox for many years to bring them good luck. Laurie is very generous with her time and is willing to pose for photographs. You can find her at her store The Cat, the Crow and the Crown, at Pickering Wharf, where she sells her paintings and does readings.

Literature with Salem as a Setting

Children's

1. *Carry On, Mr. Bowditch*, by Jean Lee Latham
2. *Early Thunder*, by Jean Fritz

Teen and Adult

1. *The House of the Seven Gables*, by Nathaniel Hawthorne
2. *The Crucible*, by Arthur Miller

Other Things to See and Do

Children's Museum, 209R Essex Street, Salem; (978) 741–1811; www.northshore childrensmuseumsalem.com. Open daily 9:00 A.M. to 5:00 P.M. year-round. Prices: $6.00 per person, $3.00 per grandparent, under 1 is free. Place for parents and children to create and learn. Hands-on.

Cry Innocent, Old Town Hall, Derby Square, Essex Street, Salem; (978) 867–4747; www.cryinnocent.com. Performances summer, fall, and the month of October. You are the jury at the trial of Bridget Bishop, the first person hanged for witchcraft in 1692. Buy your tickets early. Bridget is arrested fifteen minutes prior to the show by the fountain on Essex Street.

Dracula's Castle, 90 Lafayette Street, Salem; (978) 745–4777; www.draculathe castle.com. Haunted house open Memorial Day through November 30.

Harbor Sweets, 85 Leavitt Street, Salem; (978) 745–7648; www.harborsweets.com. Take a tour to see how delicious, preservative-free chocolates are made. Free samples.

Pickering Wharf, Wharf Street (off Derby Street), Salem. Funky shops and restaurants on the harbor near sights and attractions.

Salem Museum of Myths and Monsters, Pickering Wharf, Salem; (978) 745–7283. Open daily May through December. Yet another twist on the occult, ghosts, and witchcraft. Fee.

Salem Witch Trials Memorial, Charter Street, Salem. Thought-provoking, award-winning memorial dedicated to human rights and tolerance.

Schooner Wind Rose, Pickering Wharf Marina (in front of the Victoria Station Restaurant); (978) 526–7839 or (508) 284–4292. Prices depend on tour. Sailing June 15 through September 15.

Witch History Museum, 197–201 Essex Street, Salem; (978) 741–7770; www.witch dungeon.com. Open April through end of November 10:00 A.M. to 5:00 P.M. Witch trial stories are told through a historically accurate live presentation.

The Witch House, (ages 6 and up) 310 Essex Street; Salem; (978) 744–0180; www.salemweb.com/witchhouse. Open daily year-round with extended summer hours. Original home of Judge Jonathan Corwin, judge at the Salem witch trials. Period furniture.

Where to Eat

Bella Verona, 100 Essex Street, Salem; (978) 825–9911; www.bellaverona.com. Italian specialties of the Verona region served up with pride and care. Serving dinner. $–$$

Cats River Grill, 94 Wharf Street, Pickering Wharf, Salem. Lunch and dinner. Views of Salem Harbor and Salem Maritime National Historic Site. Seafood specialties in a fun atmosphere; children's menu. $–$$$

Engine House Pizza, 71 Lafayette Street, Salem; (978) 745–1744. Open seven days a week, 11:00 A.M. to midnight. Specialties include pizza, subs, salads, and pasta. $

In a Pig's Eye, 148 Derby Street, Salem; (978) 741–4436; www.inapigseye.com. Open for lunch and dinner. The restaurant's slogan—"Dine up—Dress down"— pretty much sums up its philosophy. Casual fare; not to be missed is Mexican night. $

Lyceum Bar and Grill, 43 Church Street, Salem; (978) 745–7665; www.lyceum salem.com. Open for lunch and dinner. Building where Alexander Graham Bell made the first phone call. Local and regional specialties. Kids welcome. $$–$$$

Museum Restaurant, Peabody Essex Museum, East India Square, Salem; (978) 740–4551; www.pem.org. Lunch only. The cafe overlooks an Oriental garden, and the tableclothed seating is in an elegant room that exhibits some of the museum's collection. Children's menu. $–$$

Reds, 15 Central Street, Salem; (978) 745–3527; www.redssandwichshop.com. Very popular with locals as well as tourists. Reasonable prices and large portions. Voted Salem's best breakfast by the *Salem Evening News,* but serves lunch and dinner too! $–$$

Whatever Floats **Your Boat**

The only floating restaurant at sea that isn't ship based is the **Rockmore Floating Restaurant** (Salem Harbor; 978–740–1001; www.rockmore.us). Take the water shuttle from Pickering Wharf, Salem, or Village Street, Marblehead. Both the water shuttle and parking are **free.** The menu includes sandwiches, hot dogs, and fried seafood. The kids get a kick out of the fish that swim up, hoping for leftover crumbs. The food is good, but the views and the ambience are what attract people here year after year. This restaurant has been a real hit with my children and their friends. They love to feed the fish, but I do worry that in their excitement, I'll be fishing them out of the water!

Amazing Salem

- Ye Olde Pepper Candy Companie of Salem is the oldest candy company in the United States.

- The Salem Maritime National Historic Site was the first place designated as a National Historic Site.

- Pioneer Village was the first outdoor museum in America.

- The first elephant to set foot in this country disembarked in Salem in the late 1700s.

- In 1650 Salem resident Anne Bradstreet became the first woman to publish a book of verse in America.

- Elias Derby became the first millionaire in America (his home is part of the Salem Maritime National Historic Site).

- The telephone was first demonstrated at Lyceum Hall by Alexander Graham Bell.

- Monopoly was produced and sold by Salem toy and game company Parker Brothers.

- The Peabody Essex Museum is the oldest continuously operating museum in the country.

Where to Stay

Amelia Payson Guest House, 16 Winter Street, Salem; (978) 744–8304; www.ameliapaysonhouse.com. Closed in winter. A small bed-and-breakfast with three rooms, all with private bath, plus a guest apartment. Period antiques. $$–$$$

The Clipper Ship Inn, 40 Bridge Street, Route 1A, Salem; (978) 745–8022. Sixty-room motel with annex. Wheelchair accessible. $–$$

Hawthorne Hotel, on the Common; 18 Washington Square West, Salem; (978) 744–4080; www.hawthornehotel.com. Designated a Historic Hotel of America, the eighty-nine-room Hawthorne has great charm and class. Restaurant serves breakfast, lunch, and dinner. $$–$$$$

Inn on Washington Square, 53 Washington Square North, Salem; (978) 741–4997; www.washingtonsquareinn.com. Great location across from the Salem Common. Historic antique inn, fireplaces, canopy beds, handmade quilts, Jacuzzi, roomy for a bed-and-breakfast. Continental breakfast served. $$–$$$

Salem Inn, 7 Summer Street, Salem; (978) 741–0680 or (800) 446–2995; www.salem innma.com. European-style inn; great location. Some rooms have canopy beds, fireplaces, and Jacuzzis. Suites available with kitchenettes. Complimentary breakfast. $$–$$$

Cut 'em off **at the Pass**

Contact **Destination Salem,** 59 Wharf Street, (978) 741–3252 or (978) 744–3663; www.salemweb.com or www.salem.org, to find out about combo tickets and special savings. These have included Salem's Best Pass and Salem Fun Pass. Ask about combination passes during **Haunted Happenings** in October.

Peabody

Brooksby Farm and Felton Junior House (all ages)
Felton Street, Peabody; (978) 531–1631 or (978) 531–7456; www.essexheritage.org.
Open year-round, but the farm stand is seasonal.

A municipally owned farm since 1976, Brooksby is a fun place to visit at almost any-time of the year. Pick your own strawberries in June, blueberries and raspberries in July and August, apples in late summer and fall; cut flowers in summer, or choose that special Christmas tree in December. A barn is home to goats, a llama, sheep, pigs, chickens, a rooster, geese, and ducks. Feeding the animals is allowed. Brooksby offers hayrides for $65 that seat twenty-five to thirty people, a great idea for a kids' party. Cross-country skiing is available for **free.** However, there is a small charge for equipment rental ($6.00) and lessons ($3.00). The trails can also be used for snow-shoeing and hiking. Ice skating is allowed on the ponds (check to see if the pond is properly frozen). A farm store sells produce from the farm and related products. The third weekend in October is Harvest Happenings, with lots of **free** events.

Owned by the Peabody Historical Society, the Felton House is fully furnished with period furniture from the 1600s. On the site is the Smith barn and the Fire Museum, which includes Peabody Engine #3. For more information and tours, call (978) 531–0805.

Peabody **Festivals**

- **International Festival,** third Sunday in September. Celebrates the diversity of the city, with ethnic food, dance, and cultural events. (978) 532–3000.

- **Harvest Happenings at Brooksby Farm,** third weekend in October. Old-fashioned fun includes apple pie–baking contests, hayrides, a horseshoe pitch, pony rides, and pumpkin decorating.

Where to Eat

Family Fare, 474 Lowell Street, Peabody; (978) 536–9049. Great Italian food in a casual atmosphere. Attentive, friendly service. $

Johnny Rocket's, Northshore Shopping Center, Peabody; (978) 532–2999; www.johnnyrockets.com. Fifties retro diner complete with a lunch counter, jukeboxes, and booths. Great burgers and shakes. $

Su Chang's, 373 Lowell Street, Peabody; (978) 531–3366. Upper-end Chinese food specializing in Cantonese and Mandarin ethnic dishes. Lovely decor. $–$$$

Where to Stay

Marriott Hotel, 8A Centennial Drive, Peabody; (978) 977–9700; www.marriott.com. Nicely appointed rooms; pool. Great daily brunches with special pricing for children. $$–$$$$

Danvers and Middleton

Endicott Park (under 10)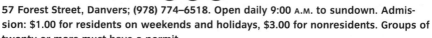

57 Forest Street, Danvers; (978) 774–6518. Open daily 9:00 A.M. to sundown. Admission: $1.00 for residents on weekends and holidays, $3.00 for nonresidents. Groups of twenty or more must have a permit.

This 165-acre park is owned by the town of Danvers. Attractions include a barn with farm animals, trails, a pond with a fishing platform, playing fields, and picnic tables. A state-of-the-art playground is a big attraction for kids. Also on the grounds are Glen Magna and the Derby Tea House, owned by the town historical society.

Rebecca Nurse Homestead (ages 5 and up)

149 Pine Street, Danvers; (978) 774–8799; www.rebeccanurse.org. Open mid-June to September, Tuesday through Sunday 1:00 to 4:30 P.M.; September and October, Saturday and Sunday 1:00 to 4:30 P.M. Open the rest of the year by appointment only. Admission: $4.00 for adults, $3.00 for kids.

If you're fascinated by tales of the Salem witch trials, you'll enjoy the original saltbox homestead of the Nurse family. The matriarch, Rebecca Nurse, was accused in 1692 of practicing witchcraft. Her accusers were a group of rebellious teenage girls who were having fits of hysteria and blaming Rebecca as one of their tormentors. Executed in July 1692, her remains were brought back to the family plot and buried in an unmarked grave. The property includes the original Nurse homestead, with seventeenth- and eighteenth-century period furnishings; a reproduction of the Olde Salem Village Meeting House (featuring a multimedia presentation); the family cemetery, with a monument to Rebecca bearing a poem by John Greenleaf Whittier; and a gift shop.

Top Ice Cream Spots

1. **Cherry Hill Farm,** 210 Conant Street, Danvers; (978) 774–0519; www.cherryfarmcreamery.com. Homemade ice cream—huge portions and a long list of flavors. For adults, there's the Sun n' Air Driving Range behind the ice cream stand to work off those excess pounds from the ice cream you just consumed. Open year-round for ice cream; seasonal golf.

2. **Putnam Pantry Ice Cream and Candies,** Route 1 North, just after the Route 62/Danvers exit, Danvers; (978) 774–2383; www.putnampantry .com. Opened in 1951, the big attraction is the make-your-own sundae bar (all the toppings and candies are made on the premises). Extremely popular with groups is the Battle of Bunker Hill, with seventeen scoops of ice cream, for $17.75. Indoor seating is reminiscent of ice-cream parlor decor of the 1940s and 1950s.

3. **Richardson's Ice Cream and Golf Country,** Route 114, 156 South Main Street, Middleton; (978) 774–5450 (ice cream) or (978) 774–4476 (golf); www.richardsonsicecream.com. Homemade ice cream, driving range, miniature golf courses, and batting cages.

Witch Hysteria Monument (all ages) 🏛
176 Hobart Street, Danvers. Open year-round. Free.

Erected 300 years after the Witchcraft Hysteria of 1692, this monument stands in solemn testimony to the memory of the twenty-five innocent people who lost their lives. It's located on town land, across from the original site of the Olde Salem Village Meeting House, where many of the accused were questioned.

Special Time

The **Danvers Family Festival** (starting the weekend prior to and ending the weekend after the Fourth of July) features road races, dog shows, a bike rodeo, Fireman's Muster, Endicott Park Day, Irish Night, a golf tournament, various band concerts, Oldies Night, and, of course, the requisite Fourth of July fireworks. Check out the Web site at www.danversfamily festival.com.

Other Things to See and Do

Plains Park Skateboard Park, 57 Conant Street, Danvers. Open dawn to dusk in season. A great place for children to practice their moves. Structures include a pyramid, a spine, the Bench, the fun box, a half pipe, a flat pyramid, steel rails, and a cement rail edge.

Where to Eat

Brothers Deli, 31 Maple Street, Danvers; (978) 750–0100. Cafeteria-style home cooking. Greek specialties. $

Danvers Yacht Club Restaurant, 161 Elliott Street, Danvers; (978) 774–8620; www.danversport.com. Save room for Gilda, the swan-shaped cream puff ice-cream dessert. Surf-and-turf specialties. $–$$

Loaf-in-a-Round, Route 1 South, 110 Newbury Street, Centre Village Plaza, Danvers; (978) 750–4321. Open weekdays 6:00 A.M. to 6:00 P.M.; Saturday 7:00 A.M. to 2:00 P.M. Closed Sunday. Specializing in a variety of homemade soups and homemade crusty hearty breads. $

Radici at the Danvers Courtyard, 275 Independence Way, Danvers; (978) 739–4478. Open for breakfast and dinner. Gourmet dining in a welcoming setting. $–$$$

Where to Stay

Danvers Courtyard by Marriott, 275 Independence Way, Danvers; (978) 777–8630; www.marriott.com. A 122-room hotel located near the Liberty Tree Mall. Seasonal outdoor pool. $$–$$$

Day's Inn, 152 Endicott Street, Danvers; (978) 777–1030; www.newengland days.com. A 130-room motel near the highway and close to mall. Free continental breakfast. $–$$

Topsfield

Ipswich River Wildlife Sanctuary (all ages)

87 Perkins Row, Topsfield; (978) 887–9264; www.massaudubon.org. **Open year-round Tuesday through Sunday, dawn to dusk, and Monday holidays. Admission: $4.00 for adults, $3.00 for seniors and children 3 to 12.**

The sanctuary has 10 miles of trails on 2,400 acres of land that are protected by the Massachusetts Audubon Society. Start your visit at the information center, where you can pick up a trail map. For families, the best trail leads to the Rockery Pond, a pile of enormous boulders. Continue around the pond (look for ducks, turtles, and frogs), then around the marsh, from which you can look over the wetlands of Topsfield and

Ipswich. In late May or June the rhododendrons around the pond are breathtakingly memorable and pulsating with color. *NOTE:* Don't bring your dog; this is a wildlife sanctuary. Do bring bug repellent, especially during the spring.

Bradley Palmer State Park (all ages)
Asbury Street, Topsfield; (978) 887–5931; www.massparks.org. Park open year-round; free. Parking for wading pool is $5.00; accessible in summer only.

Bradley Palmer, a successful attorney and friend of presidents and kings, bequeathed his mansion and grounds to the state of Massachusetts for public use. An extensive trail system is used for hiking, horseback riding, mountain biking, snowmobiling, cross-country skiing, and snowshoeing. The Ipswich River winds through the north end of the property, giving access to canoeing (rentals available at Foote Brothers in Ipswich) and fishing. It's also a great spot to teach a child to ride a bike since there is a large stretch of flat paved road. A real treat for the under-10 set is the wading pool, open from Father's Day to Labor Day. The centerpiece of the lifeguarded pool is a mushroom-shaped structure with water cascading over it.

Topsfield Fairgrounds (all ages)
Route 1 North (exit 50 off Route 95), Topsfield; (978) 887–5000; www.mafa.org or www.topsfieldfair.org.

The 83-acre fairground is home to the Topsfield Fair, an agricultural fair held every October. In addition to the Topsfield Fair, there are numerous off-season events that take place here. Some of the more popular kid-oriented events held in May and June are dog shows, the 4-H Horse Show, the Native American Festival, and the Gem and Mineral Show. Prices and schedule vary according to event; call the Topsfield Fairgrounds for more information.

It's a **Family Affair**

Topsfield Fair, Topsfield Fairgrounds, Route 1 North/exit 50, Topsfield; (978) 887–5000; www.topsfieldfair.org. Admission: $10. Free for children under 8. Parking $10 per vehicle. The Topsfield Fair, held on the Topsfield Fairgrounds, is the oldest agricultural fair in the United States. Held every October the ten days preceding the Columbus Day holiday, the fair features exhibit halls, a flower show, livestock shows, a petting zoo, a vegetable show (with the New England Giant Pumpkin contest), pig races, and a horse and ox pull. There's a midway and lots of food concessions. Local and national talent performs at the grandstand and five smaller stages. In the past there has been a figure-eight race on the final evening.

Hamilton

Myopia Hunt Club and Polo Fields (all ages)

435 Bay Road, Route 1A, Hamilton; (978) 468–7656. Polo season begins the last Sunday in May and continues to mid-October. Matches begin at 3:00 P.M.; gates open at 1:30 P.M. Admission: $10 per person; free for children under 12.

Need an activity that involves the little ones when they get antsy? During halftime spectators are asked to help prepare the field for the next half by stomping on the divots that have been dislodged by the racing polo ponies. Bring a blanket to spread out under the trees, and watch that the little ones don't run out into the field during play.

Appleton Farms and Appleton Farm Grass Rides (all ages)

Intersection of Cutler Road and Highland Street, Ipswich; (978) 356–5728; www.thetrustees.org. Open year-round 8:00 A.M. to sunset. Free.

The Appleton Grass Rides are a series of trails used for hiking, nature study, cross-country skiing, and snowshoeing. Due to the fragile nature of the trail, horseback riding is no longer allowed. One of the oldest continuously running farms in America, Appleton Farms has been newly acquired by the Trustees of Reservations and will be used to educate children on the workings of a farm. For those who enjoy birding, rare grassland birds can be observed on the Great Pasture.

Where to Stay

Miles River Country Inn Bed and Breakfast, 823 Bay Road, Hamilton; (978) 468–7206; www.milesriver.com. Lovely bed-and-breakfast with more than thirty acres of land and ten gardens. Most of the eight rooms have private baths. Open weekends only in May, June, and September. $$–$$$

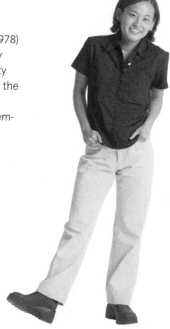

Wenham

Wenham Museum (all ages)

132 Main Street, Wenham; (978) 468–2377; www.wenhammuseum.org. Open year-round Tuesday through Sunday, 10:00 A.M. to 4:00 P.M. Closed Monday and major holidays. Admission: $5.00 for adults, $4.00 for seniors, and $3.00 for children 2 to 16.

The Wenham Museum is a social history museum that consists of a doll and toy collection, the Clafflin Richards House, a model train room, costume and textile galleries, and a room set aside for children's hands-on discovery. The Wenham Museum is often called "the doll museum" because of its enormous collection of dolls and dollhouses from around the world. Local children love to have their birthday parties here (by prior arrangement only), coupled with a visit to the Wenham Tea House for dessert.

Wenham Tea House (all ages)

4 Monument Street, Route 1A, Wenham; (978) 468–1398; www.wenhamteahouse.com. Open Monday through Saturday 9:30 A.M. to 5:00 P.M. Restaurant open from 11:30 A.M. to 2:30 P.M. for lunch, 3:15 to 4:30 P.M. for tea, and from noon to 5:00 P.M. on Sunday for tea only. Reservations suggested.

Operated by the Village Improvement Society, the tea house has a restaurant, a gourmet shop, a gift shop, a baby shop, and an adult clothing store. It's best known for its luncheon menu and afternoon tea. There is a side room for birthday parties. The tea house profits support local scholarships and playgrounds.

Beverly

Lynch Park (all ages)

55 Ober Street, Beverly; (978) 921–6067; www.bevrec.com. Open year-round from 8:00 A.M. to 8:00 P.M. in the winter, until 10:00 P.M. in the summer. Parking for nonresidents is $5.00 weekdays, $12.00 weekends and holidays.

On a windy spring day, Lynch Park is a great spot for kite flying. Once part of the Evans' estate (President Taft once summered here!), it is now the number-one choice of settings for many bridal pictures and weddings that take place in the park's beautiful rose garden. Children will delight in the extensive play structure, swings, and band shell (with summer concerts). The two small lifeguarded beaches tend to be rocky, but there's a small snack bar and kayak rentals. The annual Beverly Homecoming weeklong festival (first week in August) is centered in Lynch Park.

Children's **Theater**

- **Firehouse Theater,** 1 Market Square, Newburyport; (978) 462–7336; www.firehousecenter.com

- **Gloucester Stage Company,** 267 East Main Street, Gloucester; (978) 281–4099; www.cape-ann.com/stageco.html

- **Larcom Theatre,** 13 Wallis Street, Beverly; (978) 922–6313

- **Le Grand David and His Own Spectacular Magic Company,** 286 Cabot Street, Beverly; (978) 927–3677

- **Marblehead Little Theater,** Marblehead; (781) 631–9697; www.m-l-t.org

- **Neverland Express,** 284 Bay Road, Hamilton; (978) 468–1191; www.neverlandtheater.com

- **North Shore Music Theater,** 62 Dunham Road, Beverly; (978) 922–8500; www.nsmt.org

Marco the Magi's "Le Grand David and His Own Spectacular Magic Company" (all ages) ♫

Cabot Street Cinema, 286 Cabot Street, Beverly; (978) 927–3677. Performances are from mid-September through July, Sunday at 3:00 P.M. Admission: $18 for adults, $12 for children 11 and under. Buy tickets at the Cabot Theatre box office, Monday through Saturday, 9:00 A.M. to 9:00 P.M. Cash only.

An afternoon of family vaudeville is in the don't-miss category. Even while you're waiting for the show to start, there's plenty to watch—jugglers and puppeteers keep the kids fascinated while attendants take you to your seats. The shows are long (about two and a half hours), but don't let their length dissuade you from bringing younger kids to see the magic shows chock full of dancing, singing, and spectacular sets, all created by the dedicated resident stage troupe. Marco the Magnificent and Le Grand David have been named Magicians of the Year twice by the Academy of Magical Arts in Hollywood and by the Society of American Magicians in New York City. From October through May, on Thursdays, some holidays, and Saturdays, there's a two-hour magic show at the Larcom Theatre (13 Wallis Street, Beverly; same phone number).

North Shore Music Theater (all ages)

62 Dunham Road, Beverly; (978) 922–8500 or (978) 232–7200 for the box office; www
.nsmt.org. Call for schedule and tickets. Open year-round; snack bar and restaurant.

Professional theater in the round (every seat has a great view) featuring Broadway
musicals, celebrity concerts, one-man shows, and children's theatrical productions.
The North Shore Music Theater is extremely popular, and many shows sell out quickly.

Other Things to See and Do

Long Hill Sedgwick Gardens, 572
Essex Street, Beverly; (978) 921–1944;
www.thetrustees.org. Five acres of rare
and beautiful plantings managed by the
Trustees of Reservations.

Where to Eat

Beverly Depot and Saloon, 26 Park
Street, Beverly; (978) 927–5402; www
.barnsiderrestaurants.com. Waiters
dressed in engineers' uniforms serve your
meal in noisy but festive surroundings. Still
used as a train stop by the MBTA (be careful walking across the railroad track to get
to this restaurant). An extensive salad bar
and a variety of breads come with every
meal. If it's your birthday, notify the waiter
and you'll get a price break and a special
cake. $$–$$$

Casa de Lucca, 146 Rantoul Street, Beverly; (978) 922–7660; www.casadelucca
.com. Italian dining in a warm family
atmosphere. Pasta specials, children's
menu, and reasonable prices. $–$$

Cygnet, 24 West Street, Beverly; (978)
922–9221. Open for lunch and dinner.
Newly opened and designer-decorated by
the owner, an interior designer and owner
of the Vine and Ivy bed-and-breakfast.
Great menu, wonderfully warm and inviting
atmosphere. $–$$$

Where to Stay

Lakeview Motor Lodge, 5 Lakeview
Avenue, Route 1A, Beverly; (978) 922–
7535; www.lakeviewmotorlodge.com.
Newly refurbished suites with kitchenettes;
perfect for families. $–$$

Vine and Ivy Bed and Breakfast, 212
Hart Street, Beverly Farms; (978) 927–
2917; www.vineandivy.com. Charming five-
room inn on picturesque grounds contain-
ing vibrant gardens and a refreshing pool.
$$–$$$$

Cape Ann Region

The towns in this region include Manchester-by-the-Sea, Magnolia, Gloucester, Rock-port, and Essex. A great resource for information and brochures is the **Cape Ann Chamber of Commerce and Visitor Center,** 33 Commercial Street (978–283–1601; www.capeannvacation.com), Gloucester 01930. The Cape Ann area has a breathtaking coastline. An extremely pleasant way to meander along is by hooking up with Route 127 (Route 133 to Essex). For those more interested in getting there at a less leisurely pace, use Route 128.

Manchester-by-the-Sea

Singing Beach (all ages)

Beach Street, Manchester-by-the-Sea; www.manchester.ma.us. Free.

Manchester-by-the-Sea is home to one of the prettiest beaches on the North Shore, Singing Beach, a curving strip of sand that "sings" when the waves stroke it just right. Day-trippers from Boston take the train from North Station and walk the mile (a pleas-ant walk) to the beach. Between Memorial Day and Labor Day, beachside parking is strictly limited to residents only, so you'll have to drop the family at the beach, then drive back into town to park in one of the designated areas. At the beach you'll find a snack stand, restrooms, and changing rooms. On the way to the beach, you'll pass a grocery store that's perfectly located for last-minute picnic fixings, and there's a good ice-cream shop right next door, too, for postbeach snacking. Directions: Take Route 128 North from Boston, toward Gloucester. Take exit 15 (School Street) to the end. At the center of town, take a left through the village and follow Beach Street to the end.

Other Things to See and Do

Hiking spots with views

Agassiz Rock, School Street North toward Essex (exit 15), Manchester-by-the-Sea; www.thetrustees.com. Owned by the Trustees of Reservations. **Free.**

Coolidge Reservation, Summer Street (Route 127 North), Manchester-by-the-Sea; www.thetrustees.com. Owned by the Trustees of Reservations. **Free.**

Where to Eat

Beach Street Cafe, 35 Beach Street, Manchester-by-the-Sea; (978) 526–8049. Reasonable prices, great location. Break-fast and lunch specials. $

The Landing at 7 Central, 7 Central Street, Manchester-by-the-Sea; (978) 526–7494. Traditional New England fare, cozy and comfortable. Kids' menu. $–$$$

Where to Stay

Old Corner Inn, 2 Harbor Street (off Route 127), Manchester-by-the-Sea; (978) 526–4996 or (800) 830–4996; www.theold cornerinn.com. Open year-round. Gracious Victorian, former summer home of Danish ambassador. Rate includes continental breakfast. $$–$$$

Magnolia

Hammond Castle Museum (all ages)
80 Hesperus Avenue, Magnolia; (978) 283–7673; www.hammondcastle.org. Call for schedule. Admission: $8.50 for adults; $6.50 for seniors and students; $5.50 for children ages 6 to 12.

Built in 1926 by John Hays Hammond, an inventor, Hammond Castle Museum is an odd combination of the very old—bits of medieval French houses are built right into the building's walls—and the modern, for its day: The eight-story, 8,600-pipe organ is the largest organ in a private home in the country. Most tours include a short demonstration of the organ, which is now played by a computer. There are lots of other sights here, from a huge fifteenth-century fireplace to a glass-enclosed courtyard to a swimming pool that Hammond regularly dove into from his bedroom window. The Castle's Renaissance Fair (second weekend in July) is always a high point.

Where to Stay

The White House, 18 Norman Avenue, Magnolia; (978) 525–3642. Centrally located, charming inn with playground and sandy beach in walking distance. Rates include continental breakfast. $$

The Jaffe Family's **Favorite Beaches**

- Crane Beach, Argilla Road, Ipswich
- Good Harbor Beach, Thatcher Road, Gloucester
- Parker River Natural Wildlife Refuge and Plum Island, Newburyport
- Singing Beach, Central Street, Manchester-by-the-Sea
- Wingaersheek Beach, Atlantic Street, Gloucester

Gloucester

Gloucester is a grittier seaside village that's well known for its expert fishermen. Most members of the family will recognize the often-reproduced Fisherman's Statue, near the drawbridge. The statue, called *The Man at the Wheel,* was commissioned in 1923 to celebrate the town's 300th anniversary. Drive along the Harbor Loop to see the workings of a busy harbor.

Whale Watching

All of these whale-watching tours feature naturalists onboard and/or a touch tank. All are connected to research institutions. Sightings can include humpbacks, fin whales, and dolphins in the waters of Stellwagen Bank, a major whale feeding ground in the Atlantic. Remember to bring warm clothing, even on a hot sunny day, sunscreen, and a camera or video camera, and wear comfortable rubber-soled shoes.

- **Cape Ann Whale Watch,** Rose's Wharf, 415 Main Street, Gloucester; (978) 283–5110 or (800) 877–5110; www.caww.com or www.seethe whales.com. Claims to be the largest and fastest whale watch ship north of Boston. More than fifteen years of experience; area's best sighting record for humpbacks in the last two years.

- **Captain Bill's Whale Watch and Deep Sea Fishing,** Harbor Loop (near Capt. Carlo's Restaurant), Gloucester; (978) 283–6995 or (800) 33–WHALE; www.captainbillswhalewatch.com. All trips are narrated by the Whale Center of New England. Information collected helped Stellwagen Bank to be declared a national marine sanctuary.

- **Seven Seas Whale Watch,** Seven Seas Wharf, Rogers Street (Route 127), Gloucester; (978) 283–1776 or (888) 283–1776; www.7seaswhale watch.com. More than twenty-two years in business; featured in *National Geographic* and on the *Travelers Show* on the Discovery Channel.

- **Yankee Whale Watch and Deep Sea Fishing,** 75 Essex Avenue, Cape Ann Marina, Gloucester; (978) 283–0313 or (800) 942–5464; www .yankeefleet.com. Noted by *Charter Fishing* magazine as the best deep-sea fishing in New England, and voted by *New England* magazine as the "best bet" for whale watching.

Good Harbor Beach (all ages)

Thatcher Road, Gloucester; (978) 281–9785; www.gloucesterma.com/beaches.htm.
Parking is $25 weekends and holidays, $15 midweek (arrive early or you may not get
a spot).

Good Harbor is the most popular swimming beach in Gloucester, and deservedly so.
The beach's long white stretch of sand overlooks the Atlantic. Facilities include a
small snack stand, showers, and toilets. No dogs.

Wingaersheek Beach (all ages)

Atlantic Street (off Route 133), Gloucester; (978) 281–9785;
www.gloucesterma.com/beaches.htm. Parking is $25 weekends and holidays, $15 midweek.

Wingaersheek is a sandy ocean beach that's an especially good destination for families with young children: They love climbing on the smooth rocks and dunes that line
the shoreline. Directions: From Route 128, take exit 13. Facilities include a concession
stand, showers, and toilets. No dogs.

Moby Duck Amphibious Sightseeing (all ages)

Harbor Loop and Rogers Street, Gloucester; (978) 281–DUCK; www.mobyduck.com.
Operates weekends in May and daily Memorial Day through September, weather permitting. Price: $16 for adults, $10 for children. No credit cards.

A unique tour of Gloucester combining land and sea highlights of historical and scenic interest. The duck is an amphibious vessel on wheels.

Schooner *Thomas E. Lannon* (all ages)

Seven Seas Wharf, Rogers Street (Route 127), Gloucester; (978) 281–6634; www
.schooner.org. Operates May through October; call for a schedule. Tickets cost $30 for
adults, $25 for seniors, $20 for children 16 and under.

Sail on a 65-foot schooner past fabulous beaches, estates, lighthouses, and islands.
Special themed cruises with a flair include lobster bakes, sunset cruises, historic storytelling, music, humor, and private charters.

Recommended **Reading**

A great companion book before boarding the *Thomas E. Lannon* is
Schooner by Pat Lowery Collins. This beautifully illustrated children's
book describes the building process of the schooner as seen from the
point of view of a young boy.

Stage Fort Park (all ages)

Route 127, Gloucester; (978) 281–8865. Open year-round. Visitor center open Memorial Day through October 9:00 A.M. to 6:00 P.M. Parking fee $10.

The settlers found life too harsh at this location and eventually moved to the Naumkeag Peninsula. Ironically, this area is now a serene location for picnicking, grilling, hiking, listening to summer concerts and storytelling at the bandstand, or enjoying the two beaches (Half Moon and Cressey's Beach) and playground. Lovely harbor views.

Other Things to See and Do

Beauport, Sleeper McCann House (ages 10 and up), 75 Eastern Point Boulevard, Gloucester; (978) 283–0800; www.spnea.org. Open June 1 through mid-September. Call for schedule and prices. Whimsical summer home decorated with American and European finds by American designer Henry Davis Sleeper. Admission fee.

Ravenswood Park, Route 127, 481 Western Avenue, Gloucester; (978) 526–8687; www.thetrustees.org. Owned by the Trustees of Reservations, a 500-acre park with cross-country skiing, snowshoeing, and hiking trails. Picnicking is allowed. **Free.**

Rocky Neck, East Main Street, Gloucester; rockyneckartcolony.com. Oldest art colony in America, with many eateries and art galleries.

Where to Eat

Cameron's, Main Street, Gloucester; (978) 281–1331. A local favorite serving breakfast, lunch, and dinner. $–$$

Halibut Point Restaurant and Pub, 289 Main Street, Gloucester; (978) 281–1900. Open year-round. Good chowder that attracts lots of locals. $–$$

McT's Lobster House and Tavern, 25 Rogers Street, Gloucester; (978) 282–0950. On the waterfront. Featuring steak, seafood, pasta, and large appetizer selection. $–$$

The Rudder, 73 Rocky Neck Avenue, Gloucester; (978) 283–7967. Lunch and dinner served daily, spring through fall. A family-run restaurant whose fun-loving owners often provide unorthodox entertainment along with their excellent food. Outdoor seating overlooking Smith Cove. $$–$$$

Schooners, 50 Rogers Street, Gloucester; (978) 281–1962. Open for lunch and dinner. Specializing in seafood. The Schooner's Sampler is a great deal. $–$$$

Valentino's, 38 Main Street, Gloucester; (978) 283–6186. Voted best pizza on the North Shore for seven years running. Try the Hawaiian pizza, a pan-baked specialty, or one of the pasta dishes. $–$$

Festivals

St. Peter's Fiesta (held the last weekend in June) features a variety of events, including fireworks, races, and parades. The big attraction is the colorful "blessing of the fleet." Most events occur at the waterfront or in downtown Gloucester. Check out the Web site at www.stpetersfiesta.org.

Where to Stay

Cape Ann Motor Inn, 35 Rockport Road, Gloucester; (978) 281–2900 or (800) 464–VIEW; www.capeannmotorinn.com. Thirty-one beachfront units overlooking Long Beach with views of Thatcher Island. $$–$$$

Good Harbor Beach Inn, Salt Island Road, Gloucester, (978) 283–1489; www .goodharborbeachinn.com. Seasonal. Great location across from Good Harbor Beach. Wonderful views; family-style. $–$$

Harborview Inn, 71 Western Avenue, Gloucester; (978) 283–2277 or (800) 299–6696; www.harborviewinn.com. Six rooms, most with views of the harbor. Rate includes continental breakfast. $$–$$$

Ocean View, 171 Atlantic Road, Gloucester; (978) 283–6200 or (800) 315–7557; www.oceanviewinnandresort.com. Elegant resort and restaurant facing the Atlantic; two outdoor pools. $$–$$$$

Samarkand Guest House, 1 Harbor Road, Gloucester; (978) 283–3757; www.cape-ann.com/samarkand/. Family-oriented bed-and-breakfast across from the beach, in operation for thirty years. $–$$

Rockport

Bearskin Neck (all ages)
Corner of Dock Square and South Road.

Browse in seaside shops, restaurants, and art galleries. Don't forget to admire Motif #1 (one of the most admired scenes and painted innumerable times), a coastal shack hung with buoys.

Halibut Point Reservation (all ages)
Gott Avenue, Rockport; (978) 546–2997; www.massparks.org and www.thetrustees .org. Open daily year-round, sunrise to sunset. Parking is $2.00 Memorial Day to Columbus Day.

Halibut Point is a lovely place for walking and picnicking by the sea. It's not a sandy beach, though; the shore here is rocky, and kids should be encouraged to keep their shoes on to avoid cutting their feet on rocks or shells. Take a twenty-minute walk around the old quarry (hang onto the kids' hands), then play in the tidal pools. Bring windbreakers and warm clothes—it's usually windy—and keep an eye out for poison ivy.

The Paper House (all ages)

Route 127, 52 Pigeon Hill Street, Rockport; (978) 546–2629. Open daily April through October, 10:00 A.M. to 5:00 P.M. Admission by donation ($1.50 per person is suggested). Directions: Follow Route 127 in Rockport to Pigeon Cove. After the post office take the left onto Curtis Street and follow the signs.

Worth a stop, amazingly, everything in the house, from the walls to the furnishings, is made of paper, a twenty-year project by Elis Stenman as a leisure-time hobby!

Other Things to See and Do

Dove, T Wharf, Rockport; (978) 546–3642. Watch lobstering techniques and experience the local harbor and islands.

Northshore Kayak Outdoor Center, 9 Tuna Wharf, Rockport; www.northshore kayak.com. Tours, rentals, instructions, and overnights.

Where to Eat

Greenery Cafe and Restaurant, 15 Dock Square, Rockport; (978) 546–9593; www.thegreeneryrestaurant.com. Serving breakfast, lunch, and dinner. Delightful view of harbor. Salads, pasta, and seafood. $–$$

My Place by the Sea Restaurant, 68 Bearskin Neck, Rockport; (978) 546–9667; www.myplacebythesea.com. Open mid-April to the end of October. Panoramic view of Rockport coastline; indoor and outdoor dining. BYOB. $$–$$$$

Where to Stay

Addison Choate Inn, 49 Broadway, Rockport; (978) 546–7543 or (800) 245–7543; www.addisonchoateinn.com. Charming bed-and-breakfast minutes away from the heart of Rockport. $$–$$$

Emerson Inn by the Sea, 1 Cathedral Avenue, Pigeon Cove, Rockport; (978) 546–6321 or (800) 964–5550; www .emersoninnbythesea.com. Lovely grounds, traditional New England inn, spa, and fine restaurant. $$–$$$$

Peg Leg Inn, Beach and King Streets, Rockport; (978) 546–2352 or (800) 346–2352; www.pegleginn.com. Close to shops, restaurants, art galleries, and Front Beach. The inn incorporates a series of lovely colonial-era houses overlooking the beach, bay, and ocean. $$–$$$

Essex

Essex Shipbuilding Museum (all ages)

66 Main Street/Route 133W, Essex; (978) 768–7541; www.essexshipbuildingmuseum
.org. Open mid-May through mid-October Wednesday through Sunday noon to 4:00
P.M., mid-October to mid-May Wednesday, Saturday, and Sunday noon to 4:00 P.M., and
by appointment year-round. Admission: $5.00 for adults, $3.00 for students and seniors, under 12 free.

Reminiscent of the days when more wooden ships came from Essex than from any-
where else in the world, this excellent museum not only shows you how the ships
were built but also gives you the context you need to understand the significance of
the industry to the area. Real tools allow kids to try their hand at shipbuilding.

White Elephant (all ages)

32 Main Street, Essex; (978) 768–6901. Open daily year-round Monday through Saturday 10:00 A.M. to 5:00 P.M., Sunday noon to 5:00 P.M.

Essex is also known as an antiques-lover's haven. One of the more interesting shops
is the White Elephant, next door to the Shipbuilding Museum. The stock changes
often, but in the past it has included collections of wooden teeth, old train sets, and
wasp-waisted dresses from a hundred years ago.

Essex River Cruises and Charters (all ages)

Essex Marina, 35 Dodge Street, Essex; (978) 768–6981 or (800) RIVER–06; www.essex
cruises.com. Open May through October. Pricing: $21 for adults, $10 for children 12
and under. Charters and clambakes a specialty. Call for a schedule (seasonal).

The ninety-minute tour cruise on the *Essex River Queen* takes you past beaches,
marshes, "old money" estates, and shipbuilding yards. This is a relaxing and informative tour from a different perspective. Temperatures on the water can fluctuate; bring
a jacket.

Other Things to See and Do

Agawam Boat Charters, 21 Pickering
Street, Essex; (978) 768–1114; www.cape-
ann.com/agawam. Seasonal.

Essex River Basin Adventures, 66R
Main Street, Essex; (978) 768–ERBA or
(800) KAYAK–04; www.erba.com. Seasonal.

Stavros Reservation, Island Road (off of
Route 133), Essex; www.thetrustees.org.
Great views; hiking, picnicking, and bird-
watching.

Where to Eat

Periwinkles, 74 Main Street, Essex; (978)
768–6320; www.periwinklesrestaurant
.com. Great spot overlooking a picturesque
tidal river. $–$$

Woodman's, 121 Main Street/Route 133,
Essex; (978) 768–6451; www.woodmans
.com. According to the Woodman family,
this is where the first clam was breaded
and fried (in 1916). $–$$

North of Cape Ann

The North Shore continues up the coast to the border of New Hampshire. Main access roads are Routes 1/95 and 495. Slower going is Route 133 from Ipswich, connecting to Route 1A toward Newburyport. **Ipswich Visitor Information Center,** 36 South Main Street Route 1A; (978) 356–8540, is open Memorial Day weekend to Columbus Day.

Ipswich

Crane Beach (all ages)

310 Argilla Road, Ipswich; (978) 356–4354 (beach office) or (978) 356– 4351; www .thetrustees.org. Open year-round 8:00 A.M. to sunset. Parking fee is $5.00 to $20.00 per car, depending on time of year and day of week.

Crane Beach is a long, clean beach that's great for swimming, picnicking, and walking. During the summer there are lifeguards on duty and the bathhouse and snack bar are open. There are several pleasant, easy walks to take from the beach. One leads to Castle Hill; the other is a self-guided nature walk (trail map available) that leads you over boardwalks, through a swamp, and into a piney forest. Home to more than 200 species of resident and migratory birds, white-tailed deer, red squirrels, red fox, and opossum. *CAUTION:* Greenbug season lasts for about two weeks in midsummer and can be annoying. *NOTE:* No dogs. Directions: From Route 1A south of Ipswich, take Route 133 East. Turn left onto Northgate Road. At the end of this road, turn right onto Argilla Road, which ends at the beach.

Fun **Events**

- **Independence Day Celebration**—Castle Hill celebrates the Fourth of July with fireworks, music, and children's activities. Call (978) 356–4351 for more details.

- **Sand Blast**—Annual sandcastle contest in August at Crane Beach. Call (978) 356–4351.

Castle Hill (all ages)

290 Argilla Road, Ipswich; (978) 356–4351; www.thetrustees.org or www.craneestate
.org. Admission fee for grounds and tours; call for rates. The grounds are open 9:00
A.M. to sunset year-round.

The former home of the Crane family, for whom Crane Beach is named. Now owned
and managed by the Trustees of Reservations, a private land trust whose holdings
include many other properties listed in this book, the beautiful old mansion is the
summer home to an excellent performing arts series on Thursday nights. Audiences
sit on the sweeping lawn to hear the music or watch the play. There are other seasonal activities as well. Call or write for a schedule or visit the Web site www.crane
estate.org; tickets sometimes sell out.

Crane Islands Tour (all ages)

Argilla Road, to the right of the Crane Beach Gate, Ipswich; (978) 356–4351. Check the
summer schedule on www.thetrustees.org. Price: $12.00 for adults, $5.00 for children
3 to 12.

Tour Choate and Long Islands by hay wagon after crossing the Castle Neck River by
boat. View wildlife and the Crane Wildlife Refuge. Very scenic and chosen for the film-
ing of *The Crucible* with Winona Ryder.

Wolf Hollow (all ages)

114 Essex Road, Route 133, Ipswich; (978) 356–0216; www.wolfhollowipswich.org.
Open to the public on weekends only, 1:00 to 5:00 P.M., year-round. Admission: $6.00
for adults, $4.50 for children 17 and under.

Wolf Hollow is a wild animal refuge and educational facility dedicated to the preserva-
tion of the gray wolf. There are presentations at 1:30 P.M. year-round and at 3:30 P.M.
from March through November.

Russell Orchards (all ages) 🍁

143 Argilla Road, Ipswich; (978) 356–5366; www.russellorchardsma.com.

More than an orchard, Russell Orchards has a playground, animals in the barnyard
that are accustomed to being petted, and hayrides during the fall. In season pick your
own strawberries, blackberries, blueberries, raspberries, and apples. Don't leave without buying a few of the delicious homemade doughnuts or a bottle of their vintage
fruit wine or hard cider. Open daily from mid-May through the end of November 9:00
A.M. to 6:00 P.M. Voted Best of Boston in 1996 for farm stands north of Boston.

Foote Brothers Canoe Rental (ages 3 and up)
230 Topsfield Road, Ipswich; (978) 356–9771; www.footebrotherscanoes.com. Open
April through October, summer hours 8:00 A.M. to 6:00 P.M., spring and fall 9:00 A.M. to
5:00 P.M. Price: $25 to $40 per canoe midweek, $30 to $40 per canoe weekends and
holidays, depending upon the trip that you take.

Provides canoes and advice for families who enjoy paddling on a calm river. Shuttle
trips for longer journeys; overnight trips can be arranged.

Where to Eat

The Clam Box of Ipswich, 246 High
Street, Ipswich; (978) 356–9707; www
.ipswichma.com/clambox. Open March
through November. Cash only. Local icon
since 1935 shaped like a clam box; known
for its burgers, clams, fries, and scallops.
$–$$

White Farms Ice Cream, 266 High
Street, Ipswich; (978) 356–2633; www
.whitefarmsicecream.com. Winner of the
Best of Boston 1996 Award. Known for creative ice cream flavors like Expresso Explo-
sion, Key Lime Pie, Reverse Chip, and
Caramel Cow.

Where to Stay

Inn at Castle Hill, 280 Argilla Road,
Ipswich; (978) 412–2555; www.theinnat
castlehill.com. One of two Trustees of
Reservations' bed-and-breakfasts. Money
earned helps to preserve and maintain the
site. Open February through December.
Luxurious appointments. Views of Crane
Beach and the Ipswich River estuaries.
Continental breakfast included. $$–$$$$

Newburyport and Newbury

Newburyport is a quaint seaside town imbued with a sense of history and charm.
Imposing homes of the Federalist style line the major streets into the downtown area,
signaling the wealth of a bygone era when Newburyport was a center of commerce
and trade. Major fortunes were made in Newburyport due to its maritime industry. In
a revitalized rebirth, the community became a popular tourist destination in the '70s.
To obtain your sixty-page *Official Guide to Newburyport,* contact **Destination New-
buryport,** 38R Merrimac Street, Newburyport 01950; (978) 462–6680 or visit their
Web site at www.newburyportchamber.org/visitor.htm. For information on the three
themed Essex Heritage Trails, contact the **National Park Service's Visitor Center**
at the **Custom House Maritime Museum,** 25 Water Street, Newburyport 01950;
(978) 462–0681; www.essexheritage.org.
    A great location for family recreation is Plum Island, which is partly in Newbury
and partially in Newburyport. Both Plum Island and the Parker River Wildlife Refuge
(which is on Plum Island) are terrific places for family swimming, hiking, and biking.

Biking Shops

Biking shops for rentals in the area include:

- **Bike Shop Aries,** 96 Newburyport Turnpike (Route 1), Newbury; (978) 465–8099

- **Riverside Cycles,** 50 Water Street (The Tannery Building), Newburyport; (978) 465–5566 or (888) 465–BIKE; www.riversidecycle.com

Parker River National Wildlife Refuge (all ages)

261 Northern Boulevard, Newburyport, Plum Island; (978) 465–5753; www.fws.gov or www.parkerriver.org (special kids corner section). During the plovers' nesting season (early April through June), most of the beach is usually closed. July is limited; August through March the beach is open. Otherwise open daily year-round, dawn to dusk. Parking is $5.00 per car. A refuge pass good for the entire season costs $12.00.

Covering about two-thirds of Plum Island, the wildlife refuge is a favorite destination for Boston-area families. The refuge is operated by the U.S. Fish and Wildlife Service; it is one of the very few natural barrier beach, dune, and salt marsh complexes left on the coast of New England. Along with the abundant wildlife on view here in its natural habitat, the great attraction of Plum Island (which is what the locals call it) is the beach. Those who are in the know arrive at the refuge very early (before 8:30 A.M.), since only a few parking spots are available. There are several observation towers that are well-used by bird-watchers in March and April, the peak migration periods for ducks and other waterfowl; the views are always good, though, and there are always birds to see—300 or so species live in the area. The 6-mile-long beach is nearly always deserted. Because of the strong undertow, it's not a good place for families with young children; also, there are no lifeguards. At the extreme end is Sandy Point State Reservation (www.massparks.org) and Sandy Point, which is owned by the town of Ipswich and is a more placid place for a swim. NOTE: Don't bring pets; do bring bug spray.

Maudslay State Park (all ages)

Curzon's Mill Road, Newburyport; (978) 465–7223; www.state.ma.us/dem/parks/smaud.htm. Open year-round 8:00 A.M. to sunset. Free.

When the mansion of this 500-acre estate was taken down in the 1950s, the landscaped grounds became a state park. It's a great place on a spring or summer afternoon—picnic spots abound, and there are lots of walking trails through formal gardens, rolling meadows, woods, and an enormous stand of mountain laurel. Other popular forms of recreation here include biking, horseback riding, and cross-country skiing.

Yakity-yak, **Let's Kayak!**

Kayaking tours of the salt marshes around Plum Island and the Newburyport area can be arranged by:

- **Joppa Flats Education Center,** Plum Island Turnpike (near Ocean Avenue), Newburyport; (978) 462–9998; www.massaudubon.org

- **Plum Island Kayak Tours,** 38R Merrimac Street, Unit 102B, Newburyport; (978) 462–5510; wwwplumislandkayak.com

Other Things to See and Do

Coffin House, 14 High Road, Newbury; (978) 462–2634; www.spnea.org. Home built by the early settlers.

Cushing House Museum, 98 High Street, Newburyport; (978) 462–2681; www.newburyhist.com. Open May through October. Call for hours and fees. Depicts the history of the city and rural life.

Custom House Maritime Museum, 25 Water Street, Newburyport; (978) 462–8681; www.themaritimesociety.org. Maritime history collection. Small fee.

Merrimac Street Shops. Browsing in the quaint shops of Newburyport is a pleasant pastime.

Newburyport's Whale Watch, Hilton's Dock, 54 Merrimac Street, Newburyport; (978) 499–0832 or (800) 848–1111; www.newburyportwhalewatch.com. Whale watches, dinner cruises, charters. Will do school talks with an inflatable 55-foot fin whale. Naturalist on board.

Spencer-Pierce-Little Farm, 5 Little's Lane, Newbury; (978) 462–2634; www.spnea.org. Prominent local family's 230-acre seventeenth-century farmhouse and grounds.

Yankee Clipper, 1 Merrimac Landing #26, Newburyport; (978) 462–9316; www.harbortours.com. Historical and colorful tours of Newburyport and its waters; specializing in harbor and sunset cruises.

Where to Eat

The Black Cow, 54R Merrimac Street, Newburyport; (978) 499–8811. Water views of the Merrimac; outdoor deck seating. Daily and nightly specials, popular Sunday brunch, kids' menu. $$–$$$

The Grog Restaurant, 13 Middle Street, Newburyport; (978) 465–8008; www.thegrog.com. Newburyport's oldest historical restaurant, publike atmosphere. $–$$$

Michael's Harborside, 1 Tournament Wharf, Newburyport; (978) 462–7785; www.michaelsharborside.com. On the water overlooking the harbor. Specializing in steak and seafood. $–$$

Ten Center Street and Molly's Pub, 10 Center Street, Newburyport; (978) 462–6652. Traditional dining. Fireplaces in some of the rooms; lighter fare in the pub. $–$$$

Where to Stay

Clark Currier Inn, 45 Green Street, Newburyport; (978) 465–8363; www.clark currierinn.com. Open year-round. Classic 1803 Federal building not far from the main shopping area of Newburyport. Request a family-style room; though they're all large, not all bedrooms are appropriate for children. There's a comfortable lounge/TV room and backyard. $$–$$$

Garrison Inn, 11 Brown Square, Newburyport; (978) 499–8500; www.garrison inn.com. Bedroom lofts, working fireplaces, and views of the Merrimack River are all found at the Garrison Inn, a national historical landmark. Complimentary continental breakfast. $$–$$$$

Salisbury, Amesbury, and Merrimac

Salisbury Beach State Reservation and Camping Area (all ages)

Beach Road off Route 1A, Salisbury; (978) 462–4481; www.massparks.org. **Salisbury Beach State Reservation is open year-round and charges a $7.00 parking fee for cars Memorial Day to Labor Day.**

Close to the border of Massachusetts and New Hampshire, Salisbury Beach State Reservation, on 520 acres, abuts both the Atlantic Ocean and the mouth of the Merrimack River. A long stretch of pristine, sandy beach is lifeguarded for safe swimming from Memorial Day to Labor Day. Beautiful vistas abound, and it's a haven for boating and fishing. Other facilities include a playground, picnic area, and a concession stand. Restrooms and shower facilities are available near the campground area. The 483 campground sites have a limited number of trailer and RV hookups available. Look for the harbor seals on the rocks.

Amesbury Sports Park (ages 4 and up)

12 Hunt Road (exit 54 off Route 495), Amesbury; (978) 388–5788; www.goslide.com. Open Christmas through mid-March. Call for price and schedule; extended hours during vacation periods. Price based on day of week and time of day.

Managed by former Boston Bruins player Brad Park, this is a great place for winter tubing fun. The park has four rope tows to handle the crowds and to give you a boost up the hill. There are ten different runs at various levels; children ages 4 to 7 must be accompanied by an adult. Helmets are **free** of charge, and young children are required to wear them. There is a snack bar and cafeteria. Groups are welcome, so keep that in mind if you decide to visit during peak times. The Sports Park does snow-making to ensure snow coverage on the hill.

The new Amesbury Sports Park is offering paint ball on three levels: novice, intermediate, and expert. Call for hours, pricing, rules, and regulations.

Other Things to See and Do

Adventure Learning, 67 Bear Hill, Merrimac; (978) 346–9728 or (800) 649–9728; www.adventure-learning.com. Rock climbing for all levels.

Lowell's Boat Shop, Point Shore, Amesbury; (978) 388–0162. The country's oldest continuous boat-building business, managed by the Custom House Maritime Museum in Newburyport and part of the Essex Heritage Trail.

Where to Eat

Hodgies, Haverhill Street, Amesbury; (978) 388–1211; www.hodgies.com. Homemade ice cream, big scoops. $

The Inn at Stripers Grille, 175 Bridge Road, Salisbury; (978) 499–0400; www .stripersgrille.com. Eat outside on the spacious deck or dine in by the fireplace. Views of the Merrimack River and the Newburyport waterfront. $–$$

Where to Stay

The Inn at Stripers Grille, 175 Bridge Road, Salisbury; (978) 499–0400; www .stripersgrille.com. Twenty-one rooms, many with views of the Merrimack River and looking toward the Newburyport waterfront. $–$$$

Lowell and the Merrimack Valley

The Merrimack River winds through the valley, flowing past large cities like Lowell and Haverhill, once large mill towns, and small, picturesque, ramblin' towns like Westford and the Andovers. The major highway connecting the region is Route 495, paralleling the state line of New Hampshire just 10 to 15 miles north of the highway. For further information contact the **Greater Merrimack Valley Convention and Visitors Bureau** at (978) 459–6150 or (800) 443–3332; www.merrimackvalley.org.

Haverhill

Bradford Ski Area (ages 3 and up)
South Cross Road (off Salem Street), Haverhill; (978) 373–0071 or (866) 644–SNOW
(snow info line); www.SkiBradford.com. Open mid-December to end of March, Monday
through Saturday 8:30 A.M. to 10:00 P.M., Sunday 8:30 A.M. to 4:30 P.M. Price: Call for
prices and specials.

A great place to break a child into the sport of skiing or snowboarding (oops, no pun
intended!), Bradford, with a 250-foot vertical drop, is a family-oriented hill. Bradford
has thirteen trails accessed by two triple chairs, four rope tows, and two T-bars. The
night skiing is well lit. For the snowboard enthusiast there is a snowboard park.

Facilities include a lodge, equipment rentals, a snack bar, and a ski school.

Andover/North Andover

Outside in Andover

- **Harold Parker State Forest,** 1951 Turnpike Road, North Andover;
  (978) 686–3391; www.massparks.org. State forest covering Andover,
  North Andover, and North Reading. Hiking, biking, fishing, horseback
  riding, nature study, picnicking, swimming, camping, and interpretive
  programs.

- **Stevens-Coolidge Place and Gardens,** 139 Andover Street, North
  Andover; (978) 682–3580; www.thetrustees.org. Historic house/
  museum on ninety-five acres. Trustees of Reservations property.
  Admission is free.

- **Ward Reservation,** Prospect Road, Andover; (978) 682–3580; www.the
  trustees.org. Nice trails on 694 acres used for cross-country skiing,
  snowshoeing, hiking, and horseback riding. The highest point in Essex
  County overlooks the Solstice Stones. The Solstice Stones are
  arranged like a compass, and the spring and fall equinoxes and the
  summer and winter solstices are all aligned. Open dawn to dusk; allow
  two hours for your visit. Trustees of Reservations property. Free.

- **Weir Hill,** Stevens Street, North Andover; (978) 682–3580; www.the
  trustees.org. Activities include hiking, cross-country skiing, picnicking, and horseback riding. Great views of Lake Cochichewick.
  Trustees of Reservations property. Admission is free.

Lowell

The main tourist attraction of the Merrimack Valley is Lowell, the country's first planned industrial city, in whose enormous brick mills the world's first mass-produced cotton cloth originated. Stop by the Greater Merrimack Convention and Visitors Bureau at 9 Central Street; (978–459–6150 or 800–443–3332; www.lowell.org/lowell.php or www.merrimackvalley.org) for area information.

Lowell National Historical Park (all ages)

Visitor center at Market Mills, 246 Market Street, Lowell; (978) 970–5000; www.nps .gov/lowell. Visitor center open during the winter Monday through Saturday 9:00 A.M. to 5:00 P.M., Sunday 10:00 A.M. to 5:00 P.M. Boott Cotton Mills Museum open Monday through Saturday 9:30 A.M. to 5:00 P.M., Sunday 11:00 A.M. to 5:00 P.M. During the summer the visitor center is open from 9:00 A.M. to 5:45 P.M. Admission for Cotton Mills: $4.00 for adults, $3.00 for seniors, and $2.00 for children. The visitor center is free.

Lowell National Historic Park provides excellent presentations and tours that bring Lowell's heyday to life, in some cases, deafeningly so. Lowell was named for Francis Cabot Lowell, the man who came up with the idea (and much of the money) for a planned industrial community. He also had the idea, highly radical in its time, of employing women, who made up the majority of the workforce. Kirk Boott headed up the group of people who planned, financed, and built Lowell. The largest of the cotton mills was named for him, and today the Boott Cotton Mills Museum is the star of Lowell. Restored in 1992, the museum re-creates the work environment that the "mill girls" experienced, complete with eighty-eight looms in full operation. Earplugs are available for tourists, but there was no such thing for the workers, who spent about seventy-two hours a week here, on their feet, without the benefit of ventilation, and earning a weekly wage of $2.25. History comes to life here in more ways than one: Be sure to listen to the recorded stories of some of the workers who ran the mills.

Lots of **Locks**

Another highlight of a family trip to Lowell is the boat ride through the city's intricate canal-and-lock system. Reservations for these tours are strongly recommended; you wouldn't want to arrive in Lowell to find out that your family won't fit onto any boats that day. Tours leave from the visitor center (978–970–5000). The fee is $6.00 for adults, $4.00 for children 6 to 16, free for children under 5.

Jaffe Family **Farm Favorites**

The following is a list of area farms that have pick-your-own fruits and flowers, picnic areas, food stands, hayrides, batting cages, minigolf, farm animal viewing, or a combination of any of the above:

- **Brooksby Farm,** 38 Felton Street, Peabody; (978) 531–1631; www.essexheritage.org

- **Green Meadows Farm,** 650 Asbury Street, South Hamilton; (978) 468–3720; www.gmfarm.com

- **Ingaldsby Farm,** 22 Washington Street, West Boxford; (978) 352–2813

- **Richardson Farms Inc.,** 156 South Main Street (Route 114), Middleton; (978) 774–4476 (golf) and (978) 774–5450; www.richardsonsice cream.com

- **Smolak Farms,** 315 South Bradford Street, North Andover; (978) 682–6332; www.smolakfarms.com

- **Tendercrop Farm,** 108 High Road (Route 1A), Newbury; (978) 462–6972

American Textile History Museum (all ages)
491 Dutton Street, Lowell; (978) 441–0400; www.athm.org. Open Tuesday through Friday 9:00 A.M. to 4:00 P.M., weekends and holidays 10:00 A.M. to 5:00 P.M. Closed Mondays, Thanksgiving, Christmas, and New Year's Day. Admission: $6.00 for adults, $4.00 for children ages 6 to 16, under 6 is free.

History comes alive at the American Textile Museum, with an extremely engaging and impressive array of spinning wheels, weaving machines, 300 years of clothing and textile history, and industrial machinery. The museum, located in a historic mill building, is very well done and will amaze children.

Performing Arts for Children

Discovery Series, University of Massachusetts, 1 University Avenue, Lowell; (978) 934–4444. Price: $10 per person; reservations encouraged. Ask about discount packages. Performances have ranged from juggling, African dance, and puppetry to stories and songs and Chinese acrobats.

Lowell Festivals

- **Lowell Folk Festival** (last full weekend in July). Largest free folk festival in the country; ethnic food, music, and dance. Call (978) 970–4257 or (978) 970–5000, extension 31, for more information. You can find them on the Web at www.lowellfolkfestival.org.

- **Cambodian Water Festival** (third Saturday in August). Native Cambodian dancing and music at Sampas Pavilion. Call (978) 454–4286 or (978) 970–4257 for more information.

- **Banjo and Fiddle Contest** (third weekend in September). Premier East Coast competition at Boardinghouse Park. Call (978) 970–5000, extension 31, for more information or www.nps.gov/lowell.

Other Things to See and Do

New England Quilt Museum, 18 Shattuck Street, Lowell; (978) 452–4207; www.nequiltmuseum.org. Constantly changing exhibits (limited hanging time before the quilts start to stretch).

Revolving Museum, 22 Shattuck Street, Lowell; (978) 937–2787; www.revolving museum.org. The focus of this museum is on collaborations between artists, youth, and community members (multiple people work together to create a piece).

Whistler House Museum of Art, 243 Worthen Street, Lowell; (978) 452–7641; www.whistlerhouse.org. Birthplace of artist James McNeill Whistler, known for his painting *Whistler's Mother.* Paintings and prints from the nineteenth and twentieth centuries.

Where to Eat

Barney's Deli, 81 Middlesex Street, Lowell; (978) 452–8547. Known for its fabulous breakfasts, Barney's is open from 11:00 A.M. to 3:00 P.M. Great deli sandwiches, soup, and chowders. $

Cobblestones, 91 Dutton Street, Lowell; (978) 970–2282; www.cobblestonesof lowell.com. Historic building downtown, friendly service and architecturally interesting dining room. Unusual menu. $–$$

Ricardo's Cafe Trattoria, 110 Gorham Street, Lowell; (978) 453–2777; www.ziplink.net/~ricardos. Open Tuesday through Saturday for lunch and dinner. Ricardo has tried to model his restaurant after the small welcoming trattorias of Italy. Delicious Italian food.

For aficionados of diners, try the following:

The Club Diner, 145 Dutton Street, Lowell; (978) 452–1679. Serving breakfast all day in this remnant of a bygone era.

Four Sisters Owl Diner, 244 Appelton Street, Lowell; (978) 453–8321. Open weekends 7:00 A.M. to 2:00 P.M. and midweek from 6:00 A.M. to 2:00 P.M.

Sports

- **Lowell Locks Monsters,** 77 Merrimack Street, Tsongas Arena, 300 Arcand Drive, Lowell; (978) 458–PUCK; www.locksmonsters.com. Affiliated with the Carolina Hurricanes and the American Hockey League. Call for a schedule.

- **Lowell Spinners,** Edward A. Le Lacheur Park, 450 Aiken Street (U. Mass/Lowell Campus), Lowell; (978) 459–2255 or (978) 459–1702 (box office); www.lowellspinners.com. Farm league team of the Red Sox playing in a new 4,700-seat stadium.

Where to Stay

Doubletree Riverfront Hotel, 50 Warren Street, Lowell; (978) 452–1200; www.doubletree.com. Offers 252 guest rooms near all major attractions; cookies upon check-in; heated indoor pool. $$–$$$$

Westford, Chelmsford, and Tyngsboro

Butterfly Place at Papillon Park (all ages)

120 Tyngsboro Road, Westford; (978) 392–0955; www.butterflyplacema.com. Open daily from March 1 through Columbus Day, 10:00 A.M. to 5:00 P.M. Admission: $7.50 for adults, $5.50 for children 3 to 12.

Papillon means "butterfly" in French, and that's what your family will see at the Butterfly Place, a highly unusual farm where hundreds of butterflies flutter above and through flowering plants and weeds in an enormous solar dome. It's fun to see how many different kinds of butterflies you can identify. There's a pleasant picnic spot, too. *WARNING:* No tickets are sold after 4:30 P.M.

Nashoba Valley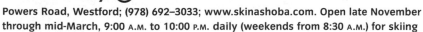

Powers Road, Westford; (978) 692–3033; www.skinashoba.com. Open late November through mid-March, 9:00 A.M. to 10:00 P.M. daily (weekends from 8:30 A.M.) for skiing and snowtubing; call for hours and rates.

Offers nine lifts (three triple chairs), seventeen trails. Facilities include a lodge, restaurant, and bar. Packages available. Special events are held throughout the winter,

Marcia's
TopAnnualEvents
for the North Shore, Cape Ann, and the Merrimack Valley

- **Strawberry Festival,** June, Russell Orchards, 143 Argilla Road, Ipswich; (978) 356–5366; www.ipswichma.com

- **Theater in the Open,** June through September, Curzon's Mill Road, Newburyport; (978) 465–2572; www.theaterintheopen.org

- **St. Peter's Fiesta,** late June, Gloucester; (978) 283–1601

- **Danvers Family Festival,** end of June, early July, Danvers; (978) 777–0001; www.danversrec.com

- **Massachusetts Maritime Festival,** mid-July, Derby Wharf (Salem Maritime National Historic Site, Salem); (978) 740–1650; www.nps.gov/stma

- **Hammond Castle Robin Hood Faire,** July, Magnolia; (978) 283–2080; www.hammondcastle.org

- **Marblehead Race Week,** late July, Marblehead; www.mheadrace.org

- **Lowell Folk Festival,** late July, Lowell; (978) 970–4257; (978) 970–5000, extension 31

- **Gloucester Waterfront Festival,** August, Gloucester; (978) 283–1601; www.castleberryfairs.com

- **Southeast Asian Water Festival,** late August, Lowell; (978) 970–4257 or (978) 970–4040

- **Schooner Festival,** Labor Day weekend, Gloucester Harbor; (978) 283–1601; www.capeannvacation.com/schooner

- **Essex Clamfest,** September, Memorial Park, Essex; (978) 283–1601; www.capeannvacations.com

- **Seafood Festival,** September, St. Peters Park, Gloucester; (978) 283–1601; www.capeannvacations.com

- **International Festival,** September, Peabody Square, Peabody; (978) 532–3000

- **Salem's Haunted Happenings,** October, Salem; (978) 744–3663 or (877) SALEMMA; www.hauntedhappenings.org

- **Spirits of the Gables,** October, House of Seven Gables, Salem; (978) 744–0991; www.7gables.org
- **Topsfield Fair,** October, Topsfield Fairgrounds, Topsfield; (978) 887–5000; www.topsfieldfair.org
- **Christmas on Cape Ann,** December, Rockport, Gloucester, Manchester, and Essex; (978) 283–1601; www.capeannvacations.com

October, and the summer. A highlight is the Halloween Celebration with three scary attractions: Vampire Village Cemetery, Nightmare Mansion, and Witches Woods Haunted Hayride.

Where to Eat

Bainbridges Restaurant, 75 Princeton Street, North Chelmsford; (978) 251–8670; www.bainbridges.com. Open Tuesday through Friday and Sunday for lunch and dinner; Saturday for dinner only. Located on the Stoney Brook Canal, Bainbridges was an old textile mill that has been rehabbed into a fine restaurant. Great views, high ceilings, and memorabilia throughout. Specialties include prime rib, seafood, and pasta. $–$$$

Kimball Farm, 400 Littleton Road, Westford; (978) 486–3891; www.kimballfarm .com. Homemade ice cream makes this a mecca for ice cream aficionados! Charming building with a country store gift shop and a small cafe. Miniature golf, bumper boats, and a nine-hole golf range. $

Where to Stay

Radisson Heritage Hotel Chelmsford, 10 Independence Drive, Chelmsford; (978) 256–0800; www.radisson.com. Five minutes from the historic heart of Lowell; indoor pool and fitness center. $$–$$$

Stonehedge Inn, 160 Pawtucket Boulevard, Tyngsboro; (978) 649–4400 or (888) 649–2474; www.stonehedgeinn.com. Luxurious, lush European-style manor with thirty rooms in French country decor—some with fireplaces. Outdoor/indoor pool and spa. The restaurant has superb cuisine and wine list (no real children's menu, but the chef will make chicken tenders with advance notice). $$$–$$$$

Greater Boston

Chock-full of history, New England's largest city seems to have a significant site on every corner. Tourism has always been part of life in busy Boston, and residents don't mind sharing their beautiful city with visitors. They appreciate the smallness of the downtown area as much as you will. What's more, many of the older areas of the North End, Beacon Hill, and the Back Bay are surprisingly compact

Marcia's
TopPicks in Greater Boston

1. The Museum of Science Campus (the Science Museum, the Omni Theater, the Hayden Planetarium, and the Laser Light Show), Cambridge

2. Museum Wharf (Children's Museum and the Boston Tea Party Ships and Museum)

3. Duckling Statues and Swan Boat ride at the Public Garden

4. New England Aquarium

5. Charlestown Navy Yard (Constitution Museum, the USS *Cassin Young*, and the USS *Constitution*)

6. Franklin Park Zoo, Jamaica Plain

7. Museum of Fine Arts

8. Boston Harbor Islands National Park and Recreation Area

9. Drumlin Farm, South Lincoln

10. Minute Man National Park, Lexington and Concord

11. Discovery Museums, Acton

12. The Prudential Skywalk Observatory

GREATER BOSTON

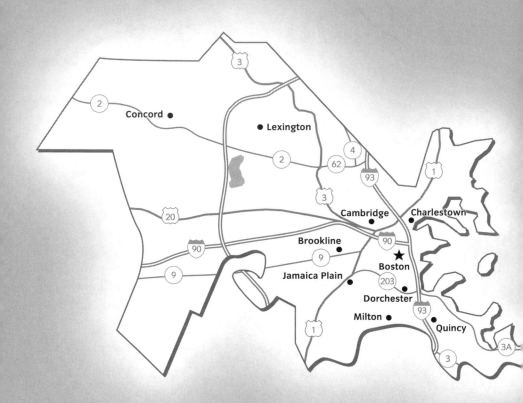

and therefore walkable for parents and kids alike. Before you arrive, contact the **Greater Boston Convention and Visitors Bureau,** 2 Copley Place, Suite 105, Boston 02116; (617) 536–4100 or (888) SEE BOSTON; www.bostonusa.com, for maps or brochures.

Avoid restricting your journey solely to the sites along the well-trafficked red line of the Freedom Trail (www.thefreedomtrail.org). Kids will also enjoy the museums of Boston, especially the Museum of Science, the New England Aquarium, and the Children's Museum. Don't miss the bronze statues of Mrs. Mallard and her brood, the heroes of *Make Way for Ducklings,* near the pond in the Public Garden. And be sure to take a day or two to explore the nearby towns of Cambridge, Lexington, and Concord.

Some Practical Information

Accommodations

Boston is an expensive place to stay. If you won't be staying with friends, plan ahead to get the best prices. The hotels listed in this chapter offer family packages throughout the year, but you must reserve ahead of time. An alternative is **Bed & Breakfast Agency of Boston** (47 Commercial Wharf, Boston; 617–720–3540 or 800–248–9262; www.boston-bnbagency.com), which maintains an extensive list of bed-and-breakfast accommodations around the city. They'll match your requirements and price range with an appropriate room, suite, efficiency, or apartment in both Boston and Cambridge. Rates are $100 to $188, double occupancy; kids stay **free.** Winter packages are great: three nights for the price of two, based on availability December 15 through January 15.

Medical

Inn-House Doctor; (617) 267–9407. Payment: credit card, check, or cash. It's no fun getting sick while you're on vacation, but lucky for you these dedicated doctors make house calls within one hour and come to more than one hundred hotels in the Boston area twenty-four hours a day. Staff includes general practitioners, pediatricians, and dentists who are affiliated with area hospitals.

Parking in Boston

Parking places are hard to come by in Boston. You'll enjoy your visit more if you leave the car in a parking garage and rely on public transportation, such as the MBTA (aka the "T"), and tour buses to get around.

Reduced-Rate Tickets

BosTix Ticket Booths offer half-price, day-of-performance tickets for theatrical and musical events. There are two locations in Boston; Copley Square and next to Faneuil

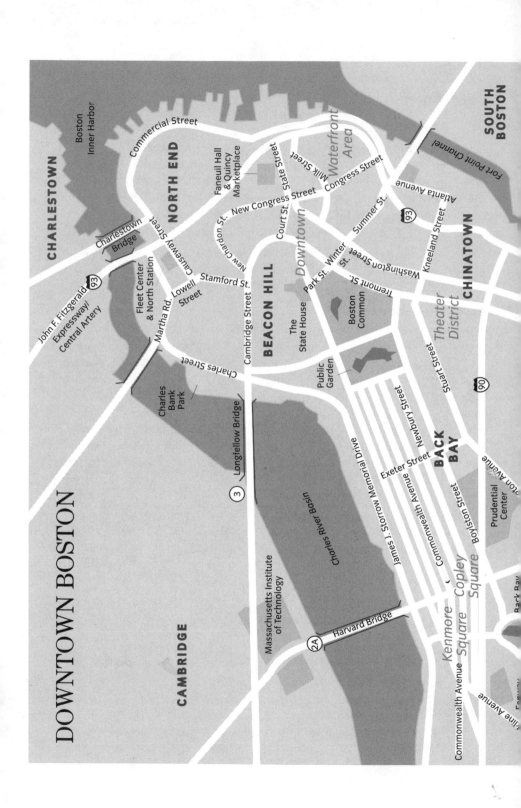

DOWNTOWN BOSTON

CHARLESTOWN

Boston Inner Harbor

Commercial Street

NORTH END

Faneuil Hall & Quincy Marketplace

State Street

Milk Street

Waterfront Area

SOUTH BOSTON

Fort Point Channel

Charlestown Bridge

New Chardon St.

New Congress Street

Court St.

Congress Street

Atlanta Avenue

John F. Fitzgerald Expressway/ Central Artery

93

Fleet Center & North Station

Causeway Street

Lowell Street

Stamford St.

Cambridge Street

BEACON HILL

The State House

Downtown

Park St.

Winter St.

Summer St.

Washington Street

Kneeland Street

93

CHINATOWN

Martha Rd.

Charles Street

Tremont St.

Boston Common

Stuart Street

Theater District

CAMBRIDGE

Charles Bank Park

Longfellow Bridge

3

Public Garden

Newbury Street

BACK BAY

Boylston Street

90

Prudential Center

Massachusetts Institute of Technology

Charles River Basin

James J. Storrow Memorial Drive

Commonwealth Avenue

Exeter Street

Kenmore Square

Copley Square

Back Bay

2A

Harvard Bridge

Commonwealth Avenue

ton Avenue

line Avenue

Hall, and only cash is accepted as a form of payment. To reach BosTix call (617) 262–8632 or www.artsboston.org. The Faneuil Hall kiosk is open 10:00 A.M. to 6:00 P.M. Tuesday through Saturday, and Sunday from 11:00 A.M. to 4:00 P.M. (closed Thanksgiving and Christmas). The Copley Square Booth has the same hours, except they are open Monday as well. The half-price tickets go on sale after 11:00 A.M.

Tours
Beantown Trolley Tours (all ages)
16 Charles Street South at the Transportation Building, Boston; (617) 720–6342 or (800) 343–1328; www.brushhilltours.com. Prices are $24.00 for adults, $22.00 for seniors and students, $7.00 for children 5 to 11, and free for children under 5. The Trolley runs from 9:00 A.M. to 4:30 P.M.

An alternative to driving, the trolleys make nineteen stops around the city, which will include most of the sites your family will want to see. Get on and off the trolley throughout the day; the entire narrated tour takes just under two hours. The trolleys are open air in the summer and heated in the winter. Tickets are sold onboard as well as at outlets around the city. (*NOTE:* Only the transportation office and select locations accept credit cards.) Also included in the price of the ticket is a forty-five-minute harbor cruise.

Cityview Trolley Tour (all ages)
Board on Beacon Street across from the State House. Buy your tickets at the Boston Common Visitor Information Kiosk (Park Street MBTA Station) or by the New England Aquarium Plaza, Boston; (617) 363–7899; www.cityviewtrolleys.com. Daily starting at 9:00 A.M. Tickets: $24 for adults, $22 for students and seniors, and $12 for children 12 and younger; under 3 free. Price includes free admission to the aquarium or a free forty-five-minute historic Boston Harbor cruise.

Each trolley tour has a different spin on visiting Boston and Cityview Trolley is no exception. Cityview's hook is video-enhanced tours of Boston, with a multimedia presentation shown on onboard monitors. The tour takes approximately one hour, and there are eight stops; Cityview doesn't stop at the hotels, just the sights.

Discover Boston Multilingual Trolley Tours (all ages)
84 Atlantic Avenue, Boston; (617) 742–1440; www.discoverbostontours.com. Offered year-round. Prices: $24 for adults, $22 for seniors and students, and $15 for children 3 to 12. The trolley runs from 9:30 A.M. to 5:00 P.M. Get off and on as often as you please.

This two-hour trolley tour features a taped "Audiomate" of the Freedom Trail to carry with you on the walking portion of your tour as well as onboard the trolley. The audio is available in six languages: English, French, German, Italian, Japanese, and Spanish. Discover Boston also includes a narrated forty-five-minute water tour leaving from Long Wharf. Special twilight and evening tours highlight little-known facts that focus on the darker side of Boston's history. This may frighten younger children, but rivet older ones.

The Duck Tour (all ages)

3 Copley Place, Suite 310, Boston (buy your tickets online or at the booth in the Prudential Center, Fanueil Hall or the Museum of Science; (617) 450–0068 for group reservations or (800) 226–7442; www.bostonducktours.com. Offered daily April through November from 9:00 A.M. to a half hour before sunset. Tours leave every half hour from the Huntington Avenue side of the Prudential Center or in front of the Museum of Science. Prices (not including 5 percent Massachusetts sales tax): $24.00 for adults, $21.00 for seniors and students, $15.00 for children; $3.00 for children under 3. This tour can fit thirty-two people on a duck.

This eighty-minute land-and-sea tour is offered on a "duck," an amphibious World War II craft that travels both on land and in the Charles River. The rain-or-shine tour is lots of fun, and you will get many friendly stares as you wind your way through the streets of Boston. Once on the Charles River, the driver/narrator will ask for volunteers to pilot the duck. Both my daughter and her boarding-school roommate from Thailand found this to be the best part of the tour. *NOTE:* A limited number of tickets are released five days prior but sell out by noon, purchased at the ticket counter or online (www.bostonducktours.com); there are no exchanges or refunds.

Boston Common and Beacon Hill

The best place to begin a Boston visit is at the corner of the Boston Common and Park Street. The Boston Common Information Booth is a few yards from here. At the booth you can collect **free** maps, brochures, and information about sightseeing tours. The central stop of the "T" (subway), Park Street, is also right here.

Boston Common is the beginning of the Emerald Necklace, the largest continuous green space through an urban center in the United States. The park system was designed by Frederick Law Olmsted in 1895 (among other acclaimed projects, Olmsted also designed New York's Central Park). From Boston Common the Necklace stretches through the Public Garden to the Commonwealth Avenue Mall, the Back Bay Fens, through the Muddy River area, to Olmsted Park, Jamaica Park, and Jamaica Pond, and on to the Arnold Arboretum and Arborway before ending at the city's largest green space, Franklin Park. Sail, row, or fish at Jamaica Pond, bike and hike through any of the parks, play golf or visit the zoo at Franklin Park, or hear concerts; there's usually something going on at one of the parks along the Necklace. For daily updates, call the **Parks and Recreation** Activities Eventline (617–635–4505; www .ci.boston.ma.us/parks).

At the foot of Beacon Hill is the **Charles River Reservation** (617–727–1300), which fronts on the Charles River. The centerpiece is the Hatch Shell on the Esplanade (not far from the Arthur Fiedler Bridge), a clamshell-shaped stage for **free** outdoor summertime concerts, ballets, performances, and films. Behind the

Holiday Happenings at the Hatch or
I'm a Yankee Doodle Dandy!

The explosive event that is the cornerstone to celebrating the Fourth of July in Boston is the Boston Pops concert at the Hatch Shell. The *1812 Overture* is always the finale—building to a crescendo—with the city's church bells sounding and cannons being fired, all signaling the start of a fabulous Fourth of July fireworks show. With a backdrop of more than a half a million people in attendance, seated in front of the stage, on Storrow Drive (the road is closed to vehicle traffic), or moored on the Charles River, this is the signature event of the summer that you don't want to miss! Good old-fashioned patriotic fun; bring a picnic and get here *many* hours before the concert begins.

Hatch Shell is a playground, a public outdoor pool with views of the Charles, lots of playing fields, and the **Community Boating Facility** (open to the public for lessons or rentals, call 617–523–1038). A unique way to tour the Charles River is with Gondola Venezia, which departs from the Hatch Shell mid-May through mid-October. Tours can fit up to six passengers, and they are private by reservation only at (617) 876–2800, (866) 2–VENICE, or www.bostongondolas.com. Lacing through the reservation is a multipurpose path used for strolling, jogging, biking, or in-line skating. . . . Keep heads up so the children won't be mowed down!

Massachusetts State House, a Freedom Trail Site (all ages)
Beacon Street, Boston; (617) 727–3676; www.state.ma.us/sec/trs. State House hours are Monday through Friday, 9:00 A.M. to 5:00 P.M.; tours, Monday through Friday, 10:00 A.M. to 4:00 P.M. (last tour is at 3:30 P.M.). Closed weekends, Thanksgiving, Christmas Day, New Year's Day, and other state and national holidays. Free.

Just up the hill from the Park Street end of the Common is the impressive gold-domed State House, built in 1798 on John Hancock's pasture. The original part of the building, which was designed by Charles Bullfinch, is in the neoclassical or Federal style. Along with the legislative chambers, the state capitol holds a collection of flags, costumes, and other remnants of the state's history. Don't forget to ask for the handout and map that explain the function and location of the different rooms in the state house, and for the booklet *The Ladybug Story,* which clearly explains to children how a bill becomes law by using an example of schoolchildren who wanted the ladybug to be the official bug of Massachusetts. Walk up the capitol's front steps and turn around to see a terrific view of the Common and the tops of the taller buildings of the Financial District; then, with the building behind you, look over to the right. You'll see a fine statue of John F. Kennedy, whom the sculptor seems to have captured in mid-stride as he left Boston for the U.S. Senate, where he served before his presidency. Of the many JFK monuments scattered around Boston, Massachusetts, and New England, this is the most human.

Boston Common, a Freedom Trail Site (all ages)

Bordered by Beacon Street, Charles Street, Tremont Street, and Park Street; www.the freedomtrail.org. Open all day, every day. Free.

On a nice day, a visit to Boston Common is worth a few hours. Tell the kids to imagine what it was like when Boston residents used this "common" area to graze their cattle, then discuss what it may have been like to live here when British soldiers used the Common as a training ground before the Revolutionary War. Nowadays, the Frog Pond is a big attraction year-round. On a hot summer's day, it's a great place for a cool dip. In the winter you can glide along on the ice. Forgot your skates? Don't worry; rentals are available for a nominal fee. At noon on any weekday, regardless of the weather, you're likely to share the park with many of the people who work in downtown offices. Bring a picnic lunch, or watch a softball game. A summer concert series attracts name talent and is popular with older kids, teens, and students. Charles Street separates the Public Garden from Boston Common.

Public Garden (all ages)

Bordered by Beacon Street, Arlington Street, Boylston Street, and Charles Street, Boston. Open year-round. Free.

The Public Garden encompasses twenty-four acres of planted landscape. Walk toward Beacon Street. Here the kids will find the bronze sculptures of Mrs. Mallard and her brood. Ask the kids to name the ducks (the first one is Jack, followed by Kack, Lack, Mack, Nack, Ouack, Pack, and Quack). Next, head for the lagoon, where your family may well see real-life cousins of the Mallard family. The **Swan Boat**

Duck, duck, duck, not goose!

Historic Neighborhoods (286 Congress Street, Boston; 617–426–1885; www.historic-neighborhoods.org) runs a *Make Way for Ducklings* tour that follows the route taken by Mr. and Mrs. Mallard. During the week it's mostly school groups; however, on Friday and Saturday during the late spring, summer, and early fall, the general public can reserve a tour. **Ducklings Day** is an annual parade held on Mother's Day at Boston Common that reenacts the *Make Way for Ducklings* tale by Robert McCloskey. Call for exact times.

(617–522–1966 [general information] or 617–591–1150 [group reservations]; www.swanboats.com) ride is a must. The boats are on the lagoon from mid-April through mid-September, open 10:00 A.M. to 4:00 P.M. The fare is $2.50 for adults, $1.00 for children under 15, under 2 **free.** It's a short fifteen minutes or so—and people-powered; a boatswain pedals the boat from his or her perch behind a wooden swan. Remember to bring a bag of crumbs or peanuts along. Before or after your ride, be sure to check out the impressive statue of George Washington astride his horse, at the Commonwealth Avenue entrance to the Public Garden. The beautiful shrubbery, trees, and plantings, along with the picturesque bridge over the swan pond, attract many budding artists.

African Meeting House (all ages)

8 Smith Court, off Joy Street on Beacon Hill, Boston; (617) 742–5415 (connects to the Museum of Afro-American History and the National Park Service; www.afroammuseum .org. Open daily Memorial Day to Labor Day 10:00 A.M. to 4:00 P.M.; tours of the Black Heritage Trail are at 10:00 A.M., noon, and 2:00 P.M. daily. From Labor Day to Memorial Day the Meeting House is open from 10:00 A.M. to 4:00 P.M. Monday through Saturday; tours are by reservation only. Suggested donations are posted.

The African Meeting House, owned by the Museum of Afro-American History, is the oldest standing African-American church in the country built by free blacks. Boston has a long history of abolitionism (Frederick Douglass spoke here); just after the Revolution, Massachusetts declared itself one of the first free states, with full citizenry extended to black residents. Before and during the Civil War, this was the headquarters of the Underground Railroad, which helped many escaped slaves leave the South and find new homes and livelihoods in the North. Puppet shows depict the Underground Railroad and the flight toward freedom for school groups.

Black Heritage Trail (all ages)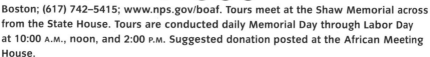

Boston; (617) 742–5415; www.nps.gov/boaf. Tours meet at the Shaw Memorial across from the State House. Tours are conducted daily Memorial Day through Labor Day at 10:00 A.M., noon, and 2:00 P.M. Suggested donation posted at the African Meeting House.

The Museum of Afro-American History and the National Park Service operate the Black Heritage Trail. The trail, covering just over 1½ miles, is a two-hour walking tour of Beacon Hill area buildings that are important to local and national black history. Along with the African Meeting House, sites include the Hayden House, an important stop along the Underground Railroad; the Charles Street Meeting House, where abolitionists Frederick Douglass and Sojourner Truth preached against slavery; and the monument to Robert Gould Shaw and the Fifty-fourth Regiment, which commemorates the first black division of the Union Army during the Civil War.

Black Heritage Trail, Boston

- Site 1: Robert Gould Shaw and the Fifty-fourth Regiment Memorial, Park and Beacon Streets
- Site 2: George Middleton House, 5–7 Pinckney Street
- Site 3: The Phillips School, Anderson and Pinckney streets
- Site 4: John J. Smith House, 86 Pinckney Street
- Site 5: Charles Street Meeting House, Mt. Vernon and Charles streets
- Site 6: Lewis Hayden House, 66 Phillips Street
- Site 7: Coburn's Gaming House, 2 Phillips Street
- Sites 8–12: Smith Court Residences, 46 Joy Street
- Site 13: Abiel Smith School, 46 Joy Street
- Site 14: African Meeting House, 8 Smith Court

Louisburg Square (all ages) 🏛

Between Pinckney and Mt. Vernon Streets on Beacon Hill, Boston. Free.

A site of interest to *Little Women* fans: Louisa May Alcott and her family lived at number 10 after her success with *Little Women* (long before Louisa's literary success, the Alcott family also lived at 20 Pinckney Street). Swedish Nightingale Jenny Lind, who toured with P. T. Barnum's circus, was married at number 14 Louisburg Square. *Make Way for Ducklings* fans will remember the book's superb overhead view of the square. Nearby is the House of Odd Windows, 24 Pinckney Street, whose facade boasts a wide variety of unusually shaped windows.

Other Things to See and Do

The Red Wagon, 69 Charles Street, Boston; (617) 523–9402. Designer kid labels at budget prices, books, and toys.

Where to Eat

Bakery Panificio, 144 Charles Street, Boston; (617) 227–4340; www.panificio boston.com. Open for breakfast, lunch, and dinner midweek, and breakfast and lunch weekends. Quaint cafe with a dozen small tables and a counter looking out on bustling Charles Street. Unusual baked breads, pastries, and sandwiches. $–$$

Bull & Finch Pub (Cheers), 84 Beacon Street, Boston; (617) 227–9605; www .cheersboston.com. Open daily, 11:00 A.M. to 2:00 A.M. The bar in the television show *Cheers* was modeled after the Bull & Finch. There's a souvenir gallery selling "Cheers" paraphernalia. Upstairs is the Hampshire House housing the library, which has a Sunday brunch September through June. $–$$$

The Hungry I, 71 Charles Street, Boston; (617) 227–3524; www.thehungryi restaurant.com. Duck your head upon entering the doorway (there is an OUCH sign that serves as a warning). Eat al fresco on a Beacon Hill private patio or dine inside in a charmingly elegant atmosphere. *NOTE:* No high chairs, but children are welcome. $$$–$$$$

Where to Stay

Beacon Hill Bed & Breakfast, 27 Brimmer Street, Boston; (617) 523–7376. This brick row house overlooking the Charles River has two large bedrooms with nonworking fireplaces and private baths. There are cots and sofa beds, but no cribs. Rates include a full breakfast. Parking, which is not included in your room rate, is in a nearby garage. For ease of movement there is a trolley stop and the MBTA nearby. $$$–$$$$

Charles Street Inn, 94 Charles Street, Boston; (617) 314–8900 or (877) 772–8900; www.charlesstreetinn.com. Great location, goldfish and chocolates upon check-in, video selection, cots and cribs for the wee ones. Beacon Hill townhouse tastefully decorated with antiques in airy, spacious guest rooms, all of which have working marble fireplaces and whirlpools. Breakfast is included and can be brought to your room. $$$$

Downtown and Financial District

If your family is hungry for information about the city, or if you'd like to join a **free** ninety-minute guided tour of highlights of the Freedom Trail, walk over to the **National Historical Park Visitor Center,** 15 State Street, Boston 02109; (617) 242–5642; (next to the Old State House). You'll find maps, books, and helpful staff. The small bookstore has an excellent collection of reasonably priced books about lesser-known people and events in Boston and New England history.

Freedom Trail Sites

- Boston Common
- State House
- Park Street Church
- Granary Burying Ground
- King's Chapel and Burying Ground
- Franklin statue and site of the first public school
- Old Corner Bookstore
- Old South Meeting House
- Old State House
- Boston Massacre site
- Faneuil Hall at Quincy Marketplace
- Paul Revere House
- Old North Church
- Copp's Hill Burying Ground
- USS *Constitution* at the Charlestown Navy Yard
- Bunker Hill Monument

Freedom Trail (all ages)
Pick up a map of the trail at the National Historical Park Visitor Center, 15 State Street, or at the Charlestown Navy Yard, (617) 242–5642 or (617) 242–5601; www.nps.gov/bost/freedom_trail.htm. Only three of the sites charge a fee: the Old State House, the Old South Meeting House, and the Paul Revere House. A fee is sometimes charged at the Charlestown Navy Yard for the Constitution Museum (the fee is currently being underwritten by an anonymous donor); the USS *Constitution* and the USS *Cassin Young* tours are free.

The Freedom Trail, a 2½-mile walking tour of the city's colonial and revolutionary landmarks, begins at Boston Common and ends at the Bunker Hill Monument. Only three of the sites are owned by the federal government; the rest are owned and operated by the city of Boston or by the state of Massachusetts, or are privately owned. The Freedom Trail is easy to follow; just look for the red line on the sidewalk. If your children are young, the walk as a whole may be too long; instead, you may wish to visit just a few of the landmarks.

Beantown for Beginners

Sing a Song of People, by Lois Lenski and Giles Larouche, has Boston as its background and gives a good overview as an introduction to Beantown for the children.

Boston by Little Feet (ages 3 and up)

77 North Washington Street, Boston; (617) 367–2345 or (617) 367–3766 for recorded
information; www.bostonbyfoot.com. Tours are offered from May through October.
Freedom Trail and downtown: Monday and Saturday 10:00 A.M., Sunday 2:00 P.M. The
Boston Underground and the Big Dig tours (recommended for ages 6 and up): Sunday
2:00 P.M. Tour price is $6.00 per person. Reservations are suggested but not required;
children must be accompanied by an adult. Meet at Faneuil Hall, the Congress Street
side, in front of the Samuel Adams statue.

Covering part of the Freedom Trail as well as other sites that are of particular interest
to kids, Boston by Little Feet (operated by Boston by Foot) is a family-oriented, one-
hour tour of the downtown area that gives kids a great introduction to Boston's history and architecture. Boston Underground is a ninety-minute tour costing $10 per
person by Boston by Foot that focuses on the underground utilities, the way the city
has grown down as well as up, and the "Big Dig," the depression of the central artery
into Boston, the largest and most expensive construction project in the country.

Old State House and the Boston Massacre Site,
a Freedom Trail Site (all ages)

Corner of Washington and State Streets, Boston; (617) 720–3291; www.bostonhistory
.org. Open daily 9:00 A.M. to 5:00 P.M. (last tourists are encouraged to be here by 4:00
P.M.); closed Christmas, New Year's Day, and Thanksgiving. Admission: $5.00 for adults,
$4.00 for seniors and students, $1.00 for children 6 to 18, under 6 free.

The brick Old State House built in 1713 is the oldest surviving public building in
Boston. It manages to hold its own against the glass skyscrapers that surround it.
Kids enjoy looking at the lion and unicorn on the building's gables. When the building
was erected, it was the seat of the British government in the colonies, and these symbols of the Crown indicated that fact. The current lion and unicorn aren't the origi-
nals; when the Declaration of Independence was read from the
building's rooftop in July 1776, Bostonians removed these symbols
of the Crown and burned them. The lion and unicorn weren't
replaced until recently. In the middle of the intersection in front of
the building (Congress and State Streets) is a star inside a ring of
cobblestones, marking the site of the Boston Massacre. On March
5, 1770, a frightened group of British soldiers fired into a crowd
of colonists who had gathered to protest recent crackdowns
on customs duties and taxes. Though it was hardly a massacre, five people were killed on this spot, including a former slave, Crispus Attucks. Thereafter Sam Adams used
the incident as a rallying point in his frequent speeches
against the British.

Old South Meeting House, a Freedom Trail Site (all ages)

Corner of Washington and Milk Streets, Boston; (617) 482–6439; www.oldsouthmeeting house.org. Open daily, year-round, from April through October, 9:30 A.M. to 5:00 P.M., and from November through March, 10:00 A.M. to 4:00 P.M. Admission: $5.00 for adults, $4.00 for seniors and students, $1.00 for children 6 to 18, free for children under 6.

The Old South Meeting House began its life in 1729 as a church but quickly became a gathering place for political and revolutionary activity. The band of colonists who participated in the Boston Tea Party in 1773 dressed as "Indians" here before they sneaked down to the harbor. Today the meeting house serves as a museum of the colonial and revolutionary period, with recordings of dramatized versions of public speeches and a re-creation of events during the period, a good gift shop, and an interesting model of Boston. Incidentally, Old South still has a political life: During campaign years politicians often use it as a venue for announcing their candidacies as well as other speaking engagements.

Granary Burying Ground, a Freedom Trail Site (all ages)

Next to the Park Street Church on Tremont Street, near the corner of Tremont and Park, Boston; www.findagrave.com. Open year-round. Free.

The Granary Burying Ground is the final resting place of Paul Revere, John Hancock, Sam Adams, the five victims of the Boston Massacre, and the famous storyteller who was known as Mother Goose. No rubbings, please.

Amazing
Massachusetts Facts

- Massachusetts has the oldest active constitution in the world. It was drafted in 1780.

- Massachusetts is one of only four commonwealths that are states (the others being Kentucky, Virginia, and Pennsylvania).

- In the first federal census (1790), Massachusetts was the only state in the Union to have no slaves.

- There are 351 cities and towns in Massachusetts.

- Symphony Hall turned 100 in October 2000.

- Harvard was founded in 1636 and was the first college in the nation, but the campus buildings date from the early eighteenth century.

Where to Eat

Cafe Marliave, 10 Bromfield Street, Boston; (617) 423–6340. Open Monday through Saturday 11:00 A.M. to 4:00 P.M. for lunch and 4:00 to 9:30 P.M. for dinner. Italian food. $–$$$

Fajitas & 'Ritas, 25 West Street, Boston; (617) 426–1222; www.fajitasandritas.com. Open Monday through Wednesday 11:30 A.M. to 9:00 P.M., Thursday 11:30 A.M. to 10:00 P.M., Friday 11:00 A.M. to 11:00 P.M., Saturday noon to 10:00 P.M.; noon to 9:00 P.M. Sunday. A good place for an informal Tex-Mex lunch. Features make-your-own fajitas, as well as chili and tacos. $

Where to Stay

Omni Parker House, 60 School Street, Boston; (617) 227–8600 or (800) 843–6664; www.omnihotels.com. An old hotel in a great location; everything, including the Common, is within a few minutes' walk from the front door. The executive suites are perfect for families; ask about the Omni kids program, where a backpack with crayons and coloring book is provided and milk and cookies are sent to the room. $$$–$$$$

Quincy Marketplace, Government Center, and the Fleet Center

Since its rebirth twenty-five years ago, Quincy Marketplace has been a mecca for both locals and tourists. Upscale shops, historic buildings, street performers, and a wide variety of restaurants add to the intrigue. Nearby Haymarket is a colorful bargain open-air market that is reminiscent of a European street market. Government Center, with its tall, modern buildings, adds architectural interest to the landscape.

Faneuil Hall (all ages)

Merchants Row, Boston; (617) 635–3105 or (617) 242–5675 (National Park Service); www.nps.gov/bost/faneuil_hall.htm. Open Monday through Saturday 9:00 A.M. to 5:00 P.M., and Sunday noon to 6:00 P.M. unless an event is scheduled. Talks are on the hour and the half hour starting at 9:30 A.M., and the last talk is given at 4:30 P.M. Free.

Faneuil Hall is a historic site, a pedestrian zone, the entry to a massive shopping area, and a food market. Faneuil Hall itself was the site of many pre–Revolutionary War meetings, which is why it's called the "cradle of liberty." National Park Service guides give a twenty-minute historic talk about the history of the hall and the painting *Webster's Answer to Haynes,* depicting Daniel Webster with Senator Haynes of South Carolina. Tell the kids to look for the gold-plated grasshopper weathervane atop the building. Made in 1742, the grasshopper has become one of Boston's symbols.

Special Events at Faneuil Hall

- **Street Performers Festival,** last weekend in May.

- **Anniversary Party of Quincy Market,** late August, **free** cake for all.

- **Furnish the Future,** September. Artists donate furniture that they've decorated, proceeds going to the homeless.

- **Holiday Lighting Ceremony,** 5:00 P.M. weekend before Thanksgiving.

Faneuil Hall Marketplace aka Quincy Market (all ages)
Between State and Congress Streets, Boston; (617) 523–1300; www.faneuilhallmarket place.com. Open Monday through Saturday 10:00 A.M. to 9:00 P.M., Sunday noon to 6:00 P.M.; closed Thanksgiving Day and Christmas. Free.

Beyond Faneuil Hall is copper-domed Quincy Market, in the center, and the North and South Market buildings on either side. The granite Greek Revival building has lived a long life as a marketplace. When it was built in 1826, the east portico was right on the edge of the harbor. The brick North and South Market buildings were built in subsequent years to accommodate the growing needs of the city's meat and produce wholesalers. In the 1970s the city hired an architectural firm to restore the buildings and their surrounding cobblestone streets into an area that would be suitable for a pedestrian shopping area. Obviously, the project was a success; many tourists now come to Boston just to see the marketplace, and many locals come here to eat lunch and people-watch. The Quincy Market building itself is mostly devoted to take-out food vendors who sell everything from frozen yogurt to overstuffed deli sandwiches to pizza-by-the-slice to raw shellfish. Once you and your family have gathered your lunch fixings, head toward the large center area, which is full of tables, chairs, and benches. The North and South Market buildings hold shops and restaurants, from the kitschy to the upscale. Outdoors, regardless of the temperature, you're likely to see several street musicians, jugglers, mimes, and other performers. It's a fun place to spend an afternoon.

Sporting around Town

Hey, sports fans—to reach the **Boston Celtics Basketball Team,** call (617) 523–6050; www.nba.com/celtics. Preseason begins in October and the regular season is from November to April. To reach the **Boston Bruins Hockey Team,** call (617) 624–1900; www.bostonbruins.com. The preseason is in September and the season begins in October and ends in April.

Haymarket Farmers Market (all ages)
Blackstone Street between North and Hanover Streets, Boston; www.foodevents.com.
Friday and Saturday 6:00 A.M. to 5:00 P.M. Free.

Walk along the east end of Quincy Market to Haymarket, an open-air market that's a sight in itself. Pick up the younger kids and walk along the narrow aisles between stands of fruit, vegetables, and seafood. Prices are excellent, and you'd have a tough time finding a better example of where the locals go: This is where many North End chefs buy their produce. Be sure to arrive early. NOTE: Before leaving the stand, check your purchase for quality and freshness.

Government Center and City Hall Plaza (all ages)
1 City Hall Plaza, Congress and Cambridge Streets, Boston; (617) 635–3911 (office of special events) or (617) 635–4505 (Wednesday night concerts by the Parks Department); www.cityofboston.gov/mayor/spevents. Free.

This is the home of the mayor of Boston and the location of several state and federal offices. It's also a great place to eat lunch on the steps or to listen to a nighttime concert sponsored by the city of Boston. The summer concert series features musical happenings on Wednesday (big bands and oldies rock 'n' roll). Call for more information and a schedule of events.

Fleet Center (all ages)
1 Fleet Center Place, Boston; (617) 624–1000 (recorded event line) or (617) 624–1050 (administrative offices); www.fleetcenter.com. Open year-round; check the schedule of events and games.

The Boston Celtics and Boston Bruins play at the Fleet Center, which replaced the venerable Boston Garden in 1995. Call Ticketmaster, (617) 931–2000, for concert tickets and (617) 931–2222 for Celtics and Bruins tickets. The Ice Capades are an annual favorite, as are other ice show extravaganzas. Concerts for the preteen and teen set are also held here.

Sports Museum of New England (all ages)
100 Causeway Street at the Fleet Center, Boston; (617) 787–7678 or (617) 624–1234; www.sportsmuseum.org. Open 11:00 A.M. to 5:00 P.M. Monday through Saturday, Sunday noon to 5:00 P.M. (admission times are on the hour). Closed major holidays. The sports museum closes two hours earlier when there is an event or game. Admission: $6.00 for adults, $4.00 for seniors and children 6 to 17, under 6 is free.

The museum has two floors of New England sports memorabilia, covering the Boston Red Sox, Boston Bruins, Boston Celtics, New England Patriots, Boston Marathon, Boston Breakers, New England Revolution, and a variety of other amateur and professional sports. Special exhibits have featured old ballparks and women's Olympic hockey. The most satisfied visitors are kids who follow the Red Sox, Celtics, or Bruins, but enthusiastic sports fans will probably enjoy looking at the collections of memorabilia, such as one-hundred-year-old baseball spikes and the life-size carved statues of Boston idols Larry Bird, Carl Yastrzemski, Bobby Orr, Ted Williams, and Harry Agganis. Budget some time to watch several of the videos of big-game highlights. *NOTE:* If you come on the morning of a night game, you might be able to peek in and get a behind-the-scenes look at the teams practicing.

Other Things to See and Do

Lenny Zakim Freedom Bridge, Interstate 93 upper and lower decks, crossing the Charles River from Charlestown to Boston. Named in memory of civil rights leader and activist Lenny Zakim. Widest cable-stayed bridge in the world.

New England Holocaust Memorial, Carmen Park, Congress Street near Faneuil Hall; (617) 457–8755; www.nehm.org. Designed by architect Stanley Stitowitz, six glass towers commemorate the deaths of six million during World War II.

Where to Eat

Durgin Park, 340 Faneuil Hall Marketplace, Boston; (617) 227–2038; www.durgin-park.com. Extremely noisy, bustling place that has had customers coming back for over 175 years. Real down-home New England fare—the original comfort food. $–$$

Ye Olde Union Oyster House, 41 Union Street, Boston; (617) 227–2750; www.unionoysterhouse.com. Open daily for lunch and dinner. Billing itself as "America's Oldest Restaurant." Delicious New England regional cooking from land and sea. Slightly overpriced but conveniently located. $–$$$$

Where to Stay

XV Beacon, 15 Beacon Street, Boston; (617) 670–1500 or (877) XV–BEACON; www.xvbeacon.com. Boutique hotel welcoming children. Upon arrival, refreshments are served followed by dessert in your room. Cots and cribs are available and there are high chairs in the gourmet restaurant. $$$$

The Millennium Bostonian, at Faneuil Hall Marketplace (on North Street), Boston; (617) 523–3600 or (866) 866–8086; www.millennium.hotels.com. Luxurious hotel across from Faneuil Hall Marketplace. Pool facilities at health club 1 block away. Ask about the "kid package" and "walking package" (complete with a Kodak camera) at time of booking. $$–$$$$

North End

North End is an Italian neighborhood with excellent restaurants, terrific cafes, and fun festivals on most summer weekends (particularly the Feast of Saint Anthony in August), as well as several of Boston's most famous historic sites, which is appropriate since it's the oldest surviving neighborhood in the city. It's an easy walk from Quincy Market (parking is tough to find on the narrow streets of North End); take the pedestrian passageway under the Fitzgerald Expressway (careful; this is a dangerous intersection!).

Paul Revere's House (all ages)

19 North Square, Boston; (617) 523–2338 or (617) 523–1676; www.PaulRevereHouse .org. Open daily from April 15 through October 31, 9:30 A.M. to 5:15 P.M.; Tuesday through Sunday from November 1 through April 14, 9:30 A.M. to 4:15 P.M. (closed Monday January through March). Closed Thanksgiving Day, Christmas Day, and New Year's Day. Admission: $3.00 for adults, $2.50 for seniors and students with ID, $1.00 for children 5 to 17; free for children 5 and under.

The oldest house in downtown Boston. Revere left from here to make his famous ride. The Paul Revere House is a great place for kids to get an upclose view of domestic life during this period. Owned and operated by the Paul Revere Memorial Association, opened to the public in 1908.

Old North Church (all ages)

193 Salem Street, Boston; (617) 523–6676 or (617) 523–4848; www.oldnorth.com. Open daily, 9:00 A.M. to 5:00 P.M., except Thanksgiving and Christmas; Sunday services at 9:00 and 11:00 A.M. and 5:00 P.M. Free, but a donation is appreciated.

In 1775 Robert Newman, the church's sexton, hung two lanterns from the belfry to alert Revere and his compatriots of the British troops' departure from Boston, by boat, on their way to Lexington and Concord to capture Sam Adams and John Hancock. This is the city's oldest remaining church. Across the street is Paul Revere Mall, with the famous statue of Revere. Behind-the-scenes tours leave hourly.

Copps Hill Burial Ground, a Freedom Trail Site (all ages)

Hull Street (near Old North Church), Boston; www.ci.boston.ma.us/freedomtrail/copps hill.asp. Free.

A great spot for a picnic, Copps Hill Burial Ground, Boston's second oldest cemetery, has the city's best view of the waterfront—Charlestown, the Navy Yard, the USS *Constitution,* and Boston Harbor. There's a nice playground here, along with picnic tables and a shaded grassy area. Enter from Hull Street, between Snowhill and Charter Streets. Pause and look across the street at the narrowest house in Boston (9 feet, 6 inches wide), at 44 Hull Street.

Where to Eat

Most Boston families think of the North End as one big restaurant. There's something for everyone here, from thin-crust pizza to fresh seafood to family-style Italian restaurants with large tables and friendly wait staff.

Bova's, 134 Salem Street, Boston; (617) 523–5601. Many North Enders say that Bova's is the best Italian bakery in town. Another reason why locals like it: It's open twenty-four hours a day. North Enders refer to Bova's as the "Beacon in the Night." $

Caffe Vittoria, 296 Hanover Street, Boston; (617) 227–7606; www.vittoria caffe.com. Open daily, 8:30 A.M. to 12:30 A.M. The decor is way over the top—faux marble tables, gilded mirrors, and garish murals of Italian seascapes—and that's all part of the scene. While the kids enjoy gelato, adults can savor espresso or cappuccino. $

Massimino's Cucina Italiana, 207 Endicott Street, Boston; (617) 523–5959; www .massiminosboston.com. Somewhat difficult to find but worth it! Known for traditional cooking and reasonable prices. $$

Mike's Pastry, 300 Hanover Street, Boston; (617) 742–3050; www.mikes pastry.com. Open Sunday and Monday 8:00 A.M. to 9:00 P.M., Tuesday 8:00 A.M. to 8:00 P.M., Wednesday 8:00 A.M. to 9:30 P.M., Thursday 8:00 A.M. to 10:00 P.M., Friday 8:00 A.M. to 10:30 P.M., and Saturday 8:00 A.M. to 11:00 P.M. Another North End institution. The kids will marvel at the selection of pastries and cookies. $–$$

Pat's Pushcart, 61 Endicott Street, Boston; (617) 523–9616. Open for dinner only, Tuesday through Saturday, 5:00 to 10:30 P.M. Upstairs is the better venue for families—the tables are larger. The red sauce is fantastic. $–$$

Pizzeria Regina, 11½ Thatcher Street, Boston; (617) 227–0765; www.pizzeria regina.com. Open Monday through Thursday 11:00 A.M. to 11:30 P.M., Friday and Saturday 11:00 A.M. to midnight, Sunday noon to 11:00 P.M. At the original Pizzeria Regina, you'll find high-backed booths, nononsense service, pitchers of soft drinks, and delicious thin-crust pizza. You may encounter a line when you get here, since there are no reservations. It's worth the wait. $–$$

Ristorante Lucia, 415 Hanover Street, Boston; (617) 367–2353; www.lucia ristorante.com. Open for lunch and dinner. Open the intricately inlaid parquet doors under the canopy to an Old World decor featuring marble everywhere and a hand-painted mural centerpiece. Attentive service. $–$$$

Ristorante Villa-Francesca, 150 Richmond Street, Boston; (617) 367–2948; www.ristorantevillafrancesca.com. Open for lunch Friday through Sunday and daily for dinner. Inviting restaurant; the front windows lift up on warm summer days to bring the street life closer. $$–$$$

Waterfront Area

The waterfront area can boast of a high concentration of kid-friendly museums and attractions. The New England Aquarium is one of the most progressive in the country; Museum Wharf features the Children's Museum and the Boston Tea Party ship. If time allows, be sure to take in a whale watch or cruise to one of the Boston Harbor Islands maintained by the National Park Service. The World Trade Center is a venue for major trade shows.

Christopher Columbus/Waterfront Park (all ages)
Atlantic Avenue across from Quincy Marketplace, Boston. Open daily year-round.

When the kids need a place to run off some energy, head to Christopher Columbus/Waterfront Park; it's one of the few places in Boston where people can actually relax on the waterfront without having to order something to eat. There's a nice playground (watch the little ones; the crow's nest is inviting, but the climb down is beyond most toddlers' abilities), as well as lots of room to stretch your legs. The rose garden is dedicated to Rose Fitzgerald Kennedy, the late matriarch of the Kennedy clan, who was born near here. *NOTE:* Along Boston's waterfront area there's no physical barrier to prevent your children from tumbling into the water. Keep a sharp eye out.

New England Aquarium (all ages)
Central Wharf, Boston; (617) 973–5200; www.neaq.org. Open Labor Day through June 30: Monday through Friday 9:00 A.M. to 5:00 P.M., weekends and holidays 9:00 A.M. to 6:00 P.M. July 1 through Labor Day: Monday through Thursday 9:00 A.M. to 6:00 P.M., Friday through Sunday and holidays 9:00 A.M. to 7:00 P.M. Admission: $15.95 for adults, $13.95 for seniors, $8.95 for children 3 to 11; free for children under 3.

One of Boston's greatest attractions is the New England Aquarium, and rightly so. Penguins, turtles, sea lions, and sharks share the stage with thousands of smaller fish, all contained in brilliantly designed tanks and pools. The four-story glass tank, wrapped by a spiral ramp, is the highlight of the aquarium. There's nothing like being eye to eye with a shark or walking up and down to follow a sea turtle's movements through the water. Plan to spend at least a couple of hours here, beginning with the harbor seal tank in front of the aquarium. Younger kids may be spooked, initially, by the dim lighting inside the aquarium; show them that the only illumination comes from the tanks, and they'll probably forget their fear and become interested in the fish. Feeding time (five times a day) in the main tank is worth waiting for: Scuba divers jump right in to feed the fish. The kids also get a kick out of the penguin feeding, and the penguin holding area is the first thing that one sees upon entering the aquarium building. On the third level is the ever-popular Edge of the Sea Tide Pool exhibit, which allows kids of all ages to touch and hold small marine creatures such as

The Orphan **Seal**

After the kids have seen the aquarium and understand the interplay between the sea and the creatures that live in it, I recommend they read *The Orphan Seal* by Fran Hodgkins and Dawn Peterson.

starfish, horseshoe crabs, and sea urchins. Don't miss the sea otter exhibit featuring two rescued animals from the West Coast that didn't have the skills to survive in the wild. Be sure to ask for the special combo aquarium and Whale Watch ticket during whale-watching season.

The Exploration Center is in a separate building. It's an ideal classroom for anything with a marine-related theme attracting preschoolers to teens; the activity center offers arts and crafts, science investigations, and different resources. This area is very popular with members and is **free** (included in your admission ticket).

Aquarium Whale Watch

(must be at least 3 years old and a minimum of 30 inches tall)

Central Wharf; (617) 973–5200 (general information) or (617) 973–5281 (reservations); www.neaq.org. Whale watch operates weekends only in April and mid- to late October; daily May through mid-October. Call for schedule since hours and times vary. Price: $29 for adults, $26 for seniors and college students with ID, $20 for children 3 to 12. Reservations are required in advance. Check in thirty minutes prior to departure. Ask about the special Family Days and members' and group rates.

The aquarium operates a whale-watching tour on the *Voyager III* from Central Wharf to Stellwagen Bank, the prime feeding grounds off the coast of Massachusetts; the trip is three and a half to four and a half hours round-trip. An alternative for those who aren't keen on being on the water too long is to travel to Provincetown and make the shorter boat trip from there (see Cape Cod chapter). For boaters, the trip down is lovely; it's a great way to cool off on a hot day while spotting whales and enjoying the harbor, coastline, and ocean. It takes approximately an hour to get to the sighting location. Profit earned helps to support research and conservation scientists at the New England Aquarium. There is a naturalist on board and a 99 percent sighting rate.

Cruising

For a short or long trip around the harbor or to nearby coastal towns, **Boston Harbor Cruises** (1 Long Wharf; 617–227–4321; www.bostonharbor cruises.com), **Massachusetts Bay Lines** (60 Rowes Wharf; 617–542–8000; www.massbaylines.com), the **Liberty Fleet of Tall Ships** (67 Long Wharf; 617–742–0333; www.libertyfleet.com), and **Boston Steamship Company** (Rowes Wharf; 617–542–8000; www.bostonsteamship.com) offer inexpensive, regularly scheduled round-trips. Bring a lunch and a sweater or jacket; even on warm days the wind can make it chilly out on the open water. The two popular dinner-cruise lines are **Odyssey Cruises** (Rowes Wharf; 800–946–7245; www.odysseycruises.com) and the **Spirit of Boston** (164 Northern Avenue at the World Trade Center; 617–748–1450; www .spiritcruises.com), featuring dancing, fine food, and a tour of the harbor.

IMAX Theater at the New England Aquarium (all ages)

Central Wharf, Boston; (617) 973–5200; www.neaq.org. Open daily Monday through Thursday 10:00 A.M. to 10:30 P.M. and Friday through Sunday 9:00 A.M. to 10:30 P.M. Price: $8.95 for adults, $6.95 for children 3 to 11.

Children always seem to enjoy IMAX theaters, and this IMAX has a giant screen that is taller than a six-story building. And what child doesn't like the special effects of a 3-D movie with those funky glasses! The great thing about IMAX is the clarity of the screen and the surround sound. Lots of underwater movies are shown here to allow visitors to see aquatic places and animals that they can't replicate in an aquarium setting.

Boston Harbor Islands (all ages)

National Recreation Area managed by the National Park Service in Boston Harbor; (617) 727–7676; www.bostonislands.com. Daily in-season departures from May through October from Heritage State Park in Lynn, Hewitts' Cove in Hingham, and Long Wharf (next to the aquarium), Boston. The islands are open daily in the summer from 9:00 A.M. to sunset and weekends in the fall and spring. There is a ranger station information kiosk at Long Wharf next to the ferry ticket booth, (617) 223–8666.

Close to this urban area is a series of more than thirty islands, each of which has its own unique flavor. Only six of these islands are reachable by public ferry; the rest are accessed by private motorcraft. The six islands are part of a hub-and-spoke system that revolves around the main island, George's Island, where there is free water shuttle service to the other five.

- George's Island: Old fort, beach, restrooms, snack bar
- Lovell's Island: Remains of a fort, lifeguarded beach, hiking, and camping

- Gallop's Island: Inhabited by rabbits, myth about buried treasure, great views of Boston skyline

- Peddock's Island: Camping, hiking, and bird-watching

- Bumpkin Island: Ruins of a farmhouse and children's hospital; camping allowed in farmhouse orchard

- Grape Island: Varied wildlife; camping allowed

- Little Brewster Island: Home of one of the oldest lighthouses in the country

Children's Museum (ages infant to 10) 🖼️

300 Congress Street, Museum Wharf, Boston; (617) 426–8855; www.bostonkids.org. Open Saturday through Thursday 10:00 A.M. to 5:00 P.M., Friday 10:00 A.M. to 9:00 P.M., and closed Thanksgiving and Christmas. Admission: $9.00 for adults, $7.00 for seniors and children 2 to 15, $2.00 for children age 1, and under 1 free. Friday night special: Admission is $1.00 per person from 5:00 to 9:00 P.M. year-round.

Families shouldn't miss the Children's Museum. It's a hands-on romp of a place with exhibits such as Playspace, a toddlers-only play area, and the ever-popular two-story climbing structure called the New Balance Climb, for kids 5 and over, a vertical maze that stretches from the second floor to the third (don't let the little ones in here; you won't be able to fit yourself inside to get them out). The old standards include Grandma's House, for a taste of the past; the Super Mercado Grocery Store, where children can act as customers or cashiers/owners; and the Recycle Bin, which is a great resource for materials to take home for those rainy day art projects. Other

Watershuttles and Taxis

- **Harbor Express** runs daily between Quincy, Logan Airport, and Long Wharf. Call (617) 222–6999 (www.harborexpress.com) for detailed departures, schedules, and prices.

- **Massport's "On Call" City Water Taxis** shuttle between harborside wharves to various locations around the city for roughly $10 per person. Operates daily, 7:00 A.M. to 10:00 P.M.; call (617) 422–0392; www .citywatertaxi.com.

- **Rowes Wharf Water Shuttle** travels between Logan Airport and Rowes Wharf for $17 round-trip (under 12 free), www.roweswharf watertaxi.com. Free bus shuttle at the airport dock links to the airline terminals. Call (617) 406–8584 or (617) 951–0255; www.massport .com/logan.

exhibits include Arthur's World (based on the books by Mark Brown). In Arthur's World, children can be on television with Arthur, play in Arthur's backyard sleepover, see the Elmwood Library, and visit Arthur's classroom. Climbing the Walls is a rock-climbing exhibit with two 2-feet-long by 8-feet-high climbing walls. Information on rock climbing and a resource center are found here. Ask at the front desk about family-oriented activities and new traveling exhibits.

Boston Tea Party Ship and Museum (all ages)

300 Congress Street, on the Congress Street Bridge, Boston; (617) 338–1773; www .bostonteapartyship.com. Closed due to fire. The fully renovated museum is sched-uled to reopen spring or summer 2005. Planned expansion will include the addition of the *Eleanor* and the *Dartmouth* as well as the *Beaver II*, an expanded museum and exhibits. After reopening, the planned schedule is from March through Memorial Day and from Labor Day through November, open daily 9:00 A.M. to 5:00 P.M.; from Memor-ial Day to Labor Day, open daily 9:00 A.M. to 6:00 P.M.; closed December, January, and February. Admission: $8.00 for adults, $7.00 for students with ID, $4.00 for children 4 to 12, under 4 free. Reenactments every thirty minutes on the hour and half hour.

Of course, it's not the real ship, but it's a good facsimile of the *Beaver,* and the "colonists" on board will retell the story that everyone knows: In 1773, to protest the high taxes imposed on tea, ninety Boston revolutionaries gathered at Old South Meeting House, and, accompanied by a large group of sympathizers, made their way to the *Beaver*, the *Dartmouth*, and the *Eleanor*. They slipped aboard and threw the ships' contents—342 chests of tea—into the harbor. If you do go on board, the kids will be able to toss "tea chests" overboard themselves.

Other Things to See and Do

FleetBoston Pavilion, 290 Northern Avenue, Boston; (617) 728–1600; www .fleetbostonpavilion.com. Seasonal (May through October) open-air covered venue with extraordinary views of Boston Harbor. Top performers from current top-pop stars (such as Jewel) to stars and bands from your childhood (past performers have been Diana Ross and Chicago)!

Women of History

The Women's Heritage Trail (get maps at Boston Common) includes the homes of Elizabeth Peabody, founder of the kindergarten movement, and Sarah Hale, the reputed author of "Mary Had a Little Lamb."

Where to Eat

Bethany's, 332 Congress Street, Boston; (617) 423–4042; www.bethany.com. Open 6:00 A.M. to 4:30 P.M. Deli catering to workers in nearby businesses and staff of the Children's Museum. There are a few tables inside, but the emphasis is on takeout. $–$$

The Chart House, 60 Long Wharf, Boston; (617) 227–1576; www.charthouse.com. National chain with great views of Boston Harbor and standard fare of seafood and grilled meats. $–$$$

The Daily Catch, 261 Northern Avenue, South Boston; (617) 338–3093; www.dailycatch.com. Fresh seafood, lobster Fra Diavlo, calamari, and squid are house specialties. $$–$$$

Jimbo's, 242 Northern Avenue, South Boston; (617) 542–5600; www.jimmysharborside.com. Associated with Jimmy's Harborside. Outdoor deck with views of water and airport. Traditional seafood, scrod, lobsters, steamers, and mussels. High chairs and kids' menu. $–$$$

The Milk Bottle, Museum Wharf, (next to the Children's Museum), Boston; (617) 451–2226 or (617) 426–8855. Open daily mid-May to October, 7:00 A.M. to 9:00 P.M. Excellent salads, sandwiches, soup, and, of course, ice cream and frozen yogurt. The bottle on display was donated to the Children's Museum in 1977 by the H. P. Hood Company, a large dairy. It can hold 50,000 gallons of milk. $

South Station, corner of Summer Street and Atlantic Avenue, Boston. Recently restored and renovated, South Station has a pleasant food court area and lots of tables. $

Where to Stay

Boston Harbor Hotel, 70 Rowes Wharf, Boston; (617) 439–7000, (617) 856–7700, or (800) 752–7077; www.bhh.com. Prestigious hotel with a good location on the waterfront. Coloring books, cookies and milk, and video games are available, 60-foot lap pool with kids' hours. $$$–$$$$

Harborside Hyatt, 101 Harborside Drive, East Boston (at Logan Airport); (617) 568–1234 or (800) 233–1234; www.hyatt.com. The 270-room Harborside, located just beyond Logan Airport, has beautiful views of the Boston harbor and skyline with slightly better pricing than downtown Boston hotels. Water shuttle service is available to Rowes Wharf. Swimming pool, health club, and spa. Great restaurant. $$–$$$$

Marriott Long Wharf, 296 State Street, Boston; (617) 227–0800; www.marriott.com. A stone's throw from the aquarium and close to Quincy Market and other area attractions. Cookies served every evening; pool, game room, and health club. $$$–$$$$

Seaport Hotel, 1 Seaport Lane, South Boston; (617) 385–4000 or (888) 982–4683; www.seaporthotel.com. Across from the World Trade Center, new deluxe hotel with pool for kids to soak in. Ask for the Children's Escape or the Vacation by the Sea packages, which include **free** passes to the Children's Museum. $$–$$$$

Chinatown, the Theater District, and Downtown Crossing

Indulge your family's senses with Chinatown's foods, smells, and sights; take in a top-notch performance in the Theater District, then head over to Boston's main shopping district, known as Downtown Crossing. Wander down the bricked-over section of the busy Washington Street shopping district, a pedestrian zone, past street vendors and performers. You're likely to see a mounted police officer or two. They're accustomed to kids' questions and the horses are very gentle, but ask first before allowing your kids to pat the horses' noses.

Chinatown (all ages)
Between Stuart and Essex Streets, Boston.

Walk through the ornate arch with the four marble Foo dogs into Boston's Chinatown for a gastronomic treat. It's hard to choose among the many restaurants. If you like to cook Chinese, this area is a great resource for Asian ingredients. Most signs in front of the shops are in both English and Chinese. A great time to expose the kids to a different culture is at the Chinese New Year celebration in late January or early February.

Filene's Basement (all ages)
426 Washington Street at Summer Street, Boston; (617) 348–7848; www.filenes basement.com. Open Monday through Friday, 9:30 A.M. to 8:00 P.M., Saturday 9:00 A.M. to 8:00 P.M., and Sunday 11:00 A.M. to 7:00 P.M. Closed Thanksgiving Day, Christmas Day, and Easter.

The original Filene's Basement is in the basement of Filene's, naturally. It's as good as you've heard; prices run the gamut from plain-old markdowns to rock-bottom, although the quality of the merchandise often suffers from overhandling. This isn't a place for young children or for anyone who isn't a die-hard shopper: Aisles can be narrow and shoppers downright rude, even to cute kids.

Other Things to See and Do

Jack's Joke Shop, 226 Tremont Street, Boston; (617) 426–9640 or (617) 426–8927; www.jackjokeshop.com or www.jacks jokes.com. Fun stop for practical jokes.

Where to Eat

Bruegger's Bagel Bakery, 7 School Street, Boston; (617) 367–4702; www .brueggers.com. Open Monday through Friday 6:00 A.M. to 6:00 P.M., Saturday 7:00 A.M. to 6:00 P.M., Sunday 7:00 A.M. to 5:00 P.M. Bagels are baked on the premises. Try one of their cream cheese mixtures; the fresh berry varieties are particularly good. Soups and salads also available. $

Chau Chow, 45 Beach Street, Boston; (617) 426–6266. Open daily from 10:00 A.M. to 3:00 A.M. One of the best restaurants in Chinatown. Specializes in seafood, but everything's good. $–$$

Jacob Wirth, 31–37 Stuart Street, Boston; (617) 338–8586; www.jacobwirth restaurant.com. Open daily at 11:30 A.M., closing at 11:00 P.M. Tuesday through Thursday, midnight Friday and Saturday, and 8:00 P.M. Sunday and Monday. For an unexpected treat in the Theater District go to Jacob Wirth, a surprisingly genuine German restaurant that has high ceilings and long tables and features a broad menu with weekly specials. $–$$$

Where to Stay

Le Meridien Boston, 250 Franklin Street, Boston; (617) 451–1900 or (800) 543–4300; www.lemeridienboston.com. Offers 326 nicely appointed rooms, a gourmet restaurant, and a pool club. A big hit with the kids is the Chocolate Buffet at Meridien's Cafe Fleuri every Saturday from noon to 2:30 P.M. mid-September to May. The buffet costs $23.00 for adults, $12.50 for kids, under 4 **free.** The Meridien also offers a kids corner station, Nintendo, a treasure chest, pool toys, a gift bag at the Sunday brunch, and a nominal rate for an extra room for the kids. $$$–$$$$

Year-round Performances
That Children Enjoy

- **Blue Man Group/Charles Playhouse (ages 5 and up).** 74 Warrentown Street in the Theater District, Boston; (617) 426–6912; www.blueman .com. Schedule varies week to week; call for tickets and schedule (Ticketmaster: 617–931–2787). Seats are from $43 to $53 per person. It's hard to explain this unusual avant-garde production with a little bit of everything (literally) thrown in except to say that it's an enjoyable treat for the whole family. Children under 5 aren't allowed to attend the show. *WARNING:* If you sit in the front rows, be sure to wear the raincoats that are provided.

- **Shear Madness/Charles Playhouse (ages 5 and up).** 74 Warrentown Street in the Theater District, Boston; (617) 426–5225; www.shear madness.com. Call the box office for tickets and schedule. Tickets are $34 per person. Boston's smash comedy whodunit is in its nineteenth year. The kids will think that it's awesome that the audience votes on the guilty party and thus influences the play's outcome.

Copley Square and the Back Bay

It's hard to imagine now, but until 1857 this part of the city was a smelly tidal flat, fronted by a failed dam, called the Back Bay (Boston itself was actually a peninsula). By the mid-nineteenth century, the city had grown so much that the marshy tidal flats became an advantageous area for expansion, and the landfill operation began. When it ended in 1890, the 450-acre area was crisscrossed with Boston's only grid system, and well over 1,000 new buildings had been built to house more people and businesses. While you're in the Back Bay area, be sure to stroll over to Commonwealth Avenue and cross into the green area, called Commonwealth Mall, that runs from the Public Garden to the Fenway. You'll see other families here, mostly locals walking their dogs and stretching their legs. As you walk west (away from the Public Garden), note that the eight streets between here and Massachusetts Avenue are named in alphabetical order: Arlington, Berkeley, Clarendon, Dartmouth, Exeter, Fairfield, Gloucester, and Hereford. The **Greater Boston Convention and Visitor's Bureau** is located at 2 Copley Place, Suite 105, Boston 02116; (888) SEE–BOSTON or (617) 536–4100; www.bostonusa.com.

John Hancock Building (all ages)
200 Clarendon Street, Boston; (617) 572–6000.

The Hancock building is a sixty-two-story rhomboid, an unusual shape for a building and one that makes it change in appearance when you see it from different angles. From Copley Square, it's a sharp, slim jab of reflective glass; from downtown, it's a wide mirror for the older Hancock building next to it. For a professional-looking photo, take a picture with the Trinity Church's reflection on the building. After September 11 the observatory at the top was closed.

Trinity Church (all ages)
Copley Square, corner of Boylston Street and Clarendon Street, Boston; (617) 536–0944; www.trinitychurchboston.org. Call for schedule.

Ranked by architects as one of the ten most important buildings in the United States because of its art and architecture. For a great view of the Trinity Church in all its glory, see the Trinity's reflection on the walls of the John Hancock building. Call for the listings of special tours and programs for children and families. Programs include special music Sundays, choirs, Friday organ concerts, and regular concerts.

Pass It On

If you're thinking of doing a lot of touring, the **Boston City Pass,** (888) 330–5008; www.citypass.com (good for nine days), includes six sites for one low price: the Hancock Building, the Isabella Stuart Gardner Museum, the Museum of Science, the Museum of Fine Arts, the New England Aquarium, and the John F. Kennedy Library. Prices for the Boston City Pass are $36.75 for adults, and $25.50 for children 3 to 17.

Boston Athletic Association's Boston Marathon Sites

(all ages)

Finish line on Boylston Street just in front of the Boston Public Library and Copley Square; www.bostonmarathon.org. Open daily. Free.

This is the most popular viewing spot during the Boston Marathon's 26-mile Hopkinton to Boston Race; on any day but Patriots Day, you too can cross the finish line. Runners come from all over the world to compete in this prestigious marathon. The Tortoise and the Hare bronze sculptures are in the Copley Square Plaza in front of Trinity Church, a heartbreaking setting for the nonwinners of the race.

The Prudential Skywalk Observatory (all ages)

Prudential Tower, 50th floor, 800 Boylston Street, Boston; (617) 859–0648; www .prudentialcenter.com. Open 10:00 A.M. through 10:00 P.M. daily. Admission: $7.00 adults, $4.00 for children 3 to 10, under 2 free. The last elevator is at 9:45 P.M.

The Skywalk Observatory offers a fabulous 360-degree view of Boston. Informative exhibits of Boston's history and facts are on the wall of the observatory. The Top of the Hub Restaurant on the fifty-second floor is open to 1:00 A.M. Sunday through Wednesday and 2:00 A.M. Thursday through Saturday and is a fantastic place for mealtime views of Boston. The shops and carts below in the Prudential Complex run the gamut from trendy to "old money" conservative.

Boston Ballet (all ages)

19 Clarendon Street, Boston; (617) 695–6950; www.bostonballet.org; for classes call (617) 456–6267.

Boston Ballet is the largest dance center in New England. The Boston Ballet's version of *The Nutcracker* is the most popular in the country; for the best seats, buy your tickets months in advance. One of the rehearsal studios is the same size as the Wang Center stage (where the troupe performs), which is one of the largest stages in the world. Tours are given by advance reservation. *NOTE:* The **Wang Center** is at 270 Tremont Street. Informances, given by the artistic director or the music director prior to the performance, deepen children's understanding and appreciation of the ballet. Call the Boston Ballet for a schedule of Informances. For Boston Ballet tickets, call Telecharge (800–447–7400) or purchase online at www.telecharge.com.

Newbury Street Shops, Art Galleries, and Restaurants (all ages)
(🍴) (🔒)

Newbury Street from Arlington Street to Massachusetts Avenue, Boston.

Newbury Street is Boston's boutique row. Designers' shops rule the roost here, though there are plenty of other businesses, running the gamut from art galleries to several excellent secondhand clothes shops to Gap and Abercrombie and Fitch to designer boutiques. Whether or not you enjoy window shopping, it's also a nice street for walking, since the sidewalks are slightly wider and there are lots of sidewalk cafes that will tempt you to rest for a while over a drink or a light meal.

Other Things to See and Do

Boston Public Library, 700 Boylston Street, Boston; (617) 536–5400; www .bpl.org. Ongoing programs include a kid's cinema, magician performances, and storyteller hours. Call for a schedule.

Clarendon Street Playground, Clarendon Street, between Commonwealth and Marlborough Streets, Boston. Center-of-the-city respite for children.

Institute of Contemporary Art, 955 Boylston Street, Boston; (617) 266–5152; www.icaboston.org. Modern art; shows rotate every few months.

Where to Eat

Abe and Louie's, 793 Boylston Street, Boston; (617) 536–6300; www.abeand louies.com. The smartly dressed chic of Boston gather here for great food and conversation. Streetside cafe reigned over by the imposing Prudential Tower Complex, as well as indoor dining. Surprisingly welcoming to children. $$–$$$$

Cactus Club Restaurant and Bar, 939 Boylston Street, Boston; (617) 236–0200; www.thecactusclubboston.com. Caribbean, Cuban, and southwestern-style food, outdoor or indoor dining, fun atmosphere. $–$$

Emack and Bolio's, 290 Newbury Street, Boston; (617) 536–7127; www.emack bolios.com. Winter hours are Sunday through Thursday noon to 10:30 P.M., Friday through Saturday noon to 11:00 P.M.; summer hours (May to September) are 11:00 A.M. to 11:30 P.M. daily. This local chain of ice cream shops specializes in unusual homemade flavors. $

Hard Rock Cafe, 131 Clarendon Street, Boston; (617) 424–7625; www.hardrock .com. Open 11:00 A.M. to midnight daily. A fun place to have lunch—the burgers are excellent. The souvenir shop sells T-shirts, pins, hats, sweatshirts, and jackets commemorating your visit. $–$$

Stephanie's, 190 Newbury Street, Boston; (617) 236–0990; www.stephanies onnewbury.com. Outdoor cafe-style dining (great people-watching location) in season, or choose to dine inside in air-conditioned comfort. Featuring comfort-food classics, pastas, and fragrant dinner entrees. $–$$$

Top of the Hub, Prudential Tower, 52nd floor, 800 Boylston Street, Boston; (617) 536–1775; www.prudentialcenter.com.

Open daily for lunch and dinner. Special Sunday brunch. On a clear day, this restaurant has a panoramic, mouth-dropping, eye-popping view of Boston; wonderful kitchen. $$–$$$$

Where to Stay

The Back Bay Hilton, 40 Dalton Street, Boston; (617) 236–1100 or (800) 874–0663; www.hilton.com. Offers excellent family packages that include discount admission passes to many city attractions (request the discount book), a lending desk of children's books and videos, a heated pool, a **free** gift for kids 12 and under at check-in, and a kids' menu in the hotel restaurant and through room service. $$–$$$$

Boston Park Plaza Hotel, 64 Arlington Street, Boston; (617) 426–2000 or (800) 225–2008; www.bostonparkplaza.com. A grande dame of a hotel. Family package rates are available. $$–$$$$

Copley Square Hotel, 47 Huntington Avenue, Boston; (617) 536–9000 or (800) 225–7062; www.copleysquarehotel.com. Great location across from Copley Place and the Prudential Complex. Owned by a local company called the Saunders Group, yet a magnet for foreign travelers. Reasonable and attractive first-class hotel. Complimentary tea every afternoon. $$–$$$$

Huntington Avenue to the Fenway and Kenmore Square

When your family is ready for another bout of museum-hopping (don't do it all in one day or you'll never have the energy for all the don't-miss exhibits), check out the Christian Science Church Campus, the Museum of Fine Arts, and the Isabella Stewart Gardner Museum. Looking for family entertainment instead? Take the kids to a performance of the Boston Pops at Symphony Hall, a baseball game at Fenway Park, or a play at Wheelock Family Theatre.

Christian Science Church (all ages)

175 Huntington Avenue, Boston. The Mother Church has had extensive renovations. (617) 450–2000; www.tfccs.com. Tours of the church are Monday through Saturday 10:00 A.M. to 4:00 P.M. Free. For concert listings of their world-famous choir and organ look on the Web site or call (617) 450–3793.

This, the international headquarters of the Church of Christ, Scientist, has several buildings of architectural note, including the 1894 original edifice and the extension, which make up the Mother Church. The fourteen-acre plaza incorporates a long reflecting pool (no wading), with a wonderful circular fountain at its eastern end. But your kids should feel free to pull off their shoes and wade in the fountain's sprinkler;

that's what it's there for. The plaza is a great place for the kids to work off any excess energy that they haven't lost during the day. When the kids have satisfied themselves with the delights of running around in the plaza and splashing in the fountain, walk through the passageway between the Colonnade building and the church to the bronze-doored Christian Science Publishing Society (where the *Christian Science Monitor* is published) and view the photo gallery. Proceed to the Mary Baker Library (see listing below) when you're done.

Mary Baker Library for the Betterment of Humanity and the Mapparium (all ages)

200 Massachusetts Avenue, Boston; (617) 450–3793, (888) 222–3711, or (800) 288–7155; www.marybakereddylibrary.org. The library is open 10:00 A.M. to 5:00 P.M. Tuesday, Wednesday, and Sunday, and until 9:00 P.M. Thursday and Friday. The library is free, but if you wish to tour the Mapparium, Quest Gallery, and Monitor Gallery, the price is $5.00 for adults, $3.00 for ages 6 to 17, free for kids under 6.

The library is dedicated to the power of ideas to inspire individuals and change. The exhibits are on life's deeper meaning. There are many interactive exhibits for children. The Quest Gallery features an adventure game that engages kids to go up a mountain, plan what they would take with them, and challenge them with a variety of choices (the challenges involve courage and joy). Another game includes interacting with colors on a wall to uncover words. Your children will love creating a page of art and displaying it off the computer. In the Hall of Ideas, a fountain in the middle of the hall bubbles up words as well as water. The words and quotes (more than 600 quotes cycle through) seem to float on the water. After the quote surfaces for about ten seconds, the words spill over onto the floor and move up a wall onto a screen. The quote is then reformed, and the source is noted as well as when and where the author lived before it dissolves. The quotes represent cultures from across the world and 3,000 years of history. Kids love to follow the words on the floor (it is actually a sleight of hand done with mirrors, but don't tell your kids!).

The Mapparium has always been a huge attraction. Originally installed at the Christian Science Publishing Society, it now has a new home in the library building. The 30-foot glass globe (that you can still walk into) is the original art from 1935 showing the map of the world as it was then. It looks like stained glass, but it's actually painted glass. There are new light panels that are customized for different shows (on Columbus Day the show illustrates where Columbus was hoping to go and where he ended up). The Mapparium always amazes.

Symphony Hall (ages 5 and up) 🎵

301 Massachusetts Avenue, Boston; (617) 266–1492 or (888) 266–1200 for the box office; www.bso.org. The BSO performs October through November and January through April. The Boston Pops performs December and May through June. Call for schedule and pricing.

Home of the Boston Symphony Orchestra (popularly known as the BSO), Symphony Hall is the most acoustically perfect auditorium in the United States. Tours are given as part of the BSO Youth Concert Series during the spring and fall and at selected times during the year. Plan ahead if you wish to attend the series: The tickets go on sale each spring for the following fall/spring series; call the Youth Activities Office, (617) 638–9300. You can get same-day discounted tickets for the BSO Tuesday and Thursday evening performances and the Friday afternoon performance at the rush ticket window: Arrive by 5:00 P.M. on Tuesday and Thursday and by 9:00 A.M. on Friday. To order tickets by phone, call Symphony Charge, (617) 266–1200 or (888) 266–1200; for online orders, check out www.bso.org. A **free** annual open house in the spring celebrates the BSO and the musical life in Boston. Also, the Boston Pops has **free** weeklong performances at the Hatch Shell timed around July 4, just before the summer series at Tanglewood. The same musicians play for the Symphony and the Boston Pops; the difference is that the Boston Pops plays a more whimsical program from Broadway hits to jazz, Latin, and swing, to classical favorites.

Museum of Fine Arts (all ages)

Avenue of the Arts, 465 Huntington Avenue, Boston; (617) 267–9300; www.mfa.org. The entire museum is open Monday, Tuesday, Saturday, and Sunday 10:00 A.M. to 4:45 P.M., until 9:45 P.M. on Wednesday, Thursday, and Friday with a voluntary donation for admittance after 4:00 P.M. The West Wing and various other galleries are open on Thursday and Friday from 5:00 to 10:00 P.M. with an admission of $13.00 for adults, $11.00 for seniors and students with ID; free for children 17 and under. The museum is closed July Fourth, New Year's, Patriots Day, Thanksgiving, and Christmas. Free tours (included with the price of admission) are given Monday through Saturday at various times. General admission: $15.00 for adults, $13.00 for seniors and students, free for children 17 and under ($6.50 on school days until 3:00 P.M.). The admission price now includes a second visit within a thirty-day period.

The Museum of Fine Arts is one of the country's great city museums, holding collections of fine art, antiquities, furniture, silver, and ceramics. Highlights include the Monet collection and the works of Corot, Renoir, Manet, Pissaro, Gauguin, and van Gogh; the famous portraits of Sam Adams and Paul Revere by John Singleton Copley; several excellent portraits by John Singer Sargent; and mummies, altars, and hieroglyphics in the Egyptian rooms (the classical Egyptian collection is the second largest in the world). Don't try to see the museum without a plan; you'll get lost and the kids will get bored. *TIP:* A good idea is to determine a meeting place before exploring the building. The museum is large and complex, and there is no paging system to find stray parents. When you arrive, go to the Information Center and ask the staff about the day's family-oriented activities (there are usually several). If your family is particularly interested in seeing certain works of art, have a staff member mark the location on a map as well as the shortest way to get there. The museum shop is an excellent source of gifts and souvenirs; allow some time for this. There is a Family Place Program on weekends (like a treasure hunt throughout the museum) geared to kids during the school year as well as art classes, workshops, and a children's room. A new summer addition is Wednesday Family Night with evening activities throughout the museum. Check the Web site or call for details. There are also other public programs, such as concerts and films geared toward all ages!

Isabella Stewart Gardner Museum (all ages)

280 The Fenway, Boston; (617) 278–5166 or (617) 566–1401; www.gardnermuseum.org. Open Tuesday through Sunday, 11:00 A.M. to 5:00 P.M.; closed on Thanksgiving, Christmas, and New Year's Day. Park at the Museum of Fine Arts garage and lot on Museum Road (there is a parking fee). There is a guided tour on Friday at 2:30 P.M.; an audio guide on selected pieces is available. The cafe is very popular, as well as the gift shop. Admission: $10.00 for adults on weekdays and $11.00 on weekends, $7.00 for seniors, $5.00 for students with ID except on Wednesday, when it's $3.00; free for children under 18. There is a $2.00 discount at the Museum of Fine Arts if you visit within two days of the Gardner Museum.

The museum was once the home of Isabella Stewart Gardner, who built Fenway Court to house her personal art collection. A New York native, Gardner shocked Boston with her short-sleeved dresses and her unorthodox habits (local lore has it that she walked her pet lions down Beacon Street on leashes, like poodles; in reality, she never owned lions). Her legacy to her adopted city is this museum. When Gardner died in 1924, she left the museum in a public trust. The heart of this 1903 Venetian-style palazzo is a glass-ceilinged, three-story courtyard that holds a lovely indoor garden. Every painting, sculpture, and piece of furniture is in the same spot where she chose to place it, nearly a hundred years ago. Much of the art collection is from the Italian Renaissance and Dutch seventeenth-century master period, but there are several fine late-nineteenth-century pieces too, notably the portrait of Gardner painted by her friend John Singer Sargent and a beautiful small seascape by James McNeill Whistler. Despite the grandness of the building and the breathtaking art collection, the museum's staff manages to preserve the museum's origins: Flowers and plants are tastefully placed throughout the museum, and staff members talk of Gardner as if she were still in charge. Art-loving families should budget at least two hours to explore the museum. To keep their interest, suggest to the kids that they try to spot the animals in many of the paintings and sculptures, and ask for the "Small Wonders" guide. A concert series is held on Saturdays and Sundays in the spring and fall.

Fenway Park and the Boston Red Sox (ages 3 and up)

4 Yawkey Way, Boston; (877) 733–7699 or (877) RED–SOX–9 (tickets), (617) 267–8661 (season tickets), (617) 482–4SOX (touch-tone), or (617) 267–8661 (information); www.redsox.com or www.bostonredsoxmlb.com. The box office is open from 9:00 A.M. to 5:00 P.M. The walk-up ticket sales office near Gate A sells the Fenway Park tours. Ask about discounted family days.

Fenway Park, opened in 1912, is the home of the Boston Red Sox. It is still a great place to take in a ball game. Even after a recent refurbishment, it's still a bit rickety, but its size (smallest in the Major League) and genuine old-time charm make it the best place in the country to watch a game. Since you're never far from the field, there's not a bad seat in the house. Opening Day is very popular with Bostonians, many of whom have not stopped smiling since the Curse of the Bambino was finally broken in 2004 and the Red Sox won the World Series for the first time in eighty-six years. Tours are offered Monday through Sunday year-round 9:00 A.M. to 4:00 P.M. and leave every hour on the hour. If there is a game, the last tour leaves three hours before game time. The tour shows the highlights of the park, including a walk around the playing field (except during inclement weather), having your picture taken in front of the Green Monster, and having a seat in the dugout! For information and pricing, call (617) 236–6666.

Jillian's (ages 7 and up)

145 Ipswich (behind Fenway Park), Boston; (617) 437–0300; www.jilliansboston.com. Open daily to children under 18 until 8:00 P.M. Price: Charges are per game; no cover charge, you pay for what you play. Restaurant on site (the Tequila Rain).

The arcade features every high-tech gadget and game to keep your child immersed for hours. This "entertainment mecca" includes 250 high-tech video games, including a giant-screen video wall arcade, and hyperbowl (virtual reality bowling game). Adult supervision is necessary to rent darts, play Ping-Pong, or use one of the fifty-five pool tables. Good luck convincing the kids to leave.

Wheelock Family Theatre (all ages)

180 The Riverway at Wheelock College, Boston; (617) 879–2147 (theater office) or (617) 879–2300 (box office). Box office opens Monday through Friday noon to 5:30 P.M.; www.wheelock.edu/wft. Productions are Friday at 7:30 P.M., Saturday and Sunday at 3:00 P.M., and selected school matinees. Price: $12 to $18 per person, depending on seat location. Reservations required.

The 650-seat theater has an excellent reputation for traditional productions and non-traditional casting, featuring multigenerational and multicultural casts. Musicals, classics, dramas, and original plays are offered from October through May.

Field of **Dreams**

Zachary's Ball, by Matt Tavares, is about the Red Sox winning the World Series.

Other Things to See and Do

Charles River Canoe and Kayak Center, Soldiers Field Road (look for the green kiosk), Boston (mailing address: 2401 Commonwealth Avenue, Newton 02466); (617) 965–5110 or (617) 462–2513; www.paddle boston.com. Offering lessons and guided trips in the Charles River and the Atlantic Ocean. Kids camp as well. Call for schedule.

Where to Eat

Burrito Max, 642 Beacon Street, Kenmore Square, Boston; (617) 266–8088. Open 11:30 A.M. to 11:00 P.M. daily. Southwestern food (Mexican and BBQ) as well as vegetarian dishes. Spicy southwestern decor meets Boston. Close to Fenway Park and Boston University. $

Cafe Belo Steak House, 636 Beacon Street, Kenmore Square, Boston; (617) 236–8666; cafebelo.com. Upscale self-serve steak house buffet with granite dining tables near Fenway Park. $

Where to Stay

Hotel Buckminster, 645 Beacon Street, Boston; (617) 236–7050 or (800) 727–2825; www.bostonhotelbuckminster.com. No-frill tourist-class hotel in Kenmore Square located near Fenway Park and Boston University. Rooms and multibed-room suites for families. Laundry and kitchen facilities (no cooking utensils provided) on every floor. The Buckminster attracts business travelers, Fenway Park visitors, families, and parents of students. $$–$$$

Hotel Commonwealth, 500 Commonwealth Avenue, Boston; (617) 933–5000 or (866) 784–4000; www.hotelcommon wealth.com. Deluxe hotel opened in the spring of 2003. Rooms overlook either Kenmore Square or Fenway Park/Mass Pike. Rooms are spacious and decorated in soothing colors with marble floors in bathroom. Great location for Fenway Park; sports packages are available. $$$–$$$$

Brookline and Jamaica Plain

Brookline is a separate city in government only; everything else about it is very much part of Boston city life. To the south of Brookline, Jamaica Plain is part of Boston proper.

Larz Anderson Park and the Larz Anderson Auto Museum
(all ages)

15 Newton Street, Brookline; (617) 522–6547 (Transportation Museum); www.mot.org. Open year-round, Tuesday through Sunday, 10:00 A.M. to 5:00 P.M. Closed July Fourth, New Year's Day, Thanksgiving, and Christmas; open on Monday during vacation weeks. Admission: $5.00 for adults, $3.00 for seniors and children 6 to 16; free for children under 5.

A pleasant family outing can be had at Larz Anderson Park (a sixty-acre park in Brookline). On the hill behind the Transportation Museum is a wonderful picnic spot that is also one of the best kite-flying hills in Greater Boston. Off to the left at the bottom of the hill are soccer fields and a baseball diamond. Next to the playing fields is a great playground with an unusual seesaw made from old telephone poles. Continue on past the playground down the hill to the duck pond and more choice picnicking sites. Housed in an 1888 carriage house that looks for all the world like a castle, the Larz Anderson Auto Museum (Carriage House, Larz Anderson Park) boasts an impressive collection of restored antique carriages (rotating exhibits) and classic cars (America's oldest collection). Don't miss the children's activity room and the climb-in car in front of the gift shop. Held most Sundays from May through October is the Outdoor Lawn Show, which includes bicycles, motorcycles, and automobiles of the past. Family programs are scheduled from January to April on Saturdays at 1:00 P.M.

Franklin Park Zoo (all ages)

One Franklin Park Road, Boston; (617) 541–LION; www.zoonewengland.org. Open October through March from 10:00 A.M. to 4:00 P.M., April through September from 10:00 A.M. to 5:00 P.M. weekdays, 10:00 A.M. to 6:00 P.M. weekends and holidays. Closed Thanksgiving and Christmas. Admission: $9.50 for adults, $5.00 for children 2 to 15; admission is free for kids under 2. Call for directions and parking instructions (parking is free).

The Tropical Rain Forest, the Australian Outback Trail, the Kalahari Kingdom, and the Savanna Exhibit of Giraffes, Serengeti Crossing, Bongo Congo, and Butterfly Landing ($1.00 per person extra in addition to the admission price) are the highlights of the seventy-two-acre Franklin Park Zoo, which is undergoing a long-term revitalization program along with the enormous Franklin Park. The three-acre rain forest is the largest of its kind in North America. It holds pygmy hippopotamuses, gorillas, ring-tailed lemurs, crocodiles, and thousands of exotic birds. The Franklin Farm has a contact area with farm animals. At the Serengeti Crossing area, your children can see zebras, ostriches, and wildebeests. Special events at the park and the zoo include the Kite Festival at Franklin Park, the third Saturday in May, and Zoo Howl, around Halloween.

The Arnold Arboretum (all ages)

125 Arborway, Jamaica Plain; (617) 524–1718; www.arboretum.harvard.edu. The grounds are open dawn to dusk year-round; the main building is open Monday through Friday 9:00 A.M. to 4:00 P.M., noon to 4:00 P.M. on weekends March through October, 10:00 A.M. to 2:00 P.M. November through February weekends. Free.

Harvard University established the 265-acre Arnold Arboretum in 1872, the first in the country. Designed by Frederick Law Olmsted, the arboretum specializes in trees, shrubbery, and vines displayed in a beautiful parklike setting. Two peak visitation times are spring, when everything is in bloom and the air is heady with the aroma of budding trees and plants, and autumn, for the vibrant colors. Passive recreational activities that are allowed on the property are cross-country skiing, snowshoeing (no groomed trails), walking, jogging, in-line skating, and biking (biking and skating on paved paths only). Dogs on a leash are allowed, but you are requested to pick up after them. To keep the arboretum pristine, there is no picnicking or food allowed on the grounds.

Other Things to See and Do

Boston's Children's Theatre, 647 Boylston Street, Chestnut Hill; (617) 424–6634; www.bostonchildrenstheatre.org. Year-round productions.

Children's Bookshop, 237 Washington Street, Brookline Village; (617) 734–7323. Appearances by local and famous authors and illustrators.

John F. Kennedy Birthplace National Historic Site, 83 Beals Street, Brookline; (617) 566–7937; www.hps.gov/jofi. Open mid-May through October.

Puppet Showplace Theatre, 32 Station Street, Brookline; (617) 731–6400; www.puppetshowplace.org. Puppet workshop held before selected shows. Puppetry for more than twenty-five years.

Where to Eat

Captain's Wharf, 356 Harvard Street, Brookline; (617) 566–5590. Open Monday through Saturday 11:00 A.M. to 9:00 P.M., Sunday noon to 9:00 P.M. Fresh seafood prepared to order. $

J. P. Licks, 659 Centre Street, Jamaica Plain; (617) 524–6740; and 311 Harvard Street, Brookline; (617) 738–8252. Open year-round. Great ice cream. $

Rubins Restaurant and Kosher Deli, 500 Harvard Avenue, Brookline; (617) 731–8787; www.rubinskosher.com. Open Sunday through Friday, closed Saturday. Best corned beef in B-town. $–$$

Where to Stay

Samuel Sewall Inn, 143 St. Paul Street, Brookline; (617) 713–0123 or (888) 713–2566; www.samuelsewallinn.com. Fourteen rooms, all with private bath. Great location near Collidge Corner, Children's Hospital, and Fenway Park. Charmingly restored by interior designer. No children under 5. Sister property of the Bertram Inn. $$–$$$

Biking in Boston and Cambridge

One of the city's many fine green spaces is the Charles River Reservation (for information call the **Division of Urban Parks and Recreation** (617–727–1300; www.state.ma.us/mdc), which borders the Charles, in both Boston and Cambridge, from Science Park all the way up to Harvard. A nice riverside bike ride (too long to walk) begins on the Boston side at the Community Boating boathouse, next to Massachusetts General Hospital. (Call Boston Bike Tours at 617–308–5902 for family bike rides with guides and rentals available along the Charles River in Boston and Cambridge—they are located on Boston Common.) Continue along the riverside area called the Esplanade, which runs below Beacon Hill and the Back Bay, past the Hatch Shell. This is where the Boston Pops performs **free** concerts during the summer (the Fourth of July concert and fireworks program regularly attracts half a million people) and, on summer Friday evenings, it's where **free** movies are shown (imagine several thousand people gathered on blankets to watch *The Wizard of Oz* outdoors). You'll find several good playgrounds in this area, too. Continue along past the lagoon up to the bridge at Massachusetts Avenue—just to confuse you, this is called the Harvard Bridge (a good spot to view the head of the Charles Regatta). On the Cambridge side, ride along the Charles between MIT and Harvard. On Sundays from April through October, Memorial Drive is closed to auto traffic between the Western Avenue Bridge and the Eliot Bridge. The drive fills with walkers, strollers, bikers, skateboarders, and in-line skaters.

Cambridge

As home to two of the country's most illustrious universities, Harvard and MIT, bustling Cambridge owes much of its vibrancy to the schools' students, faculty, and staff, who are ruthless judges of food, bookstores, museums, art galleries, fashion, film, and the performing arts. As a result, the cultural life in this relatively small city is as good as that in any other city in America. You'll find enough shopping in and around Harvard Square to satisfy the most demanding teenager, and the range of food will thrill everyone. Don't leave Cambridge without walking through Harvard Square (location of the Discovery Information kiosk) and Harvard Yard (the best place to begin a trip to Cambridge), or without driving along Massachusetts Avenue until you reach MIT. These places give you the essence of the flavor of Cambridge. Step down to the Charles River along Memorial Drive and the graceful Weeks Bridge. You'll see the Radcliffe and Harvard boathouses here, and, if you're lucky, a few oarsmen and women will carry their sculls out to the river while you're watching. Walk along the river; you'll pass the graceful sycamore trees that line Memorial Drive. Do yourself a favor and leave the car in a garage; parking is nearly impossible to find, and if you're lucky enough to find a spot, you'll have to keep running back to feed quarters into the meter (Cambridge meter maids have a sixth sense about every meter that runs out, and they are impervious to protests). For tourist information on Cambridge, contact **Cambridge Visitor's Information,** 4 Brattle Street, Cambridge 02138; (617) 441–2884; www.cambridge-usa.org.

Harvard Museum of Natural History (all ages)

26 Oxford Street, Cambridge; (617) 495–3045; www.hmnh.harvard.edu. Open Monday through Sunday 9:00 A.M. to 5:00 P.M. Admission: $7.50 for adults, $6.00 for seniors and students, and $5.00 for children 3 to 18.

Taxidermied animals from all over the world, dinosaur fossils and skeletons, the world-renowned Blaschka glass flowers, and the varied and in-depth mineralogical and geological collection of gemstones and meteors. The Peabody Museum of Archaeology and Ethnology, 1 Divinity Avenue, Cambridge; (617) 496–1027, is across the street and has some interesting totem poles and peace pipes.

Mt. Auburn Cemetery (all ages)

580 Mt. Auburn Street, Cambridge; (617) 547–7105; www.mountauburn.org. The main gate is open from 8:00 A.M. to 5:00 P.M. seven days a week. The Green House is open from 8:00 A.M. to 3:30 P.M. Monday through Friday, 9:00 A.M. to 1:00 P.M. Saturday. The office is open Monday through Friday 8:30 A.M. to 4:30 P.M., Saturday from 8:30 A.M. to 12:30 P.M. Free.

Mt. Auburn Cemetery may sound like a strange place for a family outing, but when you arrive there, you'll see why so many Cambridge and Boston families make this a weekend destination: Its 174 acres are planted with 1,000 varieties of trees, shrubs, flowers, and other plants. This was the first garden cemetery in America when it was founded in 1831; the best time to visit is during the spring, when it seems as though every plant is in bloom. Stop at the office at the main gate for a map, and ask about the day's special activities and horticultural tours. Mt. Auburn Cemetery includes the resting places of Henry Wadsworth Longfellow, Isabella Stewart Gardner, and Winslow Homer. *WARNING:* No dogs, picnicking, cycling, or in-line skating!

Harvard **Art Museums**

All museums are open Monday through Saturday 10:00 A.M. to 5:00 P.M., Sunday from 1:00 to 5:00 P.M.; closed on national holidays. Admission is $6.50 for adults, $5.00 for students, and free for children under 18. Saturday mornings are free. Call (617) 495–9400; www.artmuseums.harvard.edu. General tours are offered September through June, Monday through Friday at 11:00 A.M. at the Fogg, 1:00 P.M. at the Busch-Reisinger Museum, and 2:00 P.M. at the Sackler.

- **Arthur M. Sackler,** 485 Broadway Street. Art of Asia, the Mideast, and India.

- **Busch-Reisinger Museum,** 32 Quincy Street and Broadway. Central and Northern European art, huge focus on German-speaking countries and cultures.

- **The Fogg,** 32 Quincy Street and Broadway. French and Italian art. The Fogg also houses the Straus Center for Conservation that specializes in research and scientific evaluation of art.

MIT Museum (all ages)

265 Massachusetts Avenue, Cambridge; (617) 253–4444; web.mit.edu/museum. Open Tuesday through Friday 10:00 A.M. to 5:00 P.M., Saturday and Sunday noon to 5:00 P.M.; closed Monday and holidays. Admission: $5.00 for adults, $2.00 for students, seniors, and ages 5 to 18, under 5 free. Free the third Sunday of each month.

During the school year, the museum offers family programs the last Sunday of every month from 2:00 to 4:00 P.M. (The Sunday we were there students were racing robots that they had designed and built.) It has a fantastic holographic collection from the 1940s to the present, and a robots and artificial intelligence area.
Other MIT offerings include:

- Compton Gallery, open Monday through Friday from 9:30 A.M. to 5:00 P.M. (closed on holidays). Free. The artwork on display is not part of a permanent collection—instead there are revolving art exhibits in many media.

- Hart Nautical Gallery, Monday through Friday from 9:00 A.M. to 8:00 P.M. (closed on holidays). Free. The Hart is known for its ship model collection, autonomous underwater robots, artifacts, drawings, marine art, history of ship design and construction, and information on the MIT Ocean Engineering Department.

Museum of Science Campus (all ages)

Science Park, Cambridge; (617) 723–2500; www.mos.org. The campus is closed on Thanksgiving and Christmas. Park at the Museum of Science garage (parking fee). Many cafes with fare ranging from deli to pizza are on the main level of the museum. Ask about the Sunday Brunch package.

The museum campus consists of the Museum of Science, the Hayden Planetarium, the Omni Theater, and the Laser Show. If you want to see the museum exhibits as well as other attractions, you'll have to buy combination tickets. Buy your Omni tickets early, since it often sells out quickly, especially on winter weekends. It is highly recommended to order your tickets in advance on the Web at www.tickets.mos.org.

Museum of Science (all ages)

Open from July 5 through Labor Day, Saturday through Thursday 9:00 A.M. to 7:00 P.M., Friday 9:00 A.M. to 9:00 P.M.; between Labor Day and July 4, Saturday through Thursday, 9:00 A.M. to 5:00 P.M., Friday 9:00 A.M. to 9:00 P.M. Admission: $14 for adults, $12 for seniors, $11 for children 3 to 11, **free** for children under 3.

Straddling a dam at the mouth of the Charles River, the Museum of Science deserves its reputation as a favorite field trip for Boston-area school kids. The museum is enormous, with more than 550 interactive exhibits; bring a stroller if you have toddlers. Young kids may not want to leave the Discovery Center, which was designed (and recently renovated) with them in mind. Other favorite exhibits include the Transparent Woman, which lights up to display organs; the Live Animal Show; the Theater of Electricity; the dinosaur exhibit, which outlines the latest theory that birds and dinosaurs are closely related; and the Chick Hatchery, where you observe chicks hatching from eggs. The Computer Museum (which is now closed) gave the Museum of Science its virtual fish tank exhibit, the computer club house, and Cahner's Computer Place. On Friday nights the Gilliland Observatory is open at 7:00 P.M. in season for stargazing (on the rooftop of the museum), and it's **free!**

Let Me **Entertain You**

The street entertainers in Harvard Square are easy on the pocketbook (they depend on tips from the crowd) and diverse. Performing in the wide pedestrian area between Brattle and Mt. Auburn Streets, they offer a range of acts that can be pretty good (tell the kids that this is where singer Tracy Chapman got her start). On a warm afternoon it's nice to sit on the low brick walls, have a snack, and let the street life entertain the family for a while.

Bookstore-Hopping in Harvard Square

- **Curious George Goes to Wordsworth,** 1 John F. Kennedy Street, Cambridge; (617) 498–0062; www.wordsworthkids.com.

- **Harvard BookShop,** 1256 Massachusetts Avenue, Cambridge; (617) 661–1515; www.harvard.com.

- **The Boston Globe Store,** Church and Palmer Streets, Cambridge; (617) 497–6277; www.globecorner.com. Travel books.

- **Schoenhof's,** 76A Mt. Auburn Street, Cambridge; (617) 547–8855; www.schoenhofs.com. For foreign language books.

The Mugar Omni Theater (all ages)
For a schedule of films, call (617) 723–2500. Admission: $8.50 for adults, $7.50 for seniors, and $6.50 for children 3 to 11.

The five-story theater has stadium seating, digital screens, and surround sound. The fifty-minute films are extremely realistic and can cause motion sickness or acrophobia. Tell your kids to close their eyes if something is upsetting to them.

Hayden Planetarium (age 4 and up)
Call (617) 723–2500 for a schedule. Admission: $8.50 for adults, $6.50 for children.

Relax for your forty-five-minute introduction to the stars.

Laser Light Show (all ages)
Open Thursday through Sunday nights. Admission: $8.50 for adults, $7.50 for seniors, and $6.50 for children 3 to 11. Selected show times since it's in the planetarium. Call for information or check www.mos.org.

Laser light show set to rock music.

Other Things to See and Do

Charles River Boat Company, 100 Cambridgeside Galleria, Suite 370, Cambridge; (617) 621–3001; www.charles riverboat.com. Tours from April through November. The fifty-five-minute tour is of the lower Charles River and the major sights found alongside its riverbanks. New to the fleet is an authentic sidewheeler. Cruises depart from across the Royal Sonesta Hotel at the Cambridgeside Galleria.

Longfellow National Historic Site, 105 Brattle Street, Cambridge; (617) 876–4491; www.nps.gov/long. Open mid-May through October. Home of poet Henry Wadsworth Longfellow while he taught at Harvard and former headquarters of George Washington.

Minuteman Bikeway Trail, start at Alewife "T" stop in Cambridge; (617) 727–3180; www.minutemanbikeway.org. Ten-and-a-half-mile bike/hike trail from Cambridge through Arlington to Lexington.

Where to Shop

Cambridgeside Galleria, 100 Cambridgeside Place, Cambridge; (617) 621–8666; www.cambridgesidegalleria.com. Shopping plaza.

The Garment District, 200 Broadway in Kendall Square, Cambridge; (617) 876–5230; www.garmentdistrict.com. Used and vintage clothing of the 1960s and '70s.

HMV, 1 Brattle Street, Cambridge; (617) 868–9696. An enormous music store with an especially good selection of classical and jazz recordings.

Jasminesola, 37 Brattle Street, Cambridge; (617) 354–6043; www.jasminesola .com. Excellent clothing.

Oona's Experienced Clothing, 1210 Massachusetts Avenue, Cambridge; (617) 491–2654. One of Cambridge's best secondhand stores. Mecca for teens.

Urban Outfitters, 11 John F. Kennedy Street, Cambridge; (617) 864–0070; www .urbn.com. For clothes-hound teenagers.

Tower Records, 95 Auburn Street, Cambridge; (617) 876–3377. The best selection around.

Where to Eat

Asgard, 350 Massachusetts Avenue, Cambridge; (617) 577–9100; www.classic irish.com. Open 11:00 A.M. to 1:00 A.M. Kids feel like royalty; they love the castle-like, stately feel of the place. American and Irish specialties. $–$$

Bartley's Burger Cottage, 1246 Massachusetts Avenue, Cambridge; (617) 354–6559; www.mrbartleys.com. Features burgers and other simple fare. Students congregate here for the large helpings and low prices. $

Full Moon, 344 Huron Avenue, Cambridge; (617) 354–6699; www.fullmoon restaurant.com. A *Parent's Paper* award-winning choice: great food, children's menu, a kids' play space, and special events and lectures on child raising. $–$$$

Herrell's Ice Cream, 15 Dunster Street, Cambridge; (617) 497–2179; www.herrells .com. Opened by Steve Herrell after he sold his wildly successful chain, Steve's. $

Il Panino Express, 1001 Massachusetts Avenue, Cambridge; (617) 547–5818; www.ilpanino.com. Cheap eats—good pasta and great pizza. *NOTE:* cash only. $–$$

Johnny's Luncheonette, 1105 Massachusetts Avenue, Cambridge; (617) 495–0055 or (617) 495–0031. Fifties-style diner. Their breakfast is unbeatable! $

Koreana, 154 Prospect Street, Cambridge; (617) 576–8661. Newly reopened after extensive renovations, this Korean restaurant has great Asian food. There is a barbecue set in the middle of the table to cook your dinner. Kids love it. $–$$

Red Bones, 55 Chester Street in Somerville; (617) 628–2200; www.red bonesbbq.com. Real southern barbecue. $–$$$

Where to Stay

Charles Hotel, 1 Bennett Street, Cambridge; (617) 864–1200 or (800) 882–1818; www.charleshotel.com. Great location near Harvard Square; indoor heated lap pool (special children's hours), children's bedtime story line, and children's menu. $$$–$$$$

Royal Sonesta, 5 Cambridge Parkway, Cambridge; (617) 491–3600 or (800) SONESTA; www.sonesta.com. Across from the Cambridgeside Galleria and near the Museum of Science Campus. Ice cream is served in the lobby, bicycles can be requested from guest services (no fee charged), and you can sign up for boat rides on the Charles River. $$–$$$$

Charlestown

Charlestown has reinvented itself in the last twenty years, and the cornerstone has been both the Charlestown Navy Yard (with its crown jewel, the USS *Constitution*) and the Bunker Hill Monument and Museum. The lovely brownstone homes off City Square Park have been snapped up by the economically successful set. A great source of information on Charlestown is sponsored by the Charlestown Business Association at www.charlestownbusiness.com. *HEADS-UP WARNING:* Streets and directions change at a fast pace here, with the Big Dig project (see Boston by Little Feet) happening right in Charlestown's backyard.

The Charlestown Navy Yard (all ages)

Constitution Road, Charlestown Navy Yard, Charlestown; (617) 242–5601 (visitors center), (617) 242–5670 (USS *Constitution*-Navy), (617) 242–5653 (USS *Cassin Young*), or (617) 426–1812 (Constitution Museum); www.ussconstitution.navy.mil, (the USS *Constitution's* Web site), www.nps.gov/bost/cassin_young.htm (the USS *Cassin Young*), www.ussconstitutionmuseum.org (the museum's Web site), or www.nps.gov.bost /navy-yard.htm. The USS *Constitution* is open in the summer Tuesday through Sunday from 10:00 A.M. to 4:00 P.M. and Thursday through Sunday from 10:00 A.M. to 4:00 P.M. in the winter. Free. The USS *Cassin Young* is open from 10:00 A.M. to 4:00 P.M. winter, 10:00 A.M. to 5:00 P.M. summer. Free. The Constitution Museum is open mid-October through April 30 from 10:00 A.M. to 5:00 P.M., summer from 9:00 A.M. to 6:00 P.M. Free. Parking lot outside the main gate.

The Charlestown Navy Yard is an on-site memorial to the thousands of warships that were built here between 1800 and 1974. The highlight is a visit to the USS *Constitution.* "Old Ironsides," as it's known (for its resilience rather than its materials; it's an all-wood ship), began its service in 1797; it's still commissioned, though it leaves the dock only once a year for a turnaround so that it ages evenly. The tour of the triple-decked ship, given by navy crew members, runs approximately twenty-five minutes and is well worth planning for (try to arrive early in the day to avoid being part of a too-large group). *TIP:* If you are in a hurry, there is a speed line that gives you access to the top deck of the ship for only ten minutes. Security precautions have been implemented before boarding. To orient you to the Navy Yard, start at the visitor center/bookstore. Don't miss the Constitution Museum (www.ussconstitutionmuseum.org); the wonderful playground at Shipyard Park (beyond the Constitution Museum), which features a shiplike climbing structure; and the USS *Cassin Young*, decommissioned in 1960, representing the ships that were produced at the Charleston Navy Yard. The **free** forty-five-minute tour below deck is offered five times a day; otherwise, visitation will be restricted to the main deck.

Bunker Hill Monument and Base Lodge Museum (all ages)

Monument Square; call the National Park Visitor's Center at the Base Lodge Museum at (617) 242–5641; www.nps.gov/bost. The monument is open daily from 9:00 A.M. to 5:30 P.M. in the summer and 4:30 P.M. in the winter; closed Thanksgiving, Christmas, and New Year's Day. Free. The Base Lodge Museum is open from 9:00 A.M. to 6:00 P.M. in the summer and to 5:00 P.M. in the winter. Free.

In the center of Charlestown, the Bunker Hill Monument rises from the spot where, in June 1775, Colonel William Prescott or General Israel Putnam (there is some controversy over who uttered this famous phrase) told his revolutionary militia, "Don't fire until you see the whites of their eyes." As most schoolchildren know, the British eventually won the battle, but not until they had lost well over 1,000 soldiers to Prescott's forces; the battle was an effective morale booster to the revolutionaries in the early days of the war. Climb the grassy hill, which is actually called Breed's Hill (the Bunker part of the name comes from the bunker that the colonists built atop the hill), to reach the base of the monument. (Be forewarned: There are 294 winding steps, about a fifteen-minute climb, not an appropriate ascent for younger kids or for parents who don't want to carry them most of the way.) The museum at the monument's base has good dioramas of the battle paintings, drawings, maps, pictures, descriptions, in-depth information on the Battle of Bunker Hill, and a toy soldier display. A park ranger is available for talks on request.

Young **at Heart**

The USS *Constitution* is the flagship of the United States Navy, and it is the oldest commissioned ship afloat in the world.

Where to Eat

Figs, 67 Main Street, Charlestown; (617) 242–2229; www.toddenglish.com. An off-shoot of Olives, Todd English's first trendy restaurant, Figs is a hip spot that serves creative pizzas and pasta dishes. $$

Tavern on the Water, 1 Pier 6, Eighth Street, Charlestown; (617) 242–8040. Serving lunch, dinner, and Sunday brunch. Outdoor deck gives whopping views of the harbor, the USS *Cassin Young,* and the USS *Constitution.* $–$$$

Dorchester

Columbia Point has the showcase John F. Kennedy Library, the University of Massachusetts Boston campus, and the Commonwealth Museum, with views of the Boston Harbor and skyline. Close by are the offices of the *Boston Globe* and the Bayside Exposition Site. The area can be somewhat daunting for walking (especially at night); a car is best here.

John F. Kennedy Library and Museum (age 4 and up)

Columbia Point (next to the University of Massachusetts Campus; take Morrissey Boulevard off Interstate 93 and follow the signs), Boston (Dorchester); (866) JFK–1960 or (617) 514–1600; www.jfklibrary.org. Open daily from 9:00 A.M. to 5:00 P.M.; closed Thanksgiving, Christmas, and New Year's Day. Admission: $10.00 for adults, $8.00 for seniors and students with ID, $7.00 for ages 13 to 17, free for children under 12.

The John F. Kennedy Library and Museum is the busiest of all the presidential libraries. The library itself is rarely visited by tourists, however; for most visitors the attraction here is the museum's excellent exhibition program about JFK and his brother Robert, complete with reminiscences taped by several close friends of the Kennedy clan. The self-guided tour starts with a seventeen-minute film narrated by President Kennedy. The tour then goes to the Democratic National Convention where Kennedy was nominated. The campaign trail is re-created, including the first televised debates between John F. Kennedy and opponent Richard Nixon. Relive election night with coverage by Walter Cronkite and other famous reporters of the '60s. The tour continues with a full-length color film of the Inaugural Address, and then enters the White House with the First Family in residence. Other exhibits of interest include press conferences with President Kennedy, coverage of the first manned exploration of space, the famous televised tour of the newly redecorated White House by Jacqueline Bouvier Kennedy, and a mock White House Cabinet room with documents and pictures of Kennedy and civil rights leaders of the 1960s. The building itself, designed by I. M. Pei and completed in 1979, remodeled and rededicated in 1993, is an extraordinary sight from the expressway: Its sweeping shape captures JFK's love of the ocean and of sailing. Combine a trip to the JFK Museum with a tour of the *Boston Globe.*

Boston Globe (must be at least 9)

135 Morrissey Boulevard, Boston (Dorchester); (617) 929–2653; bostonglobe.com/community/services/tours.stm. Sixty-minute tours are given on Monday and Thursday. Reservations should be made at least two weeks in advance since tour sizes are limited to thirty people, and children must be 9 years of age or older. Tours are closed mid-July through August. Free.

Start your tour with a ten-minute film depicting the daily workings of a newspaper. Then find out what's involved in publishing a daily paper; see the room where the presses roll (the *Globe* is published at night), check out the newsroom and the advertising and classified departments, and ask lots of questions.

Other Things to See and Do

Commonwealth Museum, 220 Morrissey Boulevard, Columbia Point (between UMass and the Kennedy Library), Dorchester; (617) 727–9268; www.state.ma.us /sec/mus. Open 9:00 A.M. to 5:00 P.M. Monday through Friday, 9:00 A.M. to 3:00 P.M. on Saturday. Archaeology of the Big Dig and an exhibit on Sacco and Vanzetti highlight the museum tour.

Courageous Sailing Center, Pier 4, Charlestown Navy Yard, Charlestown; (617) 242–3821; www.courageoussailing.org. Free sailing program for Boston area kids from beginners to advanced sailors. Rent a sailboat; lessons offered.

Dorchester Heights Monument, Thomas Park, Dorchester; (617) 242–5642; www.nps.gov/bos. Open 9:00 A.M. to 5:00 P.M. Site of General George Washington's first victory over the British. Rangers are available weekends and Wednesday.

National Center for Afro-American Artists, 300 Walnut Avenue, Roxbury; (617) 442–8614. Exhibits, films, concerts, and tours.

Quincy and Milton

Just a few miles south of Boston proper is Quincy, which has the unique claim to fame of being both the birthplace and the burial place of two U.S. presidents: John Adams, the second president, and his son, John Quincy Adams, the sixth president. Milton is home to Milton Academy, one of the preeminent private secondary schools in this country. Milton is close to Boston and is more of a bedroom community.

Children's **Literature**

Why Don't You Get a Horse, Sam Adams by Jean Fritz and
Trina Schart Hyman

Adams National Historic Site (age 5 and up)
135 Adams Street (site of the Old House and the Carriage House), Quincy; (617) 770–
1175 or (617) 773–1177; www.nps.gov/adams/index.htm. Open daily mid-April through
mid-November 9:00 A.M. to 5:00 P.M. Admission: $3.00, children under the age of 16
are free. NOTE: You can visit the birthplaces only as part of a guided tour, which
lasts about two and a half hours. A free trolley from the Visitor Center (1250 Hancock Street, Quincy; 617–770–1175) goes to the birthplaces and the Old House.

The Adams National Historical Park, run by the National Park Service, is the house
and gardens of the Adams family. When John and Abigail Adams moved here in 1787,
fifty-six years after the house was built, there were only seven rooms. As their for-
tune grew, they expanded the house until it had twenty rooms. Of special note here
are the library, with its 14,000 volumes in twelve languages, and the study where
John Adams died on July 4, 1826, fifty years to the day after the Declaration of Independence was signed. Here also are the small saltbox houses where the Adams presidents were born (Franklin Street, Quincy).

United First Parish Church (all ages)
1306 Hancock Street, Quincy; (617) 773–1290 or (617) 773–0062 (tour line); www.ufpc
.org. Tours are Monday through Saturday 9:00 A.M. to 5:00 P.M. and Sunday 1:00 to 5:00
P.M. Fees: $3.00 per adult, free for children 16 and younger.

This church holds the remains of the two Adams presidents and their wives. The tour
includes a visit to the sanctuary, the president's pew (which you can sit in), and their
crypt. The building was erected in 1828 during John Q. Adams's presidency. Both
Adams presidents were members of the congregation.

Weather or Not?

The **Blue Hills Weather Observatory** has the oldest continuously operating weather observatory in the United States. In 1989 the building was
declared a national historic landmark and is now both a weather museum
and a science center observatory. Call (617) 696–1014 for weather or climate information or (617) 696–0389 for a group tour.

Blue Hills Reservation and Blue Hills Trailside Museum (all ages)

Hillside Street, Milton; (617) 698–1802 or (617) 722–5500 (for the MDC). The Blue Hills Trailside Museum is at 1904 Canton Avenue, Route 138, Canton; (617) 333–0690; www .state.ma.us/mdc/blue.htm. There is a charge for the Trailside Museum.

The Blue Hills Reservation and State Park is operated and managed by both the Massachusetts Audubon Society and the Metropolitan District Commission (MDC). The Blue Hills Trailside Natural History Museum, operated by the Massachusetts Audubon Society for the MDC, at the foot of Blue Hill, has a collection of live native animals and offers a natural history program and displays on the park.

Blue Hills Reservation, at 7,000 acres, is one of the largest metropolitan parks in the United States, with twenty-two hills. One of the highlights is the Blue Blaze Skyline Trail, which traverses over the tops of many of the hills, affording spectacular views of the countryside, the Boston skyline, the Boston Harbor, and the Atlantic. It can be done in small sections depending upon your family's hiking ability. Houghtons's Pond is considered to be Boston's busiest freshwater swimming hole, attracting thousands of locals on scorching summer days (which can be a negative if you are looking for solitude). A weather observatory (available to school groups by appointment) is maintained at the summit of the Great Blue Hill and is often cited in forecasts of Boston area weather. There are numerous ponds for boating, swimming, and fishing activities. The trails can be accessed for biking and horseback riding. Winter activities include cross-country and downhill skiing, ice skating at the MDC rink, and snowshoeing. There are programs such as maple sugaring and hayrides; ask at the visitor center. Blue Hills Reservation has year-round access and activities.

Blue Hills Ski Area (all ages)

4001 Washington Street, Route 138 (exit 2B off Route 95), Canton; (781) 828–5070; www.thenewbluehills.com. Call for hours, prices, and start- and end-of-season dates.

Operated by Ragged Mountain New Hampshire. Ski or board from early morning until late at night. Don't have your own equipment? Want to teach the kids how to ski? Rentals and youth instructional programs (as well as for the parents) are available here. Ragged has poured money into updating the snowmaking capabilities and grooming of the Blue Hill. Tubing is now available, which gives another option to family members who enjoy winter sports.

Other Things to See and Do

Quincy Quarries Historic Site, Ricciuti Drive, Quincy; (617) 698–1802 or (617) 727–4573; www.state.ma.us/mdc. Open dusk to dawn. Hike, rock climb, and picnic. Both the Applachian Mountain Club and Eastern Mountain Sports run programs here.

Where to Eat

La Paloma, 195 Newport Avenue, Quincy; (617) 773–0512; www.lapalomarestaurant.com. Open Tuesday through Saturday 11:30 A.M. to 10:00 P.M., Sunday 3:00 to 9:00 P.M. Closed Monday. Voted "Best Mexican Restaurant" in the metropolitan Boston area. $–$$

West of Boston

Just a few miles to the northwest of Cambridge are the historic towns of Lexington and Concord. The "shot heard round the world" was fired in Lexington, and the subsequent first battles of the Revolutionary War were fought there and in Concord. During the nation's first century, Concord attracted thinkers and writers such as Nathaniel Hawthorne, Ralph Waldo Emerson, Louisa May Alcott, and Henry David Thoreau, whose homes are now open to the public. Thoreau's beloved Walden Pond is a terrific spot to learn a little about Thoreau or to picnic, sun, and swim. The DeCordova Museum and Sculpture Park is another great picnic spot as well as an innovative contemporary art museum in Lincoln. Waltham is still the home of several industries, although the emphasis now is on high tech. Acton, Framingham, and Natick still manage to maintain open spaces and promote family activities. For more information, contact the **Lexington Chamber of Commerce and Visitor Information,** 1875 Massachusetts Avenue, Lexington 02421 (781–862–2480; www.lexingtonchamber.org) or the **Concord Visitor Center** (run by the chamber of commerce), 58 Main Street, Concord 01742; (978) 369–3120; www.concordmachamber.org. (The Chamber of Commerce is actually located at 100 Main Street, Suite 310–2). The Concord Visitor Center is open daily April 1 through October 31 from 9:30 A.M. to 4:30 P.M. Guided walking tours are offered seasonally Friday through Monday.

On the Road **to Liberty**

The Liberty Ride (sponsored by the town of Lexington) started in the summer of 2003 and runs July 1 through Columbus Day. This one-hour route covers major Lexington attractions and is narrated by a costumed guide—you can get off and on at the sights of your choice! Tickets are $20 for adults and $10 for students ages 5 to 17. There is free parking at the Museum of Our National Heritage and the Minute Man National Historical Park.

Path of Glory

The **Minuteman Bike Path** is a fun way to travel from northern **Cambridge through Arlington, Lexington, and Bedford.** It's a 10½-mile path that begins at the Alewife station in Cambridge (the northernmost stop on the Red Line) and follows some unused railroad tracks, ending in suburban Bedford. For more information about this trail and others in the Boston area, contact the Department of Environmental Management, 100 Cambridge Street, Boston 02202 (617–727–3180).

Lexington Battle Green/Lexington Visitor Center (all ages)
1875 Massachusetts Avenue, Lexington; (781) 862–1450; www.lexingtonchamber.org. Free.

Battle Green is the site of the first battle of the American Revolution on April 19, 1776. The visitor center, adjacent to the Minuteman Statue, has a diorama of the battle, a gift shop, and visitor information.

Museum of Our National Heritage (all ages)
33 Marrett Road (Route 2A), Lexington; (781) 861–6559; www.monh.org. New at the Museum is Heritage Cafe Restaurant and Shop. Open Monday through Saturday 10:00 A.M. to 5:00 P.M. and Sunday noon to 5:00 P.M. Free.

Exhibits on American history and culture. Diorama of excavated artifacts and revolving exhibits on Americana.

Minute Man National Historical Park (all ages)
Battle Road, Route 2A, Lexington/Lincoln line and on to Concord; (781) 862–7753; www.nps.gov/mima. Open daily from 9:00 A.M. to 5:00 P.M. Free.

Minute Man National Historical Park extends along Battle Road from Lexington to Lincoln to Concord. It was established to commemorate the events that took place along the winding, hilly road on April 18–19, 1775. Stop at the visitor center for an excellent twenty-five-minute multimedia presentation, "The Road to Revolution," that will orient you to the history and sights of the area. There's a nice 1-mile walk (follow the markers) to the ruins of the Fiske House, a farmhouse that was in the midst of the battle area. Also of interest is an entire restored colonial neighborhood centered around Hartwell Tavern. Park rangers dressed like eighteenth-century colonists offer daily musket firing demonstrations, arts and crafts events, walking tours, and historical lectures. A good book to read before arriving is *Sam the Minuteman,* by Nathaniel Benchley and Arnold Lobel.

Old North Bridge/Old North Bridge Visitor Center (all ages)
Monument Street (Old North Bridge) and 174 Liberty Street (visitor center), Concord;
(978) 369–6993. Part of the Minute Man National Historical Park.

Begin your trip to Concord at the Old North Bridge. This is the spot where the "shot heard round the world" was fired. This is why the Old North Bridge is considered to be the birthplace of the American Revolution (first shot, first day, according to the park ranger)! The current bridge is actually the fifth reproduction since the historic event. Nearby (a ten-minute walk) is the North Bridge Visitor Center on Liberty Street. Park rangers answer questions at the center and also offer good presentations at the bridge itself (from June to October, daily; spring and fall, weekends only; winter, by advance request only). The home that Louisa May Alcott grew up in and Nathaniel Hawthorne and Margaret Sidney lived in was called the Wayside and is inside the park boundaries. It is open for tours for a fee.

Orchard House (all ages)
399 Lexington Road, Concord; (978) 369–4118; www.louisamayalcott.org. Open from April through October, Monday through Saturday 10:00 A.M. to 4:30 P.M., Sunday 1:00 to 4:30 P.M.; November through March, Monday through Friday 11:00 A.M. to 3:00 P.M., Saturday 10:00 A.M. to 4:30 P.M., Sunday 1:00 to 4:30 P.M. Admission: $8.00 for adults, $7.00 for seniors and students with ID, $5.00 for children 6 to 18, free for children 6 and under. Family rates are available. Tours are on the half hour from April through October, but for other times of year, please call on that day for tour times. *TIP:* Discount coupons are found on the Web site.

Near the middle of Concord is the home where *Little Women* author Louisa May Alcott lived as an adult. The house is remarkably homey and informal; there are no ropes or fences, and there are enough recognizable items on view to make Alcott's fans feel as though she and her sisters have just left the room. Be sure to take the tour here.

Sleepy Hollow Cemetery (all ages)
Bedford Street and Court Lane, Route 62, Concord.

Remains of Ralph Waldo Emerson, Henry David Thoreau, Nathaniel Hawthorne, Louisa May Alcott, Daniel Chester French, Ephraim Wales Bull (developer of the Concord grape), and Elizabeth Peabody (founder of the kindergarten movement), among other notables.

Great Meadows National Wildlife Refuge (all ages)
Monson Road, Concord; headquarters and visitor center on Weir Hill Road, Sudbury;
(978) 443–4661. Trails are open dawn to dusk year-round. Free.

Walking trails for bird-watching and hiking along pools, rivers, and uplands. Environmental and educational programs can be set up for groups.

Walden Pond State Reservation (all ages)

915 Walden Street, Route 126, Concord; (978) 369–3254; www.state.ma.us/dem/parks /wldn.htm. Open daily; seasonal hours. Price: $5.00 parking fee in the summer; rest of the year by donation.

Walden Pond can be a crowded place, especially when the water is warm enough for swimming. It's best to come here in the off-season; otherwise, it's hard to imagine the peace that Henry David Thoreau found when he lived here alone. His cabin was taken down long ago, but in its place is a large pile of rocks that visitors have placed here as a simple tribute to the man who chose Walden Pond as his home and wrote *On the Duty of Civil Disobedience.* Ungroomed trails for cross-country skiing and snow-shoeing, canoeing, fishing, and kayaking are allowed on Walden Pond. No pets.

Discovery Museums: Children's Discovery Museum (under age 10) and Science Discovery Museum (ages 6 and up)

177 Main Street, Acton; (978) 264–4201; www.discoverymuseums.org. Call for revolving schedule and hours. Admission: $8.00 per museum or $12.00 for both, children under 1 get in free.

The Children's Discovery Museum encourages touch and exploration. A favorite is the Water Discovery exhibit, where kids can create huge bubbles and play with water. The train room with Brio trains helps kids enact fantasies of ticket selling and getting on a train to undiscovered places; the Discovery Ship, located in the attic of the Victorian house, is great fun for improvisations of walking the plank. Interactive exhibits throughout the Science Discovery Museum encourage hands-on experimentation and invention. Children particularly enjoy the Inventor's Workshop woodworking shop. The music room encourages discoveries of things that can be used to make music, such as rubber balls, tuning forks, a music wall, and an air harp, which uses beams of light to make certain sounds. The sea of clouds is a dish with fog in it that helps children understand what a cloud is like. These museums are a big hit with inquisitive, playful kids.

DeCordova Museum and Sculpture Park (all ages)

Sandy Pond Road, Lincoln; (781) 259–8355; www.decordova.org. Open year-round, Tuesday through Sunday, 11:00 A.M. to 5:00 P.M. The cafe is open Wednesday through Sunday from 11:00 A.M. to 3:00 P.M. Admission to the gallery: $6.00 for adults, $4.00 for seniors, students, and children 6 through 12, free for under 6 years of age. Free admission to the sculpture park, which is open daily dawn to dusk. The tours of the DeCordova Museum are Wednesday and Sunday at 2:00 P.M. and Saturday and Sunday at 1:00 P.M. for the Sculpture Park.

Housed in the castlelike brick mansion of a wealthy, early-twentieth-century Boston businessman, the DeCordova Museum is dedicated to promoting appreciation of contemporary art by American artists, particularly those working in the New England area. An ambitious schedule of exhibitions attracts a large, loyal audience. Outdoors on the museum's beautiful grounds, the sculpture park features permanent and temporary sculptures, some of which are musical and most of which will intrigue the kids. A fine concert series called Art in the Park is held in the outdoor amphitheater the second Sunday in June. Check the museum for a schedule of events. The DeCordova Museum also offers family education programming called First Sunday, geared for children 6 to 12 and their families.

Drumlin Farm (all ages)

South Great Road, South Lincoln; (781) 259–2200 or (800) AUDUBON; www.mass audubon.org. Nature center open March through October, Tuesday through Sunday and on Monday holidays (except Thanksgiving, Christmas, and New Year's Day), 9:00 A.M. to 5:00 P.M. Open November through February Tuesday through Sunday and Monday holidays 9:00 A.M. to 4:00 P.M. The trails are only open when the nature center is open. Admission: $6.00 for adults, $4.00 for seniors and children 3 to 12, and free for children under 3.

Drumlin Farm is a 232-acre magnet for Boston-area families with young children. It's the headquarters of the Massachusetts Audubon Society as well as a "demonstration farm," which means that the exhibits are built around what you might find on a typical New England farm: kitchen gardens, flower gardens, meadows, ponds, and, of course, lots of animals, including cows, pigs, horses, birds, and forest creatures. Excellent kid-oriented demonstrations, discussions, and walks are given on weekends at 11:00 A.M. and 2:00 P.M. *NOTE:* Picnicking is allowed in designated areas only; no dogs allowed. Special programming includes in-season sleigh rides and hayrides for $1.00 and maple sugaring from mid-February through March.

Longfellow's Wayside Inn (all ages)

72 Wayside Inn Road, Sudbury; (978) 443–1776 or (800) 339–1776; www.wayside.org.

The historic Longfellow's Wayside Inn is a pleasant place to spend a night. The red clapboard building, the oldest operating inn in the country, was built in 1702, becoming an inn in 1716; the Ford Foundation bought it and renovated it in the early 1920s. There are ten guest rooms, two of them (original to the house) reached by a narrow staircase, all with private bath. The dining room serves lunch and dinner (reservations required for dinner). On the Wayside Inn's one-hundred-acre grounds is the Red Schoolhouse, famous as the school that Mary and her little lamb attended; the Ford Foundation moved the building here from nearby Sterling, Massachusetts, during the 1920s renovation project (the schoolhouse is open daily April through November, weather permitting, noon to 5:00 P.M.). Also of interest is the gristmill on-site, which grinds the meal and flour for corn muffins and wheat rolls. It's open Wednesday through Sunday 9:00 A.M. to 5:00 P.M. April through October (it was moved at the same time as the little red schoolhouse).

Garden in the Woods/New England Wildflower Society
(all ages)

180 Hemenway Road, Framingham; (508) 877–7630 or (508) 877–3658; www.newfs.org. Open daily April 12 through June 15, 9:00 A.M. to 7:00 P.M.; June 16 through October 31, Tuesday through Sunday 9:00 A.M. to 5:00 P.M. (last admission one hour before closing). Admission: $7.00 for adults, $5.00 for seniors, $3.00 for children 6 to 16.

Largest landscaped collection of wildflowers, shrubs, ferns, and trees in New England spread over forty-five acres. More than 1,600 plants, including more than 200 rare species. Informal tours at 10:00 A.M. when the garden is open, with the exception of a 2:00 P.M. tour only on Sunday. Largest wildflower collection for sale in New England.

Gillette Stadium (formerly Foxboro Stadium) (all ages)
1 Patriot Place, Route 1, Foxboro; (508) 543–0350, (617) 931–2000, or (800) 543–1776 for tickets; www.patriots.com/stadium.

Home to both the New England Revolution and the New England Patriots. Venue site for concerts and special events. The stadium opened for the 2002 season. A modern architectural wonder, every seat has a fabulous view. It is a complete upgrade over the former stadium, which was torn down after the new state-of-the-art stadium was built.

New England Patriots (all ages)
Gilette Stadium, 1 Patriot Place, Route 1, Foxboro; (508) 543–0350 or (800) 543–1776 for tickets; www.patriots.com.

New England's professional football team, winner of the 2001–2002 and 2003–2004 Super Bowls. Preseason games are scheduled in August. The football season starts mid-September and runs through late December. The New England Patriots play in the new Gilette Stadium when at home.

New England Revolution (all ages)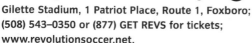
Gilette Stadium, 1 Patriot Place, Route 1, Foxboro; (508) 543–0350 or (877) GET REVS for tickets; www.revolutionsoccer.net.

Professional soccer team that has a growing following. The soccer season is from April through September.

Marcia's
TopAnnualEvents
in Greater Boston

- **Chinese New Year,** late January or early February, Chinatown, Boston; (617) 635–3485; www.cityofboston.gov

- **New England Boat Show,** February, Bayside Exposition Center, Boston; (617) 474–6000 or (800) 225–1577 (New England Boat Show); www.baysideexpo.com or www.naexpo.com

- **New England Flower Show,** March, Bayside Exposition Center, Boston; (617) 474–6153 or (617) 933–4984 (Massachusetts Horticultural Society); www.baysideexpo.com or www.masshort.org

- **Saint Patrick's Day Parade,** March 17, South Boston; (617) 268–7955

- **Boston Marathon,** Patriots Day (the third Monday in April), Hopkinton to Boston; (617) 236–1652; www.bostonmarathon.org

- **Paul Revere and Billy Dawes' Ride Reenactment,** Patriots Day, Lexington; (781) 862–2480; www.battleroad.org

- **Battle of Lexington and Concord Reenactment,** Patriots Day, Lexington; (781) 862–2480; www.battleroad.org

- **Big Apple Circus,** April and May, Boston; (617) 426–8855; www.bigapplecircus.com

- **Ducklings Day,** Mother's Day, Boston Public Garden; (617) 426–1885; www.historic-neighborhoods.org

- **Lilac Sunday,** May, Arnold Arboretum, Jamaica Plain; (617) 524–1718; www.arboretum.harvard.edu

- **Kite Festival,** May, Franklin Park, Jamaica Plain; (617) 635–4505, extension 4032; www.cityofboston.gov

- **Street Performers Festival,** Faneuil Hall Marketplace, Boston; (617) 523–1300; www.faneuilhallmarketplace.com

- **Bunker Hill Day,** June 17, Charlestown; (617) 242–5628; www.nps.gov/bost

- ***Boston Globe* Jazz and Blues Festival,** June, Newbury Street; (617) 267–2224

- **Art in the Park,** June, DeCordova Museum, Lincoln; (781) 259–8355; www.decordova.org

- **Harborfest,** end of June/beginning of July, Boston; (617) 227–1528; www.harborfest.org

- **Boston Pops Fourth of July Concert,** July 4, Esplanade, Boston; (617) 536–4100 or (617) 727–9547 (MDC); www.bostonusa.com

- **USS *Constitution* Turnaround,** July 4, Charlestown Navy Yard, Charlestown; (617) 242–5601; (visitor center), (617) 426–1812 (Constitution Museum); www.ussconstitutionmuseum.org

- **Feste (Saint's Festival),** nearly every weekend in July and August, North End; (617) 536–4100; (617) 635–3911 (mayor's office of cultural affairs); www.cityofboston.gov

- **Cambridge Carnival International,** August, Massachusetts Avenue, Cambridge; (617) 661–0457; www.cambridgeusa.org

- **Art Newbury Street,** September, Boston; (617) 267–2224

- **Head of the Charles Regatta,** October, Charles River Cambridge/Boston; (617) 864–8415 or (617) 423–1331; www.hocr.org

- ***The Nutcracker,*** November through early January, Boston Ballet, Boston; (617) 695–6950 or (800) 447–7400; www.bostonballet.org

- **Christmas Tree Lighting,** late November, Boston Common, Boston; (617) 635–4505

- **Black Nativity,** December, Museum and National Center of African-American Artists; (617) 442–8614

- **Boston Tea Party Reenactment,** December, Old South Meeting House to Boston Harbor; (617) 338–1773

- **Newbury Street Holiday Stroll,** December; (617) 267–2224

- **First Night,** December 31, Boston; (617) 542–1399; www.firstnight.org

Other Things to See and Do

Beaver Brook Reservation, Mill Street, Belmont and Waltham; (617) 484–6357; www.state.ma.us/mdc/beaver.htm. First reservation created by the MDC. A beautiful, natural habitat consisting of fifty-nine acres of ponds, meadows, forest, and marsh (look for the scenic waterfall for a perfect picnic). Great tot play area.

Cardinal Spellman Philatelic Museum, 235 Wellesley Street (at Regis College), Weston; (781) 768–8367; www .spellman.org. Open Thursday through Saturday noon to 5:00 P.M. Admission: $5.00 for adults; free for children 16 and under. Three million stamps from all over the world. Features a children's activities center, museum store, post office, and library.

Charles River Museum of Industry, 154 Moody Street, Waltham; (781) 893–5410; www.crmi.org. Open Monday through Saturday, 10:00 A.M. to 5:00 P.M. Explores the textile, watch (the Waltham Watch Company had an international reputation), bicycle, automobile, and tool industries.

Cochituate State Park, Route 30, Natick; (508) 653–9641; www.state.ma.us/ dem/parks/coch.htm.

Codman House, Codman Road, Lincoln; (781) 259–8843; www.spnea.org. The Codman family home spans 200 years of history, showing different architectural influences of residing families. Beautiful grounds.

Concord Museum, 200 Lexington Road (Cambridge Turnpike), Concord; (978) 369–9763 or (978) 369–9609 (taped information). Americana mixed with artifacts from the Revolutionary times to the days of Thoreau. Literary collection.

Danforth Museum, 125 Union Avenue, Framingham; (508) 620–0050; www. danforthmuseum.org. Open Saturday and Sunday noon to 5:00 P.M. Price is $5.00 for adults, $4.00 for students, and kids under 12 are free. Featuring American art and a junior gallery for families.

Girl Scout Museum at Cedar Hill, Patriots' Trail Girl Scout Council, 265 Beaver Street, Waltham; (781) 893–6113; www.ptgirlscouts.org/museum.htm. Girl Scout equipment and uniforms from days past on display.

Gore Place, 52 Gore Street, Waltham; (781) 894–2798; www.goreplace.org. Open mid-April through mid-November, Tuesday through Saturday, from 11:00 A.M. to 5:00 P.M. and Sunday 1:00 to 5:00 P.M. A historic mansion, farm, and gardens spread over forty-five acres. Small animal farm. Admission fee.

Great Brook Farm State Park, Lowell Road, Carlisle; (978) 369–6312; www.state .ma.us/dem/parks/gbfm.htm. A *Yankee Magazine's* editors pick for 2000. Holstein dairy cows on a working farm. Twenty miles of trails for hiking, biking, cross-country, and horseback. Great ice cream stand.

Gropius House, 68 Baker Bridge Road, Lincoln; (781) 259–8098; www.spnea.org. First home in the United States designed by William Gropius, father of the Bauhaus School of Architecture and a key figure in contemporary modern architecture of the twentieth century.

Old Manse, 269 Monument Street, Concord; (978) 369–3909; www.thetrustees .org. Trustees of Reservations property, historical sights; famous residents were Ralph Waldo Emerson and Nathaniel Hawthorne.

Rose Art Museum, 415 South Street, Waltham; (781) 736–3434; www.brandeis.edu/rose. One of the largest collections of modern and contemporary art from America and Europe in New England. Specializing in art from the last half of the twentieth century.

South Bridge Boat House, 496 Main Street/Route 62, Concord; (978) 369–9438. Canoe and rowboat rentals, lunch and dinner service on a pontoon boat.

Stone Zoo, 149 Pond Street, Stoneham; (781) 438–5100 or (617) 541–LION (5466); www.zoonewengland.com. Open year-round at 10:00 A.M., closing at 4:00 P.M. winter, 5:00 P.M. on summer weekdays, and 6:00 P.M. summer weekends and holidays. Adults are $6.00, children 2 through 15 $4.00, and under 2 **free.** Touchable barnyard and caged live wild animals.

Waverly Oaks Playground (at the Beaver Brook Reservation), Trapelo Road, Belmont; (617) 727–5380 or (617) 484–6357. Spraying fountains and pool, climbing structures, picnic tables, and hiking trails.

Where to Eat

Iguana Cantina, 313 Moody Street, Waltham; (781) 891–3039. Favorite hangout for local college students and student wannabes. Fun and hip Mexican decor, this restaurant has a great reputation for delicious Mexican food. $–$$

Mario's Italian Restaurant, 1733 Massachusetts Avenue, Lexington; (781) 861–1182. Family-style restaurant serving pasta and pizza. $–$$

Michael's Restaurant, Route 117, Concord; (978) 371–1114. Specializing in Italian dishes. $$

Rain Forest Cafe, Burlington Mall, Burlington; (781) 272–7555; www.rainforestcafe.com. You don't need raingear to eat here, but there are thunderstorms every twenty minutes, waterfalls, electronic jungle animals, and fish tanks. $–$$

Solea Restaurant and Tapas Bar, 388 Moody Street, Waltham; (781) 894–1805; www.solearestaurant.com. Open for dinner only. A communal meal can be had by ordering several hot and cold tapas dishes. Our favorite was the roasted duckling with berry sauce—ummm—mouthwatering! $–$$$

Vinny T's, 20 Waltham Street, Lexington; (781) 860–5200; www.vinnytsofboston.com. Huge portions, laid-back family atmosphere, and great Italian food. $–$$

Walden Grill, 24 Walden Street, Concord; (978) 371–2233. Casual atmosphere, Mediterranean dishes. $–$$

Where to Stay

Battle Green Motor Inn, 1720 Massachusetts Avenue, Lexington; (781) 862–6100 or (800) 343–0235 (reservations); www.battlegreeninn.com. Family-style motel just down the street from the Battle Green; heated swimming pool and **free** continental breakfast. $–$$

Colonial Inn and Restaurant, 48 Monument Square, Concord; (978) 369–9200; www.concordscolonialinn.com. On National Register of Historic Hotels; rumored to have one haunted room, which they don't rent out without the consent of the earthbound client. Close to sights, shopping, and restaurants in charming Concord Center. $$–$$$

Doubletree Guest Suites, 550 Winter Street, Waltham; (781) 890–6767 or (800) 222–TREE; www.doubletree.com. Indoor pool and sauna, game room, cookies at check-in, and kid's menu. $$–$$$$

Plymouth
and the
South Shore

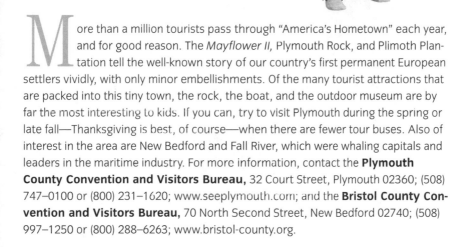

More than a million tourists pass through "America's Hometown" each year, and for good reason. The *Mayflower II*, Plymouth Rock, and Plimoth Plantation tell the well-known story of our country's first permanent European settlers vividly, with only minor embellishments. Of the many tourist attractions that are packed into this tiny town, the rock, the boat, and the outdoor museum are by far the most interesting to kids. If you can, try to visit Plymouth during the spring or late fall—Thanksgiving is best, of course—when there are fewer tour buses. Also of interest in the area are New Bedford and Fall River, which were whaling capitals and leaders in the maritime industry. For more information, contact the **Plymouth County Convention and Visitors Bureau,** 32 Court Street, Plymouth 02360; (508) 747–0100 or (800) 231–1620; www.seeplymouth.com; and the **Bristol County Convention and Visitors Bureau,** 70 North Second Street, New Bedford 02740; (508) 997–1250 or (800) 288–6263; www.bristol-county.org.

Marcia's
TopPicks in Plymouth and the South Shore

1. Plimoth Plantation, Plymouth

2. *Mayflower II*, Plymouth

3. Duxbury Beach, Marshfield/Duxbury

4. New Bedford Whaling Museum, New Bedford

5. Battleship Cove and the Fall River carousel, Fall River

6. Horseneck State Beach, Westport

PLYMOUTH AND THE SOUTH SHORE

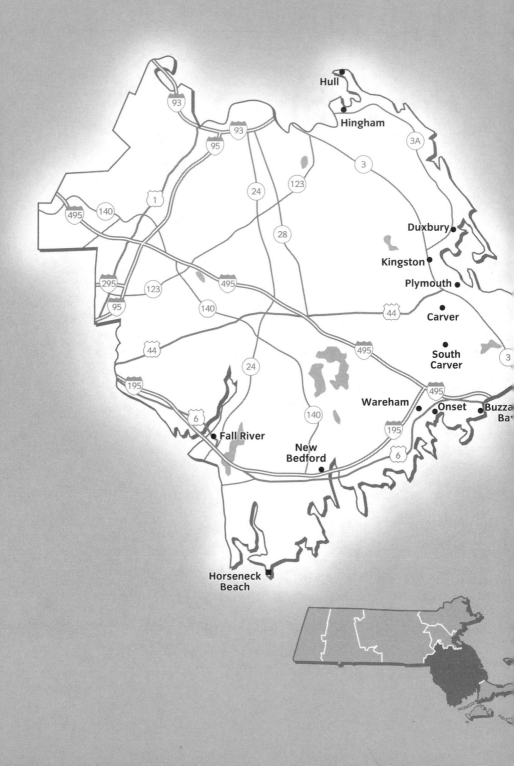

Hull, Hingham, Plymouth County

Shaped like an elbow, the west side of Hull has a commanding view of Boston Harbor and the Boston Harbor Islands, as does the neighboring more highbrow town of Hingham. World's End in Hingham was designed by Frederick Law Olmsted and is a calming respite after an active week. Lots of activities for families in this area are water-based fun. Try a canoe ride down the North River or a cruise to one of the Boston Harbor Islands.

Motion Odyssey Movie Ride (Rider must be over 40 inches tall!)

Jordan's Furniture, 100 Stockwell Drive, Avon; (508) 580–4600; www.jordansfurniture .com. Open 2:00 to 11:30 P.M. Monday through Friday (you can visit earlier if you make an appointment at 508–580–1335), Saturday from 10:00 A.M. to 9:30 P.M. and Sunday 10:30 A.M. to 5:30 P.M. Tickets are $5.00 for adults and $4.00 for children 13 and under.

The Motion Odyssey movie is a four-story-high movie screen with forty-eight seats that have flight simulator capabilities. What a clever idea to distract the kids while you shop for furniture! Proceeds earned from the ride go to charity, so everyone wins on this ride! *WARNING:* This is a high-speed, turbulent ride; if you are pregnant or have a health issue, this is not the ride for you. However, there are stationary seats for those who wish to see the movie or the laser preshow (because of the noise factor, you must be over 40 inches for the stationary seat as well).

Nantasket Beach (all ages)

Nantasket Avenue, Hull; (617) 727–8856 or (888) 925–HULL; www.hullnantasket.com or www.state.ma.us/mdc/nantask.htm. Open year-round; $2.00 parking fee.

Seven miles of clear water and clean, lifeguarded beach (in season, late June to early September) will attract your family, as will the Paragon, a vintage carousel (on Wharf Avenue) with hand-turned horses and chariots. Waterfront activities include a concert series, the Hull Heritage Days Festival, and the annual September Chowderfest. There is a new bathhouse, and the beach area has been restored.

Wompatuck State Park and World's End Reservation (all ages)

Off Route 228, Hingham; (781) 749–7160 (Wompatuck State Park) or (781) 821–2977; www.massparks.org or www.thetrustees.org. Open daily dawn to dusk. Admission to Wompatuck State Park is free. World's End admission is $4.50 for adults, children 12 and under are free.

Wompatuck State Park, named after an Indian chieftain from the colonial period who deeded the land to the settlers, covers some 3,500 acres and offers more than 250 campsites (some with trailer hookups) and shower facilities. Biking paths are threaded throughout the park, and there is a boat ramp for boating fun. Other popular forms of recreation are cross-country skiing, fishing, horseback riding, and hiking. Interpretive programs are offered. World's End Reservation at the tip of the park is managed by the Trustees of Reservations and has breathtaking panoramic views of Hingham Harbor, Hull, and the Boston skyline. This is also a great birding site, especially during the migration seasons in spring and fall.

Other Things to See and Do

Hingham Ferry to Boston and Boston Harbor Islands; (617) 227–4321 (Boston Harbor Cruises); www.boston harborcruises.com. See also the Boston Harbor Islands section in the Greater Boston Chapter.

Hull Lifesaving Museum, 1117 Nantasket Avenue, Hull; (781) 925–LIFE; www .bostonharborheritage.org. Open Wednesday through Sunday 10:00 A.M. to 4:00 P.M. year-round. U.S. lifesaving station-turned-museum.

Mary's Boat Livery, 2205 Main Street, Marshfield; (781) 837–2322. Rent a powerboat and explore the North or South River.

South Shore Music Circus, 130 Sohier Street, Cohasset; (781) 383–9850; www .musiccircus.com. Children's summer theater productions.

South Shore Natural Science Center, 48 Jacobs Lane, Norwell; (781) 659–2559; www.ssnsc.org. Programs for children, nature trails, and animal exhibits.

Winslow House, 644 Careswell Street, Route 139, Marshfield; (781) 837–5753; www.marshfield.net/winslow.general information.html. Seasonal (July through late September). Daniel Webster's law office at his former home is a national historic landmark.

Herring Runs

Sites to view the herring returning to their spawning grounds:

- **Herring Run Park,** Route 14, Pembroke
- **Island Creek** at Route 3A, Duxbury
- **Jones River** at Elm Street, Kingston
- **Town Brook** at Jenny Grist Mill, Plymouth

Duxbury and Kingston

Heading south of Boston during the summer? In their Cape-bound haste, many people miss Duxbury Beach, one of the finest barrier beaches along the Atlantic Coast. On your way there, drive or walk across the Powder Point Bridge, the longest wooden bridge on the East Coast. The pedestrian portion of the bridge is wide, allowing room for walkers to pass behind the fishing enthusiasts who gather along the bridge. Famous Pilgrims buried at the Old Burying Ground on Chestnut Street in Duxbury include Myles Standish and Priscilla and John Alden.

Duxbury Beach, aka Blakeman's Public Beach (all ages)

At the end of Route 139 (accessed through the Green Harbor section of Marshfield); (781) 837–3112. Lifeguards are on duty from late May through early September 10:00 A.M. to 4:00 P.M., weather permitting. Parking is $8.00 on weekends, $5.00 on weekdays.

This 5-mile-long stretch of sand and beach grass is a favorite of locals. The old-fashioned, full-service bathhouse is a great find for car-bound travelers. Spend the day on the beach, then wash the sand and salt water off the kids (and yourselves) before returning to the car. There's a good snack bar, lunch room, and outdoor grill.

King Caesar House (ages 8 and up)

King Caesar Road, Duxbury; (781) 934–6106; www.duxburyhistory.org. Open mid-June through Labor Day, Wednesday through Sunday, 1:00 to 4:00 P.M.; Labor Day through September 30 open Saturday and Sunday 1:00 to 4:00 P.M. Admission: $5.00 for adults, $2.00 for seniors and students.

This is the Federal-style home of Ezra Weston, a successful shipping magnate of the nineteenth century. Original wharves are located in Bumpus Park, where Ezra's ship, *The Hope,* was built. The main house has a children's room with period dolls and toys. A knot herb garden and a perennial garden are also on the property.

Other Things to See and Do

Art Complex Museum, 189 Alden Street, Duxbury; (781) 934–6634; www.art complex.com. Wednesday through Sunday 1:00 through 4:00 P.M. **Free.** Founded by the Weyerhauser family. Modern art, Asian art, and American paintings.

Blake Planetarium, Plymouth Community Intermediate School, 117 Long Pond Road, Plymouth; (508) 830–4470. Call for schedule.

John Alden House, 105 Alden Street, Duxbury; (781) 934–9092; www.alden.org. Open Monday through Saturday noon to 4:00 P.M. Price: $5.00 for adults, $3.00 ages 3 to 18, under 3 **free.** Home of *Mayflower* Pilgrims John and Priscilla Alden.

Where to Eat

Farfar's Danish Ice Cream Shop, 272 St. George Street, Duxbury; (781) 934–5152. Delicious ice cream made daily on the premises. $

Persy's Place, 117 Main Street/Route 3A, Kingston; (781) 585–5464. Diverse breakfast menu, from plain toast to catfish on eggs. Lunch also served daily. $

Plymouth

When you arrive in Plymouth, your first stop should be one of the two excellent tourist information centers. Adjacent to the highway, the **Massachusetts Tourist Information Center** (exit 5 on Route 3 South; 508–746–1150; www.seeplymouth.com), aka the Plymouth County Convention and Visitors Bureau, carries an excellent selection of books, maps, and brochures. The parking lot is large, and there are clean restrooms and picnic tables. The hard-to-stump staff is happy to answer your questions and point you in the right direction. Open year-round, daily, 8:30 A.M. to 4:30 P.M. The **Plymouth Visitor Information Center,** 130 Water Street, Plymouth 02361 (508–747–7525 or 800–872–1620) and **Destination Plymouth** (508–747–7533; www.visit-Plymouth.com) at 170 Water Street (right at the waterfront), are near most of the sites your family came to Plymouth to see. The selection of tourist literature is

Amazing
Massachusetts Facts

- America's oldest lighthouse is on Little Brewster Island off the coast of Hull.

- Old Ship Church is the oldest wooden church in the United States that has been in continuous use.

- The first canal in America was dug in the 1630s by the Pilgrims. It connected Plymouth Bay to Green Harbor in Marshfield.

- The first radio program in the world was broadcast in Marshfield on Christmas Eve 1906.

- The 1794 Court House Museum in Town Square in Plymouth is the oldest wooden courthouse in the country.

- The Forefathers Monument in Plymouth is the largest solid granite monument in the United States.

good here, the staff is helpful, and the restrooms are conveniently located (baby-changing stations in both). Open daily, 9:00 A.M. to 5:00 P.M.; extended hours in the summer and at other busy times.

Plymouth Rock Trolley (all ages)

Meets at the Plymouth Rock or at the Plymouth Visitor Center, Plymouth; (508) 747–2240; www.plymouthrocktrolley.com. Operates weekends in May and November, daily Memorial Day to Halloween and Thanksgiving through the following Sunday. Hours: 9:30 A.M. to 5:00 P.M. Price: $15 for adults, $12 for children 6 to 12; under 6 free.

For families with very young children, or families who would rather see everything quickly without having to do too much walking, the Plymouth Rock Trolley is a convenient way to get around. The trolley stops at all the major sites, from Plymouth Rock to the *Mayflower II*, during each forty-five-minute trip. You can get on and off the trolley as many times as you like. During the summer the trolley ride is extended to Plimoth Plantation, Long Beach, and most of the hotels in the center of town.

Colonial Lantern Tours (ages 6 and up)

5 North Street, Plymouth; (508) 747–4161 or (800) 698–5636; www.plimouth.com. Offered from April through November. Two public tours nightly; reservations recommended. (Halloween tours by reservation only). Price: $15 for adults, $12 for children 6 to 18, under 6 free. Family rates available for four or more at $12 per person.

As you carry your punched-tin lantern through the streets of town, you are given a glimpse of Plymouth past and present. This guided walking tour, given the much coveted AAA rating, covers about a mile circuit about town and lasts for an hour and a half. Special themed tours are given at Halloween and Thanksgiving; daily tours give the history of the town (the Lantern Tour) or recount spine-tingling tales of Plymouth (the Legends and Lore Tour).

Plymouth Rock (all ages) 🏛

Water Street, Plymouth. Open year-round dawn to dusk. Free.

As any schoolchild in America can tell you, the first European settlers in Plymouth stepped off the *Mayflower* onto this rock in 1620. Considering its prominence in American history, the size of the rock may disappoint you; it's a rather ordinary-looking boulder. Nevertheless, it's the number-one tourist attraction in Plymouth.

Mayflower II (all ages)

State Pier, Water Street, Plymouth; (508) 746–1622; www.plimoth.org. Open April 1 through the Sunday following Thanksgiving 9:00 A.M. to 5:00 P.M. Admission: $8.00 for adults, $6.00 for children 5 to 12; free for children under 5. Special rates if you visit the boat and Plimoth Plantation on the same day ($22 for adults, $14 for children).

Near Plymouth Rock is the *Mayflower II*, a reproduction of the original boat that brought the Pilgrims to Plymouth. The costumed staff knows all sorts of facts about the boat, which seems astonishingly small when you think about the 102 people who crowded onto it during its first journey from England to America. Self-guided tour; allow approximately one hour to see everything.

Plimoth Plantation (all ages)

Route 3A/Warren Avenue, Plymouth; (508) 746–1622; www.Plimoth.org. Open April through November, daily, 9:00 A.M. to 5:00 P.M. Admission: $20 for adults, $12 for children 6 to 12; free for children under 6. Special rates if you visit the *Mayflower II* and Plimoth Plantation on the same day ($22 for adults, $14 for kids). Plimoth Plantation is 2½ miles south of the *Mayflower*. Free parking.

One of New England's best living museums is Plimoth Plantation. Budget at least half a day to see this remarkable reproduction of a 1627 Pilgrim village. It is populated by authentically costumed people who play, convincingly, the parts of the residents. Ask them questions about their clothes, their chores, what they do for fun, what they eat, how they survive without indoor plumbing—whatever comes to mind.

Hobbamock's Homesite, comprising a longhouse and a weetu, is interpreted by native Wampanoag guides dressed in traditional garb. Massasoit, the Wampanoag chief, had sent Hobbamock and his family to live near the Pilgrims, to teach them to survive, to translate and interpret, and to keep track of their doings.

At the Carriage House Craft Center, artisans re-create crafts using the same materials and many of the same tools that were used in the 1600s.

The Nye Rare Breeds Barn features rare and minor breeds of farm animals. Petting of the animals is allowed when the animals are on site.

The best day of the year to visit the plantation is Thanksgiving, of course; call ahead for a meal reservation. The gift shop has a large stock of books about Plymouth and the Pilgrims' lives and times. Call for the calendar of events and brochures; ask about children's activities and dining events.

Recommended Children's Books on
Plymouth and the Pilgrim Story

- *The First Thanksgiving*, by Jean Craighead George, illustrated by Thomas Locker
- *The Pilgrims of Plimoth*, written and illustrated by Marcia Sewall
- *Sarah Morton's Day: A Day in the Life of a Pilgrim Girl*, by Kate Waters

Boat Excursions in Plymouth

- **Captain John Ferry and Harbor Cruises,** State Pier; (508) 747–2400 or (800) 242–2469; www.captjohn.com. Operates daily from June through September. Ninety-minute boat ride from Plymouth to Provincetown, or seventy-five-minute cruise of Plymouth Harbor. Price: Provincetown round-trip: $30 for adults, $20 for kids under 12. Harbor Cruises: $12.00 for adults, $8.00 for kids under 12 (discount coupon on Web site).

- **Captain John Whale Watch and Deep Sea Fishing,** Town Wharf; (800) 242–AHOY; www.captainjohn.com. Floating classroom (in springtime only), with naturalist on board with every whale watch. Whale watch tour price: $29 for adults, $18 for children under 12. Discount coupon on Web site.

- **Lobster Tales,** Town Wharf; (508) 746–5342; www.lobstertalesinc .com. Harbor tour of historic Plymouth, followed by hauling of lobster traps and examination of the catch (crabs, fish, and lobster). Touch tank on board. Price: $12 for adults, $10 for children under 12. Discount coupon on Web site.

- **Lobster Tales Pirate Adventure,** east end of Route 44, Town Wharf; (508) 746–5342; www.lobstertalesinc.com or www.piratefun.com. Kids don pirate hats, bandannas, and makeup, follow a treasure map to find buried booty, have a battle at sea with an enemy pirate vessel, and eventually may win the treasure chest. The loot is divvied up, and a celebration ensues with buccaneer brew, dancing, music, and singing. Price: $14.00 for adults and $8.00 for children under 4. Discount coupon on Web site.

- ***Pilgrim Belle,*** State Pier; (508) 746–2643; www.plymouthharbor cruises.com. Only authentic paddlewheeler in New England; meals served on select cruises. Prices vary depending upon the cruise. Discount coupon on Web site.

- **Splashdown Amphibious Tours,** Harbor Place; (508) 747–7658 or (800) 225–4000; www.ducktoursplymouth.com. One-hour land-and-sea tour of historic Plymouth. Price: $17.00 for adults and $11.00 for children 3 to 12; under 3 is $3.00. Discount coupon on Web site.

Beaches in Plymouth

- **Nelson Street Beach,** off Water Street, just north of Cranberry World. Good swimming, free parking, and a playground.

- **Plymouth Beach,** Route 3A. Lifeguarded beach with snack bar and bathhouse.

- **Stephen's Field Park,** 1 mile south of Plymouth Center, just off Route 3A. Free parking, a small duck pond, a beach, tennis courts, picnic tables, and a playground.

Pilgrim Hall Museum (all ages)
75 Court Street, Plymouth; (508) 746–1620; www.pilgrimhall.org. Open daily, 9:30 A.M. to 4:30 P.M., closed in January and on Christmas Day. Admission: $6.00 for adults, $3.00 for children 6 to 16 (family rate of $16.00). Free parking.

In operation since 1824, the Pilgrim Hall Museum holds the largest existing collection of Pilgrim possessions, including a portion of the *Sparrow-Hawk,* one of the ships that brought the earliest European migrants to Plymouth. The only known contemporaneous painting of a *Mayflower* passenger, Edward Winslow, is here, too.

Plymouth National Wax Museum (all ages)
16 Carver Street, Plymouth; (508) 746–6468. Open daily from March through November, with extended summer hours; call for the schedule. Admission: $7.00 for adults, $2.75 for children 5 to 12; free for children under 5.

This museum will probably seem cheesy to grown-ups, but kids love the life-size wax figures of prominent Plymouth residents. More than 180 characters tell the Pilgrim story from 1601 to 1627.

Mayflower Society Museum and Library (all ages)
4 Winslow Street, Plymouth; (508) 746–3188 (library); www.mayflower.org. The museum is open Friday through Sunday from Memorial Day to the end of June and Labor Day through Columbus Day weekends only, then daily July 1 through Labor Day. Hours: 10:00 A.M. to 4:00 P.M. The library is open year-round Monday through Friday from 10:00 A.M. to 3:30 P.M. except weekends and holidays. Admission for the museum is $4.00 for adults, $1.00 for children under 12. The library fee is $2.50 for the day.

The museum, a beautiful white building with a sweeping double staircase, offers a mother lode of history. The original owner of the house (built in 1754) was Edward Winslow, who fled to Canada along with other Tories when the Revolutionary War began. The author and transcendentalist Ralph Waldo Emerson was married in the front parlor in 1835, and seven years later ether was discovered here. The *Mayflower* Society Library, just down the driveway from the museum, is a wonderful resource if you're interested in researching your family's history. The building is the headquarters of the General Society of *Mayflower* Descendants, who have extensive archives and libraries of information that are open to the public.

Watch for the Pilgrim Progress every Friday in August at 6:00 P.M., when a costumed group, representing the Pilgrims that survived the first winter, parade through many historic locales in Plymouth.

Richard Sparrow House (all ages)

42 Summer Street, Plymouth; (508) 747–1240; www.sparrowhouse.com. Open April through December 10:00 A.M. to 5:00 P.M. every day except Wednesday, when it is closed. Admission: $2.00 for adults, $1.00 for children 6 to 16.

Built in 1640, the Richard Sparrow House is now Plymouth's oldest surviving wooden frame house. The sparsely furnished house gives visitors a view of early Pilgrim life in an authentic setting.

The Jabez Howland House (all ages)

33 Sandwich Street, Plymouth; (508) 746–9590; www.mayflowersociety.org. Open Memorial Day through Columbus Day, then Thanksgiving weekend, 10:00 A.M. to 4:30 P.M. Admission: $4.00 for adults, $1.00 for children age 6 to 12, under 6 free.

The Jabez Howland House is the only surviving house in Plymouth that is known to have been inhabited by *Mayflower* passengers John and Elizabeth Howland.

Priscilla Beach Theatre (all ages)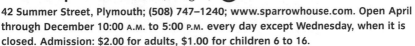

796 Rocky Hill Road, Manomet; (508) 224–4888; www.priscillabeachtheatre.com. Open June through mid-September.

The Priscilla Beach Theatre is the country's oldest summer-stock playhouse. Children's shows are presented from June through mid-September. The theater also runs a performing arts day camp (one- and two-week programs). Call ahead for show schedules and for more information about the day camp.

Other Things to See and Do

Jenney Grist Mill Museum and Shoppe, 6 Spring Lane, Plymouth; (508) 747–4544; www.jenneygristmill.com. Idyllic site. Tour the working mill, then relax on the deck with a snack while observing the wildlife on the pond.

1749 Spooner House, 27 North Street, Plymouth; (508) 746–0012. Open Thursday through Saturday 10:00 A.M. to 4:00 P.M. early June to early October. Mid-eighteenth-century home occupied by generations of the same family for more than 200 years.

1677 Harlow Old Fort House, 119 Sandwich Street, Plymouth; (508) 746–0012. Seventeenth-century period Pilgrim home open Tuesday through Friday 11:00 A.M. to 2:00 P.M. early July through the end of August. Colonial home skills and crafts are represented and interpreted.

Little Shoes, 359 Court Street, Plymouth; (508) 747–2226. Good selection of specially priced shoes below regular retail.

Middleboro Historical Museum, Jackson Street, Middleborough; (508) 947–1969. Mr. and Mrs. Tom Thumb of circus fame donated their collection of miniatures. Seven-building complex is open Wednesday through Saturday 1:00 P.M. to 4:00 P.M. by appointment.

Where to Eat

Crow's Nest, 170 Water Street, Plymouth; (508) 747–4000. Steaks, pasta, and seafood dishes; children's menu, outdoor patio and deck. $–$$

Lobster Hut, Town Wharf, Plymouth; (508) 746–2270. Lobster in the rough with great views of the Plymouth Bay breakwater. $–$$

Peaceful Meadow's Ice Cream, 170 Water Street (Village Landing Marketplace), Plymouth; (508) 746–2362. Homemade ice cream. $

Star of Siam, Route 3A, Manomet; (508) 224–3771. An excellent take-out Thai restaurant (with a few tables outside) in the Manomet area of Plymouth, just a few miles south of Long Beach. $–$$

Where to Stay

The John Carver Inn, 25 Summer Street, Plymouth; (508) 746–7100 or (800) 274–1620; www.johncarverinn.com. A large hotel/motel in the middle of town, with a themed Pilgrim pool and a restaurant. $$–$$$$

Mayflower B & B, 25 Mayflower Street, Plymouth; (888) 718–0093. Children of all ages are welcome, video library, picturesque setting close to town and adjacent to Jenney Pond in a restored New England farmhouse. $$–$$$

Pilgrim Sands, 150 Warren Avenue/ Route 3A, Plymouth; (508) 747–0900 or (800) 729–SANDS; www.pilgrimsands.com. On Long Beach, near the Plimoth Plantation. Call ahead to request an efficiency apartment. There are two pools—one indoors, one outdoors. $$–$$$

Carver/South Carver

Along Route 58 in Carver (and on many back roads in the area as well), your family may see some of the state's cranberry bogs. Half of the country's cranberry crop comes from the marshy, sandy bogs in this area, and cranberries are Massachusetts's number-one agricultural product. When it's harvest time (mid-September through early November), the farmers use machines to literally shake the berries from their vines. They corral the berries into large crimson islands, then use enormous vacuum hoses to scoop the harvest into trucks.

Edaville Railroad (under 10)

Route 58, 7 Eda Avenue, South Carver; (508) 866–8190 or (877) EDAVILLE; www.edaville .org. Call for schedule or look on the Edaville Railroad Web site. Price: Adults $16; ages 3 and up are $14 per person; children under 3 are free.

Ellis D. Atwood, whose initials E.D.A. gave birth to the name Edaville, built the railroad to run 5 miles into cranberry country to serve his cranberry business in the forties. A regional landmark from the fifties through the nineties, Edaville has been revived as a vacation destination for families (my own parents have pictures of my brother and me standing in a caboose at Edaville back in the sixties!). Don't miss the half-hour ride through the cranberry bog, lakes, and countryside. Today there is a family amusement park with trains, rides, a carousel, and a museum; the newest attraction is Cranberry World, located in the Cran Central Junction Building sponsored by Ocean Spray. Hungry? There are plenty of venues to fill up at; try the cafe, barbecue picnic area, or one of the many snack bars.

Myles Standish State Forest (all ages)

Cranberry Road, South Carver; (508) 866–2526; www.state.ma.us/dem/parks/mssf.htm. The camping fee of $12 per night includes showers.

Bike, hike, fish, or swim at Myles Standish State Forest, just a twenty-minute drive from Plymouth. The 14,635-acre park was Massachusetts's first state forest when it was created in 1916. There are miles of quiet walking trails, bike and horseback riding paths, fifteen ponds (two are designated for swimming; the rest are for fishing), and lots of picnic spots in the forests and meadows. There are 416 tent/RV sites (no hookups) with restrooms and hot showers, plus fireplaces and picnic tables at each site. For reservations call (877) I–CAMP–MA or (877) 422–6762.

Onset and Wareham

Onset, the "thermometer capital of the world," is a charming village that is part of Wareham. Onset Beach enjoys the warm waters that the Cape is known for and is a lovely spot to hear a musical concert at the bandstand on a warm summer's evening.

Porter Thermometer Museum (all ages)

49 Zarahemia Road, Onset; (508) 295–5504; www.members.aol.com/thermometerman. Open daily year-round; call for an appointment (the museum is in Porter's home). Free.

Dick Porter's motto for his museum (the world's only) is "Always open and always free with over 4,600 thermometers to see." This retired Lexington schoolteacher will amaze you with tidbits about his unusual collection, the largest in the world (he is in both the *Guinness Book of World Records and Ripley's Believe It or Not*). Porter has been featured on countless television shows and articles, and he is in great demand on the lecture circuit (he has given more than 700 lectures). Given his popularity, he is very interested in imparting his knowledge to every visitor and converting you into a "thermometermaniac." Some of the thermometers that he is most proud of are the pill-size thermometers swallowed by John Glenn on his NASA shuttle mission. This is a fun and educational experience. The Plymouth County Convention and Visitor's Bureau awarded the Thermometer Man its Hospitality Award for Tourism in 1998 as well as the Science Educator of Cape Cod for 1998.

Other Things to See and Do

Cape Cod Canal Cruises, Onset Pier, Wareham; (508) 295–3883; www.hy-linecruises.com. Narrated cruise on the canal May through October.

Onset Beach, Onset Avenue (Cranberry Highway/Routes 6 and 28 to Onset Avenue), Wareham.

Water Wizz, Route 28, 3031 Cranberry Highway, Wareham; (508) 295–3255; www.waterwizz.com. Open mid-June through Labor Day 10:00 A.M. to 6:30 P.M. Water park.

Greater New Bedford and Greater Fall River

The entire downtown area of New Bedford seems to be a monument to the city's world-famous whaling days. The New Bedford National Historical Park includes the Whaling Museum and the schooner *Ernestina*. Though it's inland, Fall River is a major seaport, and Battleship Cove is a magnet for those who enjoy touring warships and other vessels. To contact the **New Bedford Office of Travel and Tourism** at 52 Fisherman's Wharf, Pier 3, New Bedford 02740, call (508) 979–1745 or (800) 508–5353; www.ci.new-bedford.ma.us. To contact the **Fall River Office of Tourism** at 1 Government Center, Fall River 02720, call (508) 324–2028 or go to www.fallriverma.org.

New Bedford Whaling Museum (all ages)

18 Johnny Cake Hill, New Bedford; (508) 997–0046; www.whalingmuseum.org. Open daily year-round, 9:00 A.M. to 5:00 P.M., Thursday until 9:00 P.M. Memorial Day through Labor Day, closed Thanksgiving, Christmas, and New Year's Day. Admission: $10.00 for adults, $6.00 for children 6 to 14; free for children under 5.

Kids are justifiably awed by the tools of the trade: enormous hooks, harpoons, and a 90-foot-long whaling bark that they are welcome to climb on. The scrimshaw collection is remarkable for its quality and depth—among the 2,000 items are a sled and a birdcage carved from whalebone. Be sure to watch the twenty-two-minute vintage orientation film, *The City That Lit the World*. A new display is the 66-foot skeleton of a blue whale—one of three in the United States, one of six in the world. The latest exhibit, "Portrait of a Port," shows New Bedford at its height and narrates the history of whaling. The museum's Saturday at Sea program, where kids can make crafts and sing chanteys from the whaling era, is fun for the entire family; also of interest is the annual reading of the classic tale of *Moby-Dick* by Herman Melville, which takes place on January 3 (Melville was a crew member on a whaler that departed from New Bedford). Don't forget to ask for the family guide, which gives activities that tie into major exhibitions. Also, the museum tries to incorporate kid-friendly activities during school holiday and summer vacation periods.

Buttonwood Park Zoo (under 10)

425 Hawthorn Street, New Bedford; (508) 991–6178 or (508) 991–4556; www.bpzoo. org. Open daily 10:00 A.M. to 5:00 P.M. (closed Thanksgiving, Christmas, and New Year's Day). Admission: $5.00 for adults and $2.50 for children 3 to 11, under age 3 is free. A family plan admits two adults and any number of children for $15.00.

All the animals (cougar, black bear, bald eagle, bobcat, etc.) in the Buttonwood Zoo are indigenous to Massachusetts (the theme encapsulates the Berkshire Mountains to Buzzard's Bay) and represent the diversity of the wildlife in our state, with the exception of the Asian elephant exhibit. There is also a farm area that features

- **St. Patrick's Day Parade,** March, Scituate; (781) 545–8741

- **Taunton Riverfront Festival,** early June, Taunton; (508) 821–9347; www.weircorp.org

- **Fall River Hot Air Balloon, Craft, and Antique Car Festival,** June, Fall River; (508) 324–2028

- **Tweeter Center for the Performing Arts,** summerlong concerts, Mansfield; (508) 339–2333; www.tweetercenter.com

- **Plymouth Philharmonic Concerts and Orchestra,** October through May; (508) 746–8008 for schedule or check www.plymouthphil harmonic.com

- **Strawberry Thanksgiving,** late June, Plimoth Plantation, Plymouth; (508) 745–1622; www.plimoth.org

- **New Bedford Summerfest,** early July, New Bedford; (508) 999–5231 or (800) 508–5353; www.newbedfordsummerfest.com

- **New Bedford Whaling Blues Festival,** end of July, Fort Tabor Park, New Bedford; (508) 990–1425; www.whalingblues.com

- **Waterfront Festival,** mid-July, Plymouth; (508) 830–1620; www.seeplymouth.com

- **Whaling City Festival,** mid-July, Buttonwood Park, New Bedford; (508) 996–3348; www.whalingcityfestival.com

- **Brockton Fair,** July, Brockton Fairgrounds; (508) 586–8000; www.brocktonfair.com

- **Feast of the Blessed Sacrament,** end of July/August, New Bedford; (508) 992–6911; www.portuguesefeast.com

- **Onset Blues Festival,** August, Onset, Buzzards Bay; (508) 295–7072; www.onsetvillage.com

- **Fall River Celebrates America Festival,** August, Fall River; (508) 676–8226; www.fallrivercelebrates.com

- **Illumination Night,** mid-August, Onset Harbor; (508) 295–7072; www.onsetvillage.com

- **Marshfield Fair,** late August, Marshfield Fairgrounds; (781) 834–6629; www.marshfieldfair.org

- **King Richard's Faire,** late August–October, Carver; (508) 866–5391 or (952) 238–9915; www.kingrichardsfaire.net

- **Great Feast Holy Ghost,** end of August, Kennedy Park, New Bedford; (508) 324–2028; www.fallriverma.org

- **Cranberry Harvest Festival,** October, Edaville Railroad, South Carver; (877) 332–8455; www.edaville.org

- **Edaville Railroad Christmas Festival,** early November through January, South Carver; (508) 866–8190; www.edaville.org

- **Plimoth Plantation's Thanksgiving Celebration,** November, Plymouth; (508) 746–1622 or (800) USA–1620; www.seeplymouth.com

- **La Salette Festival of Lights,** Thanksgiving through early January, Attleboro; (508) 222–5410; lasalette.shrine.tripod.com

- **Fall River Christmas Open House,** Thanksgiving to December 31; (508) 324–2028; www.fallriverma.org

- **Holiday Festival of Light,** November through January, Edaville Railroad, South Carver; (877) EDAVILLE; www.edaville.org

- **Fall River First Night,** December 31; (508) 324–2028; www.fallriver ma.org

domestic rare-breed animals such as Randall Lineback cows and Suffolk Punch Draft horses. The Buttonwood Zoo is a nice, gentle introduction to animals for young children, and parents like it because the scale is very manageable. Set aside one to two hours to take in the zoo, and when you're through with your touring, get a snack in the Bear's Den Cafe.

Seaman's Bethel (all ages)
15 Johnny Cake Hill, New Bedford; (508) 992–3295. Donations accepted.

Chapel visited by Herman Melville and described in *Moby-Dick*. The chapel is a memorial to those who were lost at sea. The schoolroom on the bottom floor was used to teach the seamen reading, writing, and arithmetic, and to improve their navigational skills. The school was run by the New Bedford Port Society, which was largely composed of Quakers.

Demarest Lloyd State Park (all ages)

Barney's Joy Road, South Dartmouth; (508) 636–3298 (seasonal phone); www.state.ma
.us/dem/parks/dem/parks/deml.htm. From Memorial Day through Labor Day, parking is
$7.00 per car. Directions: Take Route 24 south to Route 195 east to the Faunce Corner
exit. Turn right onto Faunce Corner Road; cross Route 6 onto Chase Road and follow
the signs.

Not far from New Bedford is South Dartmouth and Demarest Lloyd State Park, a
beautiful beach with calm water, long sandbars, great hiking trails, restroom facilities,
and lots of picnic tables in a shady area. Considering how pleasant this beach is,
there are surprisingly few people midweek (during the weekends the gates close as
soon as the parking lot fills up—usually by 10:00 A.M.). *WARNING:* watch the kids at
low tide; the sand bars drop off suddenly.

Horseneck State Beach (all ages)

John Reed Road, (Westport Point), Route 88, Westport; (508) 636–8816; www.state.ma
.us/dem/parks/hbch.htm. From Memorial Day through Labor Day, parking is $2.00 per
car. Directions: Take Route 24 south to Route 195 east to Route 88.

Just to the west of Dartmouth is Westport, site of another gorgeous beach. Horseneck
State Beach is a 3-mile-long stretch of sand. There's a bathhouse, a snack bar, picnic
tables, a 100-site campground adjacent to the beach, hiking, and good swimming.

New Bedford Oceanarium Corporation (all ages)

1 Compass Place, 128 Union Street, New Bedford; (508) 994–5400; www.nbocean.org.

Slated to open March 2005. Planned to be one of the largest aquariums in the
world, the site will focus on the interrelationship and dependency between humans
and the sea. A former power plant by the harbor is being retrofitted to house the
new aquarium.

Battleship Cove (all ages)

Exit 7 off Route 24, 5 Water Street, Fall River; (508) 678–1905 or (508) 678–1100; www
.battleshipcove.org. Open daily year-round, 9:00 A.M. to 5:00 P.M.; closed Thanksgiving,
Christmas, and New Year's Day. Admission: $12.00 for adults, $7.00 for children 6 to
14; free for children under 6.

Today Battleship Cove holds six U.S. Navy warships from the World War II era, including a submarine. The USS *Massachusetts* is the biggest, by far, and probably the
most interesting to the kids, who will avail themselves of the opportunity to clamber
throughout the ship's nine decks (you don't have to take a tour in order to explore
the ship). The *Massachusetts* was moved here in 1965 to stand as a permanent
memorial to the more than 18,000 Massachusetts men and women who gave their
lives in service during World War II, Vietnam, Korea, Desert Storm, and September
11. Be sure to pick up a brochure when you arrive; it's easy to get lost. Try out the

hammocks that served as the sailors' bunks, climb the turrets, and admire the enormous main deck. Next, check out the Soviet-built missile Corvette built in 1984 and acquired by Battleship Cove in 1997. Other National Historic Landmark designees at Battleship Cove are the destroyer *Joseph P. Kennedy Jr.*, the submarine *Lionfish,* and PT boats 617 and 796. There is a growing aircraft collection such as the Cobra Attack Helicopter. A marvelous history lesson is an overnight encampment program offered to organized youth and school groups ($40 per person). The participants speak to former crew members, get to tour all the ships, have a knot-tying lesson, eat sailor's grub, and sleep in the sailor's bunks throughout the ships. Since Battleship Cove preserves the world's largest collection of historical naval ships, the experience is educational besides being fun!

Fall River Carousel (all ages)

Fall River; (508) 324–4300. Open year-round; seasonal hours. Rides are three for $1.00.

Also at Battleship Cove is the Fall River Carousel, a restored merry-go-round that was moved here from Dartmouth in the early 1990s. The horses are hand-carved and hand-painted. Bring a picnic lunch; there's a nice grassy area next to the carousel.

Fall River Historical Society (all ages)

451 Rock Street, Fall River; (508) 679–1071; www.lizzieborden.org. Open April through November Tuesday through Friday 9:00 A.M. to 4:00 P.M. (hourly tours 9:00 A.M. to 3:00 P.M.) and weekends June through September 1:00 P.M. to 5:00 P.M. (hourly tours 1:00 to 4:00 P.M.). Admission: $5.00 for adults, $3.00 for children.

Lizzie Borden took an axe, gave her mother forty whacks, when she saw what she had done, she gave her father forty-one—every girl remembers this jump rope song. At the Fall River Historical Society, there are more than 10,000 items related to the Lizzie Borden trial, the largest collection in the United States. The Lizzie Borden collection is just a small part of this museum, which offers a tour of the former mill owner's mansion, nautical exhibits, paintings and furnishings, as well as 2,000 items of clothing and costumes in a revolving exhibit.

Other Things to See and Do

Attleboro Industrial Museum, 42 Union Street, Attleboro; (508) 222–3918; www.industrialmuseum.com. Call for schedule. Free. Artifacts, photos, tools, and machinery related to the industrial history of Attleboro.

Brockton Rox, 1 Lexington Avenue, Brockton; (508) 559–7000; www.brockton rox.com. Professional independent minor league baseball team. The Rox play in Brockton's Campenelli Stadium.

Capron Park Zoo, 201 County Street, Attleboro; (508) 222–3047; www.capron parkzoo.com. Many Asian, African, and American species are represented. Nocturnal building for nighttime animals.

Cuttyhunk Boat Lines, Pier 3, Fisherman's Wharf, New Bedford; (508) 992–1432; www.cuttyhunk.com. Visit Cuttyhunk (part of the Elizabeth Islands 14 miles off the coast of New Bedford) aboard the M/V *Alert II.*

Easton's Children's Museum, The Old Fire Station, 9 Sullivan Avenue, North Easton; (508) 230–3789; www.childrens museumineaston.org. Open Tuesday through Sunday noon to 5:00 P.M. $5.00 per person admission (under 1 is free). Hands-on kids' activities.

Fuller Art Museum, 455 Oak Street, Brockton; (508) 588–6000; www.fuller museum.org. Open daily 10:00 A.M. to 5:00 P.M. Price: Adults are $5.00, and ages 12 and under are free. Art and gardens on more than thirteen acres. Teahouse and cafe open from noon to 2:00 P.M.

Golf Museum, 300 Arnold Palmer Boulevard, Norton; (774) 430–9100. Open Monday through Friday 10:00 A.M. to 5:00 P.M. Free. Opened in 2002, it traces the history of golf in Massachusetts.

Hetty Green Museum, 52 Union Street, New Bedford; (888) 554–3889; www.hetty green.com. This museum is dedicated to the richest (and most frugal) woman in the world at the turn of the century, Henrietta Green.

Marine Museum at Fall River, 70 Water Street, Fall River; (508) 674–3533; www.marinemuseum.org. *Titanic, Andrea Doria,* and *Fall River* line exhibits and artifacts.

New Bedford Art Museum, 608 Pleasant Street, New Bedford; (508) 961–3072; www.newbedfordartmuseum.org. Vintage bank turned museum. Local, national, and international artists are on display. Contemporary and historic art.

New Bedford Fire Museum, 51 Bedford Street, New Bedford; (508) 992–2162. Open July through Labor Day 9:00 A.M. to 4:00 P.M. Monday through Saturday. Restored fire trucks and related exhibits.

Old Colony and Fall River Railroad Museum, Battleship Cove, Central and Water Streets, Fall River; (508) 674–9340. Open Saturday noon to 4:00 P.M. and Sunday 10:00 A.M. to 4:00 P.M. New England railroad memorabilia and historical displays.

Rotch-Jones-Duff House and Garden Museum, 396 County Street, New Bedford; (508) 997–1401; www.rjdmuseum .org. Mansion of whaling magnate William Rotch Jr.

Schooner *Ernestina*, New Bedford State Pier, New Bedford; (508) 992–4900; www .ernestina.org. The schooner was a Grand Banks fisher, Arctic expedition vessel, and a survey and trade ship.

Seekonk Speedway, 1710 Fall River Avenue, Seekonk; (508) 336–9959; www .seekonkspeedway.com. Open April through October every Saturday at 6:00 P.M. Nascar track.

Spindle City Ballet, 288 Plymouth Avenue, Fall River; (508) 677–2130; www.spindlecityballet.org. Highlighting locally trained classical dancers.

Zeiterion Theater, 684 Purchase Street, New Bedford; (508) 994–2900; www.zeiterion.org. The Zeiterion, an old vaudevillian theater, has a full schedule of concerts, theater, movies, choirs, and ballets.

Where to Eat

Abbey Grill (at the International Institute for Culinary Arts), 100 Rock Street, Fall River; (508) 675–9305 or (888) 383–2665; www.iicaculinary.com. Open for lunch Monday through Friday 11:00 A.M. to 2:30 P.M.; Tuesday through Saturday evening 5:00 to 10:00 P.M. for dinner. Running the gamut from pizza to rack of lamb to grilled swordfish Mediterranean. $–$$$

Audrey's Restaurant, Johnson and Wales Inn, 213 Taunton Avenue, Seekonk; (508) 336–4636; www.jwinn.com. Johnson and Wales University students ply their craft in an award-winning setting. $$

Bittersweet Farm Restaurant and Tavern, 438 Main Road, Westport; (508) 636–0085; www.lafrancehospitality.com. Country setting for fine dining halfway between Fall River and New Bedford. $–$$$

Davy's Locker, 1480 East Rodney French Boulevard, New Bedford; (508) 992–7359. Great seafood, good quality, reasonable prices. $–$$

Sagres, 181 Columbia Street, Fall River; (508) 675–7018. Highly regarded family restaurant specializing in Portuguese dishes. $–$$

Water Street Cafe, 36 Water Street, Battleship Cove, Fall River ; (508) 672–8748; www.waterstreetcafe.com. Views of the water, near Battleship Cove. $–$$

Where to Stay

Hampton Inn Hotel, Hampton Way, Fairhaven; (508) 990–8500; www.hamptoninn.com. Pool and Jacuzzi. $$$

Johnson and Wales Inn, 213 Taunton Avenue, Seekonk; (508) 336–8700; www.jwinn.com. Run by students from Johnson and Wales University; the staff is eager to please. $$–$$$

Lizzie Borden Bed & Breakfast, 92 Second Street, Fall River; (508) 675–7333; www.lizzie-borden.com. Five-room inn and museum (former home of the infamous Borden family). One-and-a-half-hour guided tour (the general public gets only a half-hour tour, so it's a bonus to stay overnight here!), videos, and snacks. $$–$$$$

Melville House Bed and Breakfast, 100 Madison Street, New Bedford; (508) 990–1566; www.melvillehouse.net. Built in 1855, the house was home to Herman Melville's sister, so Herman would come to stay quite often. This charming colonial, on a quiet street close to sights, features two rooms. Gourmet, all-natural continental breakfast. $$

Paquachuck Inn, 2056 Main Road, Westport Point; (508) 636–4398; www.Paquachuck.com. On the National Register of Historic Places; small boat dock available to guests. Seven bedrooms overlook the water. Welcoming well-behaved children and their parents. $–$$

Cape Cod, Martha's Vineyard, and Nantucket

Cape Cod

Shaped like a bent arm and stretching 60 miles into the Atlantic, the peninsula of Cape Cod offers nearly 300 miles of beaches, along with acres of nature preserves, dozens of pretty villages, and an abundance of top-notch inns and restaurants that welcome families. Route 6A was designated a national scenic byway and runs almost 35 miles from Bourne to Orleans. Known as the King's Highway, it has evolved from a Native American pathway to a colonial road to the scenic byway that is one of the main routes for vehicle traffic today. For **free** information on the Cape, contact the **Cape Cod Chamber of Commerce** at (508) 862–0700 or (888) 33–CAPECOD; www .capecodchamber.org. For information on the weather go to www.gocapecod.org

Marcia's TopPicks on Cape Cod, Martha's Vineyard, and Nantucket

1. Cape Cod National Seashore

2. Nauset Beach, East Orleans

3. Cliffs at Gay Head, Martha's Vineyard

4. Children's Beach, Nantucket

5. National Marine Fisheries Science Aquarium, Woods Hole

6. Flying Horses Carousel, Martha's Vineyard

7. Whale-watching trips from Provincetown

8. Chatham fish pier

9. Pilgrim Tower, Provincetown

CAPE COD, MARTHA'S VINEYARD, AND NANTUCKET

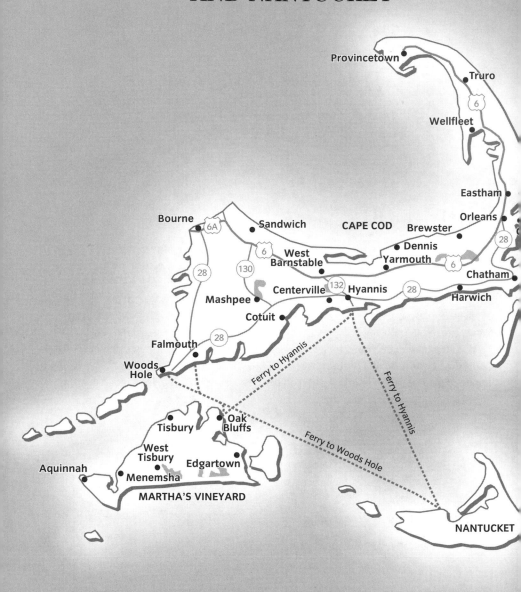

and click on the **Cape Cod Weather Forecast.** At the fist of the Cape's arm, pulsating Provincetown surrounds the Pilgrim Monument, a replica of the Campanile in Siena. The spectacular view of the curving Cape and the surrounding ocean and bay is worth the climb up the tower's 116 steps. Regardless of the season, visit one or more of the first-class beaches along the Cape's eastern edge. A fun way to keep kids interested during the short drives from town to town is to make the trip into a lighthouse tour. There are seven working lighthouses on the Cape, from Province-town all the way to Woods Hole. **Bed & Breakfast Cape Cod** is a great reservation service connecting you to outstanding properties on the Cape and the Islands (800–541–6226; www.bedandbreakfastcapecod.com).

Bourne and Sandwich

When you drive over the Sagamore Bridge, you end up on Route 6 in Sandwich. Few visitors stop here; most zip on by on their way to the beaches and cottages of the outer Cape. Considering how much there is to see and do here, try not to overlook this area. For further information on this area, contact the **Canal Region Chamber of Commerce,** 70 Main Street, Buzzards Bay 02532; (508) 759–6000; www.capecod canalchamber.org. You can travel to Sandwich by train from Hyannis, tour the village's family-oriented attractions, and travel back, all in an afternoon.

Adventure Isle (all ages)

343 MacArthur Boulevard, Bourne; (508) 759–2636 or (800) 535–2787; www.adventure isle.com. Open 10:00 A.M. to 11:00 P.M. daily in the summer and on an abbreviated schedule in the late spring and fall. The laser tag is open all winter. Summer price: $12.95 per person for an all-day pass that includes all activities, the arcade, the driving range, and the jousting room. Discount coupons on the Web site.

Kid paradise to the max. How awesome is this? Laser tag, go-karts, bumper boats, giant slide, kiddie land, American Gladiator jousting room, roller skating, arcade, bumper cars, and miniature golf. Fun for all ages!

National Marine Life Center (all ages)

120 Main Street (edge of Cape Cod Canal), Buzzards Bay; (508) 743–9888. Interim facility; fund-raising in progress for permanent facility.

The highest concentration of strandings in the United States for whales, seals, dolphins, and sea lions is on Cape Cod Bay, Nantucket Sound, and the coast of Maine. When opened, the National Marine Life Center will be a clearinghouse to address the needs of these marine animals through hospitalization and rehabilitation for future release. A Marine and Science Center will be created as well, and open to the general public.

Cape Cod Canal Bike Trail (all ages)

Access points along the Cape side of the canal: in Sandwich, at the Sandwich Marina; in Sagamore, from Pleasant Street; from the Bourne Bridge at Scusset Beach State Reservation; and at the Buzzards Bay Recreation area next to the Bourne Bridge; (508) 759–4431; www.recreation.gov. Free.

The well-maintained Cape Cod Canal Bike Trail (maintained by the Army Corps of Engineers) is a service road that borders the canal on both banks. The 6.8-mile-long trail along the Cape side is less hilly and further removed from auto traffic than the 7.2-mile-long mainland-side trail. Families should avoid crossing either bridge with children, either on foot or on bicycle. If you must cross the canal on your bikes, use the Sagamore Bridge (its sidewalk is safer), and don't ride—walk. Because the bridges' auto lanes are so narrow, drivers aren't looking out for pedestrians or bikers—they're avoiding cars in adjacent lanes. Kids get a charge out of following the ships up close from the bike path as they go through the canal on their way to the open sea.

Scusset Beach State Reservation (all ages)

Scusset Beach Road, Bourne and Sandwich. Located north of the Cape Cod Canal; (508) 888–0859; www.state.ma.us/dem/parks/scus.htm. Open year-round 8:00 A.M. to 8:00 P.M. Parking is $7.00 per car.

On Cape Cod Bay at the east end of the Cape Cod Canal, Scusset Beach is a 380-acre park/beach area, which remains reasonably populated in the summer months. Facilities include restrooms, access to the Cape Cod Canal Bike Trail, a snack bar, picnic tables, and 98 campsites. To reserve a campsite contact Reserve America at (877) 422–6762; www.reserveamerica.com.

Green Briar Nature Center and Jam Kitchen (all ages)

6 Discovery Hill Road, East Sandwich; (508) 888–6870; www.thorntonburgess.org. Open year-round, mid-April through December Monday through Saturday 10:00 A.M. to 4:00 P.M. and Sunday 1:00 to 4:00 P.M., January through mid-April Tuesday through Saturday 10:00 A.M. to 4:00 P.M. and Sunday 1:00 to 4:00 P.M. Admission is by donation.

Two miles from the Burgess Museum (see entry below) is the Green Briar Nature Center and Jam Kitchen, founded in 1903. The nature center building is adjacent to the Briar Patch and a small wildflower garden, and houses natural history exhibits and a collection of small live animals. The fifty-seven acres of forests are laced with easy walking trails. The Thornton W. Burgess Society runs a full program of nature walks and natural history classes, mostly geared to children and families, throughout the year. After you explore the nature center, stop in at the Jam Kitchen, an old-fashioned kitchen in a pondside building that looks like it's right out of one of Burgess's stories. The Jam Kitchen sells natural jams, jellies, and pickled goods. Ask about classes on the fine art of making jam. The Cape Cod Cranberry Day in September is quite popular.

Heritage Museums & Gardens (formerly Heritage Plantation)

(all ages)

Grove and Pine Streets, Sandwich; (508) 888–3300; www.heritagemuseumsandgardens
.org. Open November through April 10:00 A.M. to 4:00 P.M. Wednesday through Saturday, noon to 4:00 P.M. Sunday (closed Monday except holidays), and from May through
October, 9:00 A.M. to 6:00 P.M. Monday through Saturday, and Sunday noon to 6:00 P.M.
Dan'l Webster Cafe open 11:30 A.M. to 4:00 P.M. in season with dining al fresco under a
green and white striped tent (call for off-season hours). Admission: $12.00 for adults,
$6.00 for children 6 to 16, free for children under 5.

Heritage Museums & Gardens holds an interesting collection of antique cars in mint
condition exhibited in a replica of a round Shaker stone barn (if you want to see the
real thing, visit the Hancock Shaker Village near Pittsfield; see the Berkshires chapter).
The Cape Cod Baseball League Hall of Fame is housed in the American history
museum. Catch a ride on the restored antique carousel at the art museum. Gardening
enthusiasts and kids with lots of energy love to roam the one hundred acres of meticu-
lously tended paths that wind through fantastic flower gardens and blooming shrubs.
There are many activities geared for kids during the summer at the Museum. One of
my favorites is the Kids' Garden Club, where the children learn to grow annuals, vegetables, and herbs at weekly meetings, and it's open to all ages. In the Sizzling Summer Step Out program, there are creative craft activities tied to themes in the different
exhibits. Fridays in July and the first Friday in August is Fridays Live at the Heritage
Museum. There are live performances for kids and families which run the gamut from
storytellers to giant puppets from 10:30 to 11:30 A.M. As a parent, I really appreciate
the many interactive displays for hands-on fun throughout the museum. Extensive holiday program during the month of December celebrates Chanukah, Kwanzaa, and
Christmas.

Hoxie House and the Dexter Grist Mill (all ages)

18 Water Street, Sandwich; (508) 888–1173. Open June to September, Tuesday through
Saturday 10:00 A.M. to 5:00 P.M. Admission: $2.50 for adults, $1.50 for children 5 to 18;
free for children under 5. A combination ticket for Hoxie House and the Dexter Grist
Mill is $4.00 for adults, $2.00 for children 5 to 18; free for children under 5.

This Cape Cod saltbox, restored to its original 1675 interior, contains furnishings on
loan from the Boston Museum of Fine Arts. The Dexter Grist Mill was built in 1640
and is still in operation. Demonstrations of corn being ground into flour are fascinating to children. Scenic Shawme Pond on the property attracts swans, ducks, and
Canada geese (bring bread to feed them). For the past one hundred years, the town
of Sandwich has celebrated the Illumination Boat Parade at Shawme Pond on the
Fourth of July. The evening begins with an old-fashioned band concert. Participants
affix Japanese lanterns to their boats to outline elaborate displays—pirates, dragons,
or whatever they can conjure up.

Sandwich Glass Museum (all ages)

129 Main Street, Town Hall Square, Sandwich; (508) 888–0251; www.sandwichglass museum.org. Open daily April through December 9:30 A.M. to 5:00 P.M.; February through March, Wednesday through Sunday, 9:30 A.M. to 4:00 P.M.; closed Thanksgiving, Christmas Day, and January. Admission: $4.50 for adults, $1.00 for children 6 to 16, free for children under 6.

On a bright day the Sandwich Glass Museum is a colorful sight to behold. Since much of the museum's collection is displayed in front of windows, sunlight is very much a part of the installation. Sandwich is internationally known for its glassware, made mostly during the nineteenth century. An excellent video and a diorama explain the glass-making process. New is a furnace for daily glassblowing demonstrations, which kids can participate in. Kid activities include a treasure hunt throughout the museum (ask for the family guide—when the hunt is done, turn the guide in for a prize) and a theatrical presentation of the people of Sandwich from the past.

Thornton W. Burgess Museum (under 10)

4 Water Street, Sandwich; (508) 888–6870; www.thorntonburgess.com. Open from April through October (and the first two weekends in December for Christmas) Monday through Saturday 10:00 A.M. to 4:00 P.M., Sunday 1:00 to 4:00 P.M. Admission by donation.

The cottage by a duck pond is the Thornton W. Burgess Museum, which houses books and memorabilia of the renowned author (he wrote the *Mother West Wind* stories about Reddy Fox, Peter Cottontail, and Paddy the Beaver). Thornton Burgess stories are enduring classics that focus on our delicate ecology and the love of nature and its creatures. Thornton's aunt Arabella Burgess lived in this house and he was a frequent visitor (Thornton never had a permanent home; he boarded in ten different houses across town with his widowed mother). The 10:30 A.M. story hour ($1.00 per person) takes place Monday, Thursday, and Saturday in July and August and on some holidays and school vacations. The annual Peter Rabbit's Fair is held the second Wednesday in August.

Other Things to See and Do

Aptucxet Post, 24 Aptucxet Road, Bourne; (508) 759–9487; www.bourne historicalsoc.org/aptucxet.htm. Open Tuesday through Saturday 10:00 A.M. to 4:00 P.M. and Sunday 2:00 to 5:00 P.M. Pilgrims and Wampanoags traded here. Re-creation of a trading post with a collection of artifacts.

Pairpoint Glass Works, 851 Sandwich Road, Sagamore; (508) 888–2344 or (800) 899–0953; www.pairpoint.com. Watch glassware being made using methods that have been passed down for generations.

Sandwich Fish Hatchery, Route 6A, Sandwich; (508) 888–0008; www.state.ma .us/czm/wpfacil.htm. Free. Trout farm. Kids will love feeding the fish.

Where to Eat

Bayberry's, 271 Cotuit Road, Sandwich; (508) 477–4094. Log cabin setting with great food and large portions. Kids' menu and activity book. $–$$

The Marshland, 109 Route 6A, Sandwich; (508) 888–9824. Open Tuesday through Saturday 6:00 A.M. to 9:00 P.M. for dinner, Sunday for breakfast from 7:00 A.M. to 1:00 P.M., Monday 6:00 A.M. to 2:00 P.M.

for breakfast and lunch. Picturesque views of the marshes, great food. $–$$

Where to Stay

Daniel Webster Inn, 149 Main Street, Sandwich; (508) 888–3622 or (800) 444–3566; www.danlwebsterinn.com. A traditional inn with four-poster beds and fireplaces in some of the rooms. Pool; restaurant. $$–$$$$

Falmouth, Mashpee, and Woods Hole

West of the town of Barnstable is Falmouth, a pleasant New England village that pulses with visitors throughout the summer. Its Nantucket Sound coast is lined with guest houses, hotels, and summer homes. The downtown area has some good shopping and a few ice-cream parlors, but the main attraction of Falmouth is its coastline: The beaches are terrific, and the many inlets provide lots of space for private boat mooring. Of the four beaches that are open to nonresidents, the best are South Cape Beach, Surf Drive Beach, and Old Silver Beach. Woods Hole is home to the Woods Hole Oceanographic Institute, the National Marine Fisheries Science Aquarium, and the Steamship Authority. The village of Woods Hole is part of Falmouth; it's a fun place for kids to watch the boats going in and out of Eel Pond, which serves as a harbor and town center, of sorts. Walk around the pond to see the village's sites: the aquarium, St. Mary's Bell Tower and Garden, the harbor, and the drawbridge. Many families see little more of Woods Hole, however, than the Steamship Authority parking lots and waiting area. For more information on Falmouth, contact the **Falmouth Chamber of Commerce,** 20 Academy Lane, Falmouth 02540; (508) 548–8500 or (800) 526–8532; www.falmouth-capecod.com. For information on Mashpee contact the **Mashpee Chamber of Commerce,** Falmouth Road, Mashpee 02649; (508) 477–0792 or (800) 423–6274; www.mashpeechamber.com.

Sneak This One In . . .

If you're in the Falmouth–Woods Hole area in mid-August, cheer on the runners in the **Falmouth Road Race,** an annual 7-mile race that attracts participants from all over New England. For more information, call (508) 540–7000; www.falmouthroadrace.com.

Ashumet Holly Wildlife Sanctuary (all ages)

286 Ashumet Road, East Falmouth; (508) 362–1426; www.massaudubon.org/nature-connection/sanctuaries/ashumet_holly. Trails open dusk to dawn. Admission: $3.00 for adults, $2.00 for children 3 to 12, free for children under 3.

Enjoy nature trails that wind among holly trees (more than sixty-five varieties) on more than forty-nine acres. The sanctuary sponsors ecology cruises to Cuttyhunk and other Elizabeth Islands; call for the schedule.

Barnstable County Fair (all ages)

Barnstable County Fairgrounds, Route 151, East Falmouth; (508) 563–3200; www .barnstablecountyfair.org/tickets.htm. Admission: Adults are $8.00, children 12 and under are free.

In late July bring the kids to Barnstable for a real old-time county fair (since 1866). All profits are used to improve the fairgrounds, and scholarships for agricultural and food-related careers. You'll enjoy livestock shows, oxen pulls, baking contests, a midway, and lots of great food.

Cape Cod Children's Museum (under 10)

577 Great Neck Road South, Mashpee; (508) 539–8788; www.capecodchildrens museum.pair.com. Open Monday through Saturday 10:00 A.M. to 5:00 P.M., Sunday noon to 5:00 P.M. Memorial Day to Labor Day. From Labor Day to Memorial Day open Monday through Wednesday 10:00 A.M. to 3:00 P.M., Thursday through Saturday 10:00 A.M. to 5:00 P.M., and Sunday noon to 5:00 P.M. Admission: $5.00 for ages 5 to 59 and $4.00 for children under 5.

The Cape Cod Children's Museum is a good place to spend a rainy day. It has a tree house, a puppet theater, a shadow room, and a 30-foot pirate ship (especially popular with toddlers). Visit the toddler castle in the toddler play area, the star lab planetarium (with planetarium shows on selected days in the summer), and the science workshops. The newest exhibit features native Cape Cod artifacts such as a wetu (summer hut used by Native Americans), animal hives, and prints. The arts-and-crafts workshops, field trips, and monthly museum activities are fun for everyone. Children under 13 must be accompanied by an adult.

Island Queen (all ages)

Falmouth Heights Road (off Route 28), Falmouth; (508) 548–4800; www.islandqueen .com. Operates late May to mid-October to Oak Bluffs. Price: $12.00 for adults, $6.00 for children 3 to 12, free for children under 3. Bicycles cost $6.00 to transport. Passenger ferry only; there is no car transportation.

If your family is in the mood for a pleasant boat ride, an alternative to the Steamship Authority ferries to and from Martha's Vineyard is the *Island Queen,* which departs from its own dock in Falmouth's Inner Harbor. Park the car at the *Island Queen* parking lot on Falmouth Heights Road, and take the thirty-five-minute ferry over to the Vineyard for the day; it's less expensive and the boat is smaller and more comfortable than the Steamship Authority boats. No reservation is needed, but do try to get there a half hour before departure to get the departure that you want.

National Marine Fisheries Science Aquarium (all ages)

166 Water Street at Albatross Street, Woods Hole; (508) 495–2001; www.nefsc.nmfs .gov/omi/aquarium. Open year-round, Monday through Friday 11:00 A.M. to 4:00 P.M.; closed federal holidays. Free.

The National Marine Fisheries Science Aquarium preserves living sea creatures that are native to the Cape's waters. The touch tanks are low to the ground so that even toddlers can reach in and feel the crabs, lobsters, turtles, and other sea creatures. The whole place is child-oriented, and the helpful staff love to answer kids' questions. A real treat is to watch the seal feedings at 11:00 A.M. and 4:00 P.M. at the seal tank in front of the building.

Nobska Light (all ages)

Nobska Road, Woods Hole; www.lighthouse.cc/nobska. Open year-round.

Nobska Light sits on a bluff above winding Nobska Road between Woods Hole and Falmouth, overlooking Martha's Vineyard, Vineyard Sound, and the Elizabeth Islands. The lighthouse building that stands on this site today was built in 1876. Flashing every six seconds, Nobska's fixed-beacon light provides precise information to mariners: Seen head-on, the beam is white, indicating the safest route into Woods Hole Harbor; seen from either side, the red beam warns mariners against routes that could force them to go aground against the shoals. The light guides thousands of ships each year through the treacherous waters that lead to Woods Hole. For coast guard tours of the lighthouse check www.navmark.com/capecod/woodshol/nobska.

Fair **Play**

The Barnstable County Fair is the largest annual event on the Cape. Weeklong attendance exceeds 120,000 visitors every year.

Family Fun Night

Free summer musical concerts in July and August on Thursday nights at the Main Street Kiosk in Falmouth.

Shining Sea Bike Path (ages 8 and over)

Depot Avenue in Falmouth to Locust Street, Woods Hole Harbor; www.state.ma.us/mhd/paths/websea.htm. Open year-round. Free.

The Shining Sea Bike Path is a 3½-mile trail between Falmouth and Woods Hole that's named for the last line of Falmouth native Katherine Lee Bates's beloved song, "America the Beautiful." The path can be crowded in the summer, and it's hilly in a few spots. Pick it up on Palmer Avenue in Falmouth. From here it winds through forests, goes past Nobska Lighthouse, and ends at Woods Hole Harbor.

South Cape Beach (all ages)

Great Oak Road, Mashpee; (508) 539–3288 or (508) 457–0495; www.state.ma.us/dem/parks/socp.htm or www.mass.gov/dem/parks/socp.htm. Parking is $7.00.

Located between Waquoit Bay and Vineyard Sound, South Cape Beach is part of South Cape Beach State Park, which has several nice nature trails. The beach is the attraction here, though: It's a 2-mile-long barrier beach with a bathhouse, a snack shop, and a big parking lot that rarely fills. The park is jointly managed by the State of Massachusetts Department of Environmental Management and NOAA, which oversees the Waquoit Bay National Estuaries Research Reserve (of which South Cape Beach is a subset).

Powwow

The **Wampanoag Powwow** is held at the Tribal Grounds (483 Great Neck Road South) the first weekend in July in the Upper Cape. This three-day event features native crafts and foods. Native drumming, dancing, and singing demonstrations and contests are key to this colorful festival. A highlight is the clambake dinner held on the last day. Admission is $8.00 for adults, $5.00 for seniors and children 12 and under. For more information, call the Mashpee/Wampanoag Indian Tribal Council Office (508–477–0208).

Whisked **Away**

The **Whoosh Trolley** (800–352–7155; www.capecodtransit.org) operates between Falmouth and Woods Hole with stops in between from late June to September 1 ($1.00 for adults, 50 cents for children 6 to 17, under 6 **free**).

Steamship Authority (all ages)

Woods Hole; (508) 477–8600, (508) 693–9130, or (508) 548–5011; www.islandferry.com or www.steamshipauthority.com. Directions: Follow the signs to the Woods Hole Steamship Authority off Route 28. Parking is $10 a day in season. Passengers and vehicles are accepted. Call for passenger, bikes, and vehicle rates.

If you want to visit Martha's Vineyard without a car, park in one of the Steamship Authority's parking lots and take the **free** shuttle bus to the harbor. You don't need a reservation if you're traveling without a car; simply purchase tickets for each person. The trip takes approximately forty-five minutes for Martha's Vineyard, and there are numerous ferry departures for both Oak Bluffs and Vineyard Haven. The vehicle reservations for the Steamship Authority ferries go fast; the reservation lines open in mid-March, so plan early.

Surf Drive Beach (all ages)

Off Main and Shore Streets, Falmouth; (508) 548–8623. Parking is $10.

On Vineyard Sound, Surf Drive Beach is popular with sailboarders and sea kayakers, some of whom have beachside "garages" for their boats and gear. It's west of the main part of Falmouth, which keeps much of the summer crowd away.

Other Things to See and Do

Edward's Boatyard and Waquoit Kayak Co., 1209 East Falmouth (Route 28), East Falmouth; (508) 548–2216 or (508) 548–9722; www.edwardsboatyard .com. Open in season 8:00 A.M. to 4:30 P.M. Canoe or kayak on the Child's River or Waquoit Bay. Guided tours are offered as well as lessons.

Old Indian Meetinghouse, Meetinghouse Way near the Route 28 Intersection, Mashpee; (508) 477–0208. Built in 1684 for the Mashpee/Wampanoag tribe, the Old Indian Meetinghouse is the oldest surviving meetinghouse on the Cape.

Spohr's Garden, on Fells Road, off Oyster Pond Road, Falmouth. A three-acre garden that's a lovely spot. Donations accepted.

Woods Hole Film Festival, late July through early August; (508) 495–FILM; www.woodsholefilmfestival.com. Look for animation and comedies. None of the films are rated, so use caution in your choices.

Woods Hole Theater Company, 68 Water Street, Woods Hole; (508) 540–6525; www.woodsholetheatercompany .org. Comedic and dramatic productions.

Where to Eat

Box Lunch Gourmet Deli, 781 Main Street, Falmouth; (508) 457–7657; www.boxlunch.com. Great takeout. Try their kidwiches. $

Coonamessett Inn, 311 Gifford Street, Falmouth; (508) 548–2300. Fine dining in a country inn overlooking a pond. Appealing kids' menu. $$–$$$$

Landfall Restaurant, Luscombe Avenue, Woods Hole, (508) 548–1758. Waterfront location next to the island ferry. The restaurant used recycled material from old buildings and shipwrecks. Specializing in seafood. Large selection of desserts for those with a sweet tooth. $–$$$$

Pie in the Sky, 10 Water Street, Woods Hole; (508) 540–5475. Open daily year-round for breakfast, lunch, and dinner. Great muffins, juice, coffee, and sandwiches. $

Where to Stay

Coonamessett Inn, 311 Gifford Street, Falmouth; (508) 548–2300. Fine country inn in picturesque setting; children welcome. $$–$$$$

Sea Crest Resort, 350 Quaker Road, Falmouth; (508) 540–9400 or (800) 225–3100; www.seacrest-resort.com. Two-hundred-room resort on the beach. $–$$$$

Woods Hole Passage, 186 Woods Hole Road, Woods Hole; (508) 548–9575 or (800) 790–8976; www.woodsholepassage .com. Open May through October. Quiet bed-and-breakfast in the northern part of Woods Hole. Rooms are spacious and comfortable, and the full breakfasts are delicious. Children welcome with notification. $$–$$$

West Barnstable, Centerville, Cotuit, and Hyannis

Barnstable is the Cape's largest town: Its 60 square miles include the villages of Barnstable and West Barnstable along Cape Cod Bay, and Cotuit, Marstons Mills, Osterville, Centerville, and Hyannis along Nantucket Sound. These villages differ greatly. Hyannis is the commercial center of the Cape, as well as its most crowded town. If you're coming to the Cape to get away from crowds, malls, and traffic, you should avoid Hyannis. If you like the bustle of a busy harbor town, however, you'll enjoy Hyannis—but be sure to get out into the quieter villages that border it on the north and west. By the way, while you're in Hyannis, don't bother looking for Kennedys: When they're at their private compound on the town's western edge, they're on vacation, too, and they keep well out of sight. The **Hyannis Chamber of Commerce** can be reached at 1471 Route 132, Hyannis 02601; (508) 362–5230 or (877) HYANNIS; www.hyannis.com.

Cape Cod Central Railroad (all ages)

The train leaves from the station at 252 Main Street in downtown Hyannis; (508) 771–3800 or (888) 797–RAIL; www.capetrain.com. Open April through December, call for a schedule and prices.

The ride on the Cape Cod Central Railroad, an air-conditioned train from Hyannis to Sandwich, is fun for kids. Views of the Cape's forests and cranberry bogs line the route, and the small village of Sandwich is a nice place to stroll for a couple of hours before you catch the train back to Hyannis. The scenic train is only in the summer; the rest of the time it is the dinner train or the family supper train. *TIP:* A pretty time to take the ride is at sunset.

Cape Cod Potato Chip Factory (all ages)

Independence Drive, off Route 132 to 100 Breeds Hill Road, Hyannis; (508) 775–3358 or (508) 775–2808; www.capecodchips.com. Open weekdays year-round, 9:00 A.M. to 5:00 P.M. Free.

One of the highlights of a trip through busy Hyannis is a self-guided tour of the Cape Cod Potato Chip Factory, followed by lots of **free** samples. As you approach, you can smell the chips. Cape Cod Potato Chip Factory produces potato chips, popcorn, pretzels, and tortilla chips.

Craigville Beach (all ages)

Craigville Road, Barnstable; (508) 790–9888; www.town.barnstable.ma.us/ departments_01/recreation/beaches.htm. Parking is $10 weekdays, $12 weekends.

On Nantucket Sound, Craigville Beach is a busy place that's popular with teenagers as well as families with young children. The water is warmer here than on the north or east coasts of the Cape. Craigville Beach has lots of parking, changing rooms and showers, restrooms, and a snack bar (and plenty of clam shack–type eateries within a few minutes' walk of the beach).

Kalmus Park Beach (all ages)

End of Ocean Street, Hyannis; (508) 790–9884; www.townbarnstable.ma.us/ departments_01/recreation/beaches.htm. Parking is $10 weekdays, $12 weekends.

Wide, scenic Kalmus Park Beach is a good spot for families. There are gentle waves, fine sand, fishing areas, lots of seashells to collect, and a sheltered area for toddlers, as well as restrooms and a snack bar. Kalmus juts out into Lewis Bay and Nantucket Sound (one of the largest windsurfing areas on the Cape and in the country).

Hyannis **Ferries**

Fast ferries from Hyannis to Nantucket take approximately one hour and can zip along at a faster rate because they are smaller vessels, carry fewer people (in a more luxurious setting), and don't accept vehicles. The traditional Martha's Vineyard and Nantucket ferries take approximately two hours, with only the Steamship Authority accepting vehicles. All of the ferries offer restrooms, a snack bar, free shuttle service from their parking lots in Hyannis, and onboard carriage of bikes for a fee. Arrive forty-five minutes before departure. Call for prices and hours.

- **Hy-line Cruises,** Ocean Street and Route 28, Ocean Street Dock, Hyannis; (508) 778–2600 or (800) 492–8082; www.hy-linecruises.com. Fast ferry to Nantucket only, traditional ferry service to both Nantucket and Martha's Vineyard, Oak Bluffs dock. The ferry ride takes one hour and three quarters on the traditional service to either Martha's Vineyard or Nantucket. The speed ferry to Nantucket takes only one hour. No cars accepted (passengers only). A charge of $15 per calendar day for parking is collected when you pick up your car.

- **Steamship Authority,** corner of Pleasant Street and South Street, South Street Dock, Hyannis; (508) 477–8600 or (508) 693–9130; www.steamshipauthority.com or www.islandferry.com. Choice of traditional or fast ferry service to Nantucket; passage to Martha's Vineyard is from Woods Hole only. Cars are accepted with reservations on the traditional ferry. Parking is $10.00 a day on-site, $8.00 a day off-site in season.

Sandy Neck Beach (all ages)
Sandy Neck Road, off Route 6A, West Barnstable; (508) 362–8300; www.town .barnstable.ma.us/departments_01/recreation/beaches.htm. Parking is $10 weekdays, and $12 on weekends.

At Barnstable's lovely beach on Cape Cod Bay, the dunes of 6-mile-long Sandy Neck Beach protect Barnstable Harbor from heavy surf. They also form one of the Cape's finest barrier beaches, and one that's rarely crowded. There's an adjacent parking lot, restrooms, changing rooms, and a snack bar.

Veterans Park Beach (all ages)

Ocean Street, at the end of Gosnold Street, Hyannis; (508) 790–9885; www.town.
barnstable.ma.us/departments_01/recreation/beaches.htm. Parking is $10 weekdays,
and $12 on weekends.

Adjacent to the John F. Kennedy Memorial, Veterans Park Beach has lots of picnic
tables, grills, a bath house, playgrounds, snack bar, and volleyball, and is lifeguarded
from 9:00 A.M. to 4:30 P.M.

Other Things to See and Do

Cahoon Museum of American Art,
4676 Falmouth Road, Cotuit; (508) 428–
7581; www.cahoonmuseum.org. Open
Tuesday through Saturday 10:00 A.M. to
4:00 P.M. Closed in January. Price: $3.00 for
adults, **free** for children under 12. Featuring the home and the art of Ralph and
Martha Cahoon, antique dealers who
painted primitives on furniture and other
mediums.

Cape Cod Melody Tent, 21 West Main
Street, Hyannis; (508) 775–5630 (office) or
(508) 775–9100 (box office); www.melody
tent.com. Theater productions showcasing
nationally known casts. Children's theater
productions on Wednesdays during the
summer.

John F. Kennedy Hyannis Museum,
397 Main Street, Hyannis; (508) 790–3077.
Open Monday through Saturday 9:00 A.M.
to 5:00 P.M. and Sunday noon to 5:00 P.M.
Price: $5.00 for adults, $2.50 for kids 10 to
16, under 10 **free.** Not as impressive as
the one in Dorchester, but worth a look.

**Simmons Homestead Inn and Toad
Hall Classic Car Museum,** 288 Scudder
Avenue, Hyannisport; (508) 778–4999 or
(800) 637–1649; www.simmonshome
steadinn.com/ToadHall. Open daily year-
round from 11:00 A.M. to 5:00 P.M. Admission: $8.00 for adults, kids 16 and under

are **free.** Collection of more than fifty
cars in mint condition all in neon RED!

Sturgis Library, Route 6A, 3090 Main
Street, Barnstable; (508) 362–6636;
www.capecod.net/~sturgis/. Oldest public
library building in the United States.

The West Parish Meetinghouse, Corner of Route 149 and Meetinghouse Way,
West Barnstable; (508) 362–4445. Second
oldest surviving meetinghouse on the Cape.

Where to Eat

Four Seas, 360 South Main Street, Cen-
terville; (508) 775–1394; www.fourseasice
cream.com. Open mid-May through mid-
September only. Rated number one in New
England by *Gourmet* magazine. Serves
some of the best ice cream on the Cape,
along with sandwiches and lobster rolls. $

Gringo's, 577 Main Street, Hyannis; (508)
771–8449. Features seafood, pizza, and
Mexican dishes. Children's menu. $–$$

Paddock Restaurant, 25 West Main
Street, Hyannis; (508) 775–7677. Steaks
and seafood specialties. $–$$$$

Tugboats, 21 Arlington Street, Hyannis
Marina, Osterville; (508) 775–6433; www
.tugboatscapecod.com. Outside dining on
a covered deck, great views of Hyannis
harbor. Kids will love watching the harbor
activity (especially the passing of the
steamship). $–$$$

Land and Sea Tours in the Hyannis Area

- **Cape Cod Duckmobile,** 437 Main Street, Hyannis; (508) 790–2111 or (888) 225–3825; www.duckmobile.com. Open in season 10:00 A.M. to 5:00 P.M. daily. Tours are on the hour. Price: $16.00 adult, $12.00 students and kids over 5, $5.00 for kids 5 and under. Land-and-sea tour of Hyannis on an amphibious duckmobile.

- **Catboat *Eventide*,** Ocean Street Dock, Hyannis Port; (508) 775–0222; www.catboat.com. Harbor and sunset cruises; the price for children ninety pounds and under is $10, adults are $25. Sailings daily April through Columbus Day. Look for discount coupons on the Web site.

- **Hy-Line Hyannisport Harbor Cruises,** Ocean Street Dock, Hyannis; (508) 778–2600, (888) 778–1132, or (800) 492–8082; www.hy-line cruises.com. Specializing in Lobster Lunch cruises; Sunday Ice Cream "Float" cruises, and jazz and blues cruises. Children sail for **free** on early morning and late afternoon family cruises. Price: $12.00 for adults, $6.00 for ages 3 to 11 (prices change for theme cruises).

Where to Stay

Anchor-In, 1 South Street, Hyannis; (508) 775–0357; www.anchorin.com. The only hotel in Hyannis with its own boat-docking facilities; harborside pool. Family-friendly. $–$$$$

Captain Gosnold Village, 230 Gosnold Street, Hyannis; (508) 775–9111; www .captaingosnold.com. Open May to October. Large cottages with fully equipped kitchens. Pool, basketball hoop, lawn-game equipment, and gas grills. $–$$$$

Centerville Corners, 1338 Craigville Beach Road, Centerville; (508) 775–7223 or (800) 242–1137; www.centerville corners.com. Near Craigville Beach. Indoor heated pool, two saunas, large lawn, and croquet and badminton equipment. Renovated all rooms in 2003. Pet friendly. $–$$$

Yarmouth, Dennis, and Harwich

Yarmouth, Dennis, and Harwich cover both the bay and the sound coasts of the mid-Cape, as well as the congestion of Route 28 and the peaceful residential areas north of Route 6A and south of Route 28. The **Yarmouth Chamber of Commerce** is at 424 Route 28, West Yarmouth 02673; (508) 778–1008 or (800) 732–1008; www.yarmouth capecod.com. To contact the **Dennis Chamber of Commerce** (242 Swan River Road, West Dennis 02670) call (508) 398–3568 or (800) 243–9920; www.dennischamber .com. The **Harwich Chamber of Commerce** (P.O. Box 34) is located at 532 Main Street, Harwichport 02646; (508) 430–1165 or (800) 442–7942; www.harwichcc.com.

The Cape Cod Rail Trail (all ages)

Running from Route 134 in South Dennis to Locust Road in Eastham. To pick up the trail, take exit 9 off Route 6 in Dennis, turn south on Route 134, and travel approximately ¼ mile. The trail ends in Wellfleet, just east of Route 6, near the Wellfleet Chamber of Commerce information booth. The Web site is www.state.ma.us/dem /parks/ccrt.htm. Free.

The Cape Cod Rail Trail is a 25-mile-long asphalt biking path that follows the old (discontinued) railroad tracks that cut a swath through six towns (Dennis, Harwich, Brewster, Orleans, Eastham, and Wellfleet), Nickerson State Park, and the Cape Cod National Seashore. The trail is fairly flat and safe; however, there currently are some short sections of the trail that are on roads. There are lots of places to pull over for beach fun, buy a hard-earned snack, or use a restroom.

Cape Cod Waterways (all ages)

16 Route 28 (¼ mile east of Route 134) on the Swan River in Dennisport; (508) 398–0080. Rent by the hour; price depends on boat chosen and number of participants.

Paddleboat or canoe, which to choose? Luckily, the rental is by the hour and the owner allows you to change boats midstream. Our decision was to canoe the route to South Village Beach and change over to the paddleboat for the northerly trek to Swan Pond. The paddleboats can be electronically operated to help navigate the changing tidal currents, or you can switch over to manual and use foot power to propel you on your way.

The Holy Grail **of Trails**

The Cape Cod Rail Trail is Massachusetts's longest paved rail trail.

Freedom Cruise Line (all ages)

702 Main Street, Route 28, Saquatucket Harbor Dock, Harwichport; (508) 432–8999; www.nantucketislandferry.com. Operates late May through mid-October, three times a day. Price: $48 for adults, $38 for children 2 to 12, $6.00 for children under 2. Parking is free for day-trippers only.

Ninety-minute cruise from Harwichport to Nantucket. Freedom Cruise Line's appeal is its location mid-Cape—and there is less hustle and bustle here than leaving from Hyannis. Reservations are recommended; bikes allowed onboard for an extra fee. No vehicles accepted. For overnight parking the charge is $12 per night.

Gray's Beach (all ages)

Off Centre Street from Route 6A, Yarmouth; (508) 398–2231 or (508) 775–7910. Open parking, no fee.

A fine beach for families, Gray's Beach has another attraction—the long wooden Bass Hole Boardwalk, which stretches over a salt marsh. Kids love to scamper along the elevated walkway; it's also fun to peer out over the marshy grasses and flowers. The beach has calm water, picnic tables, restrooms, and a playground. *NOTE:* There is a strong current beyond the swimming area.

Pirate's Cove (all ages)

728 Main Street (Route 28), South Yarmouth; (508) 394–6200; www.piratescove.net. Open daily April through November from 10:00 A.M. to 7:00 P.M., with extended hours from late June through Labor Day (9:00 A.M. to 11:00 P.M.). Admission: $7.50 for adults, $6.50 for children 12 and under.

Among the many miniature golf courses that line Route 28, the most inventive is Pirate's Cove. The two eighteen-hole courses are laid out around a pirate ship that sits in a lagoonlike pond, surrounded by cliffs and waterfalls. To round out your experience there is an arcade, a gift shop, a marketplace, and a snack bar.

Amazing
Massachusetts Facts

- It is the law in Massachusetts for children 12 and under to wear protective helmets when operating or riding as a passenger on a bicycle.

- The tallest all-granite structure in the United States is the Pilgrim Tower in Provincetown.

Zooquarium (all ages)

674 Route 28, West Yarmouth; (508) 775–8883; www.zooquariumcapecod.net. Open mid-February to late June and Labor Day to the end of November 9:30 A.M. to 5:00 P.M., open late June through Labor Day daily 9:30 A.M. to 6:00 P.M. Admission: $9.50 for adults and $6.50 for ages 2 to 9, free for children under 2.

Not overwhelming in size, the Zooquarium is an eclectic mix of native wildlife and rare-breed farm animals. The zoo adopts animals (placed by agencies) that were injured and rehabilitated but can no longer be reintroduced into the wild. Some of the rare-breed farm animals that are maintained by the zoo are Irish Dexter cattle and Navajo Churro sheep. There is a killer sea lion show, which your family will find most entertaining. At the Zoo Theater, a daily Zoo-rific Presentation can be anything from cockroaches to bobcats—it's very hands-on; your family is allowed not only to see and learn but also to touch the animal that is being presented. A Touch Pool of marine and aquatic animals and fish also allow one-on-one interaction and greater understanding of the world around us. At the Children's Discovery Center kids can find out how zookeepers prepare the animals' diets. For some reason the Scoop on Poop exhibit is very popular with little boys. The boys seem to find it very amusing when they find out these little-known facts:

- Llamas have a communal dung pile.
- Sea lions' poop is very greasy because they eat a lot of fish.
- A mouse's skeletal structure can be re-created from an owl's pellets because owls don't digest bones.
- Early settlers' diets were discovered from the privies dug up by the Big Dig in Boston.

A nice take-in for the whole family; set aside two to three hours to explore the Zooquarium.

Scargo Tower (all ages)

Route 6A, to Old Bass River Road, take the first left onto Scargo Hill Road, Dennis.

Scargo Tower isn't that tall a tower—only 28 feet—but the high hill it sits on makes it a great place to take in a terrific view of Cape Cod Bay and the Cape's midsection.

West Dennis Beach (all ages)

Off Davis Beach Road, West Dennis; (508) 760–6162; www.dennisrecreation.com. Parking is $11.

One-mile-long West Dennis Beach, bordering a flat salt marsh and several tidal streams, is a busy place in the summer. The eastern end is for Dennis residents only; the rest of it is taken over by families who park in the enormous parking lot—so big that it rarely fills (unusual for a good Cape beach). Enjoy the beach and its many facilities—good swimming, lots of lifeguard stations, restrooms, showers, play areas with swing sets, and a snack bar.

Other Things to See and Do

Barbara's Bike Shop, 430 Route 134, South Dennis; (508) 760–4723; www.barbs bikeshop.com. Rental shop located at the beginning of the Cape Cod Rail Trail.

Cape Cod Storyland, 68 Center Street, Hyannis; (508) 778–4339. Minigolf and bumper boats. Ice-cream shop on premises.

Cape Museum of Fine Arts, Route 6A, on the grounds of the Cape Playhouse, Dennis; (508) 385–4477; www.cmfa.org. Work by Cape Cod artists. Special treasure hunt for children.

The Cape Playhouse, Route 6A, Dennis; (508) 385–3911; www.capeplayhouse.com. Many of the famous thespians of today cut their teeth here. The playhouse bills itself as "America's Oldest Professional Summer Theater." Friday morning live children's productions.

Cape Symphony Orchestra, Fiddler's Green, 712A Main Street, Yarmouthport; (508) 362–1111; www.capesymphony.org. Third largest orchestra in Massachusetts. Performances are at the Barnstable High School Performing Arts Center on 744 West Main Street, Hyannis.

Captain Bangs Hallet House, 11 Strawberry Lane (off Route 6A), Yarmouthport; (508) 362–3021; www.hsoy.org. Fifty-acre sea captain's house and estate; hiking trails.

Harwich Junior Theatre, 105 Division Street, Harwich; (508) 432–2002; www.hjt capecod.org. Summer theater productions for kids. Previous pieces performed have

been *The Wind in the Willows* and *The Secret Garden*.

Seaview Playland, 475 Lower County Road, Dennisport; (508) 398–9084; www .seaviewcapecod.com. Spacious indoor arcade, miniature golf, and par-three golf.

Where to Eat

Black Rock Tuscan Grille, 633 Route 28, South Yarmouth; (508) 771–1001; www.blackrocktuscangrille.com. Black Angus steaks, salads, Tuscan dishes. Western riding gear decor. $$–$$$

Breakfast Room, 675 Main Street, West Dennis; (508) 398–0581. Open seasonally for breakfast and lunch. Always a line, very popular. Kids' menu. $

Clancy's, 175 Route 28, West Yarmouth; (508) 775–3332; www.clancyscapecod .com. Seafood, steaks, kids' menu. Irish music singalongs. $$

Lobster Boat, 681 Main Street, West Yarmouth; (508) 775–0486. Waterfront dining overlooking the Parker River and the marina. Lobster and other seafood dishes, as well as hamburgers, fried chicken, and the like. $$–$$$

Marshside Restaurant, 28 Bridge Street, East Dennis; (508) 385–4010. Serving breakfast, lunch, and dinner. Lots of bird activity in the many birdhouses that are in the marsh, keeps kids' attention. $–$$$

The Sundae School, 387 Lower County Road (off of Route 28), Dennis; (508) 394–9122. Homemade ice cream and sundaes. $

Where to Stay

All Seasons Motor Inn, Route 28, South Yarmouth; (508) 394–7600 or (800) 527–0359; www.allseasons.com. Indoor and outdoor pool; TV, VCR, restaurant, fitness center, sauna and refrigerator in every room. $–$$$

Edgewater Beach Resort, 95 Chase Avenue, Dennisport; (508) 398–6922; www.edgewatercapecod.com. Suites, some oceanfront and some efficiencies. Indoor and outdoor pools. $–$$$$

Holiday Hill Motor Inn, 352 Main Street, Route 28, Dennisport; (508) 394–5577 or (800) 333–2569; www.holidayhill motorinn.com. Ice-cream shops, video game room, bumper cars, minigolf, and pool on premises. Modest rooms are easy on the pocketbook (with many amenities). $–$$

The Lighthouse Inn, 1 Lighthouse Road, West Dennis; (508) 398–2244; www.light houseinn.com. Family-oriented resort on Nantucket Sound, near the Bass River. Accommodations include single rooms and cottages scattered across nine well-maintained acres. On-site attractions include a working lighthouse, tennis courts, a pool, miniature golf, shuffleboard, a private beach, and lots of planned activities for kids. Breakfast included in rate. $$$$

Travelodge, 99 Main Street, Route 28, West Dennis; (508) 394–8870 or (800) 578–7878; www.travelodge.com. Each child gets a teddy bear and travel pack with crayons and stickers upon check-in. Outdoor pool. $–$$

Chatham

Chatham is a village of shingled cottages, with a delightful Main Street full of shops and cafes and a variety of top-level summer accommodations for families. There are several attractions that are in the don't-miss category for families: the Fish Pier, Chatham Lighthouse, the Friday-evening band concerts at Kate Gould Park, and the Railroad Museum. Contact the **Chatham Chamber of Commerce,** P.O. Box 793, Chatham 02633; (508) 945–5199 or (800) 715–5567; www.chathaminfo.com.

Chatham Light and Chatham Break (all ages)
On Main Street between Shore Road and Bridge Street.

Chatham Light sits across from a small parking lot, several sets of coin-operated binoculars, and a breathtaking view of the Chatham Break. The break was formed during a ferocious winter storm in 1987, when storm-pounded waves broke through the barrier beach that stretches south from Nauset Beach, forming a separate island (now called South Beach) and a break in the barrier that had protected Chatham's harbor and coastline from the full brunt of the Atlantic. The break is a spectacular example of the power of weather, wind, and ocean. The present structure is one of a pair of towers that was built in 1877 (the light's twin was moved to Nauset in 1923). Chatham's original lighthouses were built in 1808. Heavy erosion, which is still a problem in Chatham, forced the Coast Guard to move the lights back from the coast to the spot where the light stands today. Chatham Light flashes two times every ten seconds.

Chatham Railroad Museum (all ages)

Depot Road, Chatham; (508) 945–5199 (Chamber of Commerce). Open mid-June through mid-September, Tuesday through Saturday, 10:00 A.M. to 4:00 P.M. Free; donations accepted.

The restored depot building of the Chatham Railroad Museum, with its Cheerio-like architectural details, holds an impressive collection of thousands of model trains. Thomas the Tank Engine fans will enjoy the old caboose, which is most kids' favorite object. *TIP:* There's a great playground across the street.

Hardings Beach (all ages)

Hardings Beach Road, Chatham; (508) 945–5100. Parking is $10 per day, $50 per week, and $85 for the season. Pay by the day at the beach, or obtain a sticker at the permit department at Town Hall.

The best family beach in Chatham is Hardings Beach. It's a long beach with small dunes, restrooms, a snack bar, and a large parking lot (arrive early; it can fill up before noon in the summer).

Kate Gould Park (all ages)

On Main Street, Chatham. Every Friday night from early July through early September. Free.

Every Friday night there's a band concert at the bandstand in Kate Gould Park. Thousands of visitors and locals show up for these evenings to dance to old standards, Sousa marches, and the like.

Down by **the Sea**

A variety of water tours in Chatham can be arranged by contacting one of the following boat tour operators:

- **Beachcomber** (508–945–5265; www.sealwatch.com)
- **Chatham Water Tours** (508–432–5895; www.chathamwatertours.net)
- **Outermost Harbor Marine** (508–945–2030; www.outermostharbor.com)
- **Rip Rider** (508–945–5450; www.monomoyislandferry.com)

Safety Tip

The road between Chatham and Orleans can be busy; take the time to drive the kids to the beach rather than allowing them to walk.

Monomoy National Wildlife Refuge (all ages)

Morris Island Visitor Center, Morris Island; (508) 945–0594; www.friendsofmonomoy .org (literature and maps of Monomoy). If your family would like to tour Monomoy, you'll need to arrange a guided tour with one of two organizations: either the Cape Cod Museum of Natural History (508–896–3867 or www.ccmnh.org. for information and reservations) or the Wellfleet Bay Wildlife Sanctuary (508–349–2615 or www.well fleetbay.org). Open year-round.

One of the true adventures left for Cape visitors is a trip to Monomoy Island Wildlife Refuge, a 2,700-acre wilderness area on two islands (although the refuge extends beyond the islands to the waters around it, and it consists of 5,000 acres) that serve as a resting area for migratory birds and a home for as many as 300 species of seaside birds. In addition, an amazing number of gray and harbor seals call the sandbars off this island home. On your tour of the islands (North and South Monomoy), you'll see acres of true seaside wilderness: There are no roads, no buildings (except for the light keeper's cottage on South Monomoy), and no electricity.

For a unique experience stay at the light keeper's cottage on South Monomoy for an overnight; kids 12 and up are welcome. If you don't have time for a guided tour or an overnight stay, visit the Monomoy Island Wildlife Refuge Visitor Center on Morris Island. They offer self-guided and guided tours, and the helpful staff will provide you with plenty of literature and will point you and the kids toward the ¾-mile self-guided interpretive tour around Morris Island. The Morris Island Visitor Center also offers birding and naturalist hands-on programs and special family fun days. Leashed dogs only, please. Directions to the Monomoy Island Visitor Center on Morris Island: From Main Street in Chatham, make a right onto Shore Road, take the first left after Chatham Light. Take the first right; follow Morris Island Road to the visitor center (508–945–0594). *TIP: The Disappearing Island* by Corinne Demas and Ted Lewin is a great book about this area.

Catch as **Catch Can**

Watch the day's catch being unloaded from the observation deck at **Chatham Fish Pier** between 2:00 and 6:00 P.M. It's just north of town, on the corner of Bar Cliff Avenue and Shore Road.

Breaker's **Beach**

If you're looking for a deserted beach, try **South Beach,** which is the part of Nauset Beach that was separated by the Chatham Break. There are no lifeguards and no facilities here; pack a lunch and plenty of water. You'll share the beach with lots of shorebirds, the overflow from Monomoy Island.

Other Things to See and Do

Atwood Museum, 347 Stage Harbor Road, Chatham; (508) 945–2493; www.chathamhistoricalsociety.org or www.atwoodhouse.org. Maritime and American antiques, shell collections, artwork by local artists, China trade, bird carvings by nationally known Elmer Crowell, an eighteenth-century furnished house, and paraphernalia make for an eclectic museum.

Cabbages and Kings Bookstore, 595 Main Street, Chatham; (508) 945–1603; www.chathambookstore.com. Toys, games, and adult and children's books are among the dizzying array found here.

Cape Cod Aerial Tours, Inc., 240 George Ryder Road, Chatham Airport; (508) 945–2363; www.chathamairport .com. Sightseeing rides to view Monomoy Island seals or Provincetown.

Grist Mill, Chase Park, Shattuck Place, Chatham. Original old mill.

Where to Eat

Buffy's Ice Cream, 456 Main Street, Chatham; (508) 945–5990. Homemade ice cream made fresh daily. $

Chatham Bars Inn, Shore Road, Chatham; (508) 945–0096; www.chatham barsinn.com. Meals are served in spacious, elegant dining rooms; clambakes take place on the beach once a week. $$–$$$$

Chatham Candy Manor, 484 Main Street, Chatham; (508) 945–0825 or (800) 221–6497; www.candymanor.com. Hand-dipped chocolates and unusual candies.

The Cloud Nine Cafe, 240 George Ryder Road, at Chatham Airport, Chatham; (508) 945–1144; www.chathamairport.com. Serving breakfast and lunch. Open year-round. $

Where to Stay

Chatham Bars Inn, Shore Road, Chatham; (508) 945–0096 or (800) 527–4884; www.chathambarsinn.com. Select from suites, cottages, and rooms with balconies; there are 205 rooms in all on the twenty-two-acre property. The inn has a private beach just across Shore Road, with planned complimentary activities (including all-day children's programs). $$$–$$$$

Horne Family Cottages, off Morris Island Road, Chatham; (508) 945–0734. Cottage and a house on the nicest private beach in Chatham. Clean and beautifully maintained. $$$–$$$$

Monomoy Point Lighthouse Keepers House/Monomoy Island Wildlife Refuge, Reservations made through the Cape Cod Museum of Natural History (508–896–3867). Open last week of June to the end of August for prearranged tours. A forty-five-minute boat shuttle takes you to Monomoy Island. Overnight accommodations are in the keeper's house (which sleeps up to eight people). Rate includes dinner and breakfast. Children must be at least 12. Expect to pay upwards of $200 per person for this unique experience.

Pleasant Bay Village, Route 28, 1191 Orleans Road, Chatham; P.O. Box 772, Chatham 02633; (508) 945–1133 or (800) 547–1011. Open the end of April through the end of October. Large complex of buildings (58 bedroom suites) set on beautifully maintained grounds with five waterfalls. Efficiency units have well-equipped kitchens. Heated pool and adult spa. $$–$$$$

Brewster

Brewster was home to dozens of ship captains during the nineteenth century, many of whom built beautiful homes along what is now Route 6A. Today, when the tide is out, Brewster's beaches along the bay—Sea Street Beach, Paines Creek Beach, and Point of Rocks Beach on Cape Cod Bay—are fun spots for kids to explore the miles and miles of sun-warmed tidal pools and skittering seaside animals, birds, and bugs. If you need further information, contact the **Brewster Chamber of Commerce** at 74 Locust Lane (P.O. Box 1241), Brewster 02631; (508) 396–3500; www.brewstercapecod.org.

Cape Cod Museum of Natural History (all ages)

869 Route 6A, Brewster; (508) 896–3867; www.ccmnh.com. Open daily from June through September 10:00 A.M. to 4:00 P.M., on weekends only from October through December from 10:00 A.M. to 4:00 P.M., and Wednesday through Sunday 10:00 A.M. to 4:00 P.M. April through May. Admission: $7.00 for adults, $3.50 for children 5 to 12, free for children 4 and under.

The Cape Cod Museum of Natural History does a terrific job of teaching kids (and their parents) about the Cape's fragile ecology. The museum also runs tours of Monomoy Island Wildlife Refuge (see the description under Chatham in this chapter). There are three nature trails (guided trail walks to Wing Island are a treat and can take one and a half hours) and marine tanks with live indigenous salt- and freshwater creatures. The touch tanks feature crabs, mollusks, fish, turtles, frogs, and other local species. Set aside about one hour to completely digest the museum. The museum also sponsors canoe and kayak day trips for a nominal fee. Other family activities include seal cruises through the summer and a day camp for kids that runs from three days to a week.

Row, Row, **Row Your Boat!**

Jack's Boat Rental can fix you up with canoes, kayaks, surf bikes, seacycles, Sunfish, and paddleboats.

New England Fire and History Museum (all ages)

1439 Main Street, Route 6A, Brewster; (508) 896–5711. Open July through August 10:00 A.M. to 4:00 P.M. Monday through Saturday, noon to 4:00 P.M. Sunday, Memorial Day to July 1 hours vary, so call ahead, and Labor Day to Columbus Day Saturday and Sunday noon to 4:00 P.M. or by appointment. Admission: $7.00 for adults, $3.00 for children 5 to 12, $1.00 for children 4 and under.

The six buildings of the New England Fire and History Museum hold a variety of exhibits, including historic firefighting equipment, a 50-foot exhibit entitled *Boston Burns in 1872,* a life-size reproduction of Benjamin Franklin's firehouse, a blacksmith shop, an apothecary, and a fireboat that kids can climb on. The museum claims to have the largest fire equipment collection in the world. Picnic sites are available.

Nickerson State Forest (all ages)

3488 Main Street and Route 6A, Brewster; (508) 896–3491; www.state.ma.us/dem /parks/nick.htm. Free.

If your family would rather not swim in salt water, Nickerson State Forest, Cape Cod's largest park, is a great place for you—it has several large freshwater ponds with a small beach at one of the ponds. The park also features hiking trails, fishing, bike trails, boating, summertime interpretive programs, and camping. (Call Reserve America at 877–422–6762; www.reserveamerica.com). Jack's Boat Rental (508–349–9808 or 508–896–8556) is located at both Flax's and Cliff Ponds in Nickerson State Forest. Skating and cross-country skiing (conditions permitting) are popular in the winter.

Other Things to See and Do

Barbara's Bike Shop, 3430 Main Street, Brewster; (508) 896–7231; www.barbsbike shop.com. Rental shop located outside the entrance to Nickerson State Park in Brewster. Close access to the Cape Cod Rail Trail.

Stony Brook Grist Mill and Museum, 830 Stony Brook Road, Brewster; (508) 896–1734. Corn mill still in use. Demonstrations and artifacts.

Where to Eat

Brewster Fish House, 2208 Main Street, Brewster; (508) 896–7867; www.brewster fishhouse.com. Chowders, pasta, and seafood. Highly regarded by the locals. $$–$$$

The Brewster Teapot at the Beechcroft Inn, 1360 Main Street, Brewster; (508) 896–9534 or (877) 233–2446; www.beechcroftinn.com. Open 11:00 A.M. to 5:00 P.M. serving lunch and afternoon tea. English floral decor; only nine tables, come early or miss out! $–$$

Chillingsworth Bistro, 2449 Main Street, Route 6A, Brewster; (508) 896–3640; www.chillingsworth.com. Don't confuse the bistro with the restaurant of the same name, unless you're up for a seven-course dinner in an antique-filled setting (not a good idea with kids). The bistro specializes in grilled food, has a contemporary setting with lots of glass and skylights, and will gladly do a pasta dish for the kids. $$–$$$

Where to Stay

Ocean Edge Resort and Golf Club, 2907 Main Street, Route 6A, Brewster; (508) 896–9000 or (800) 343–6074 (for room reservations); www.oceanedge.com. Located on a private beach with two indoor and four outdoor pools, tennis, bike trails, kids' program, and four dining rooms (the most family friendly are The Reef and Mulligan's). You can opt to stay in a hotel room or a one-, two-, or three-bedroom villa. $$$$

Old Sea Pines Inn, 2555 Main Street, Brewster; (508) 896–6114; www.oldsea pinesinn.com. Family suites, cozy fireplace in the main area, inviting porch with rocking chairs. Step back in time to a slower pace. Reasonable rates include a full breakfast. $–$$$

Orleans and East Orleans

For families, Orleans's main attraction is actually in East Orleans—Nauset Beach. Other recreational opportunities take advantage of water locations. Orleans is bounded on the east by the Atlantic and on the west by Cape Cod Bay. For more information contact the **Orleans Chamber of Commerce** (P.O. Box 153), 44 Main Street, Orleans 02653; (508) 255–1386 or (508) 865–1386; www.capecod-orleans.com.

Nauset Beach (all ages)

Beach Road, East Orleans; (508) 240–3775 or (508) 240–3780 (beach office); www.town .orleans.ma.us. Nonresident's fee: $10; you can park at both Nauset and Skaket (see entry below) Beaches for the same price and try two beaches in one day! Directions: From exit 12 off Route 6, turn right onto Eldredge Park Way, right onto Main Street, then left onto Beach Road, which leads to Nauset Beach. Nauset Beach has two beach chairs for the handicapped (no charge).

Nine miles long and backed by high dunes, this is one of the Cape's best beaches. If you're willing to walk a bit, Nauset Beach is so long that you will be able to stake out your own territory even on the busiest summer weekends. If you want to stay near the lifeguards, however, keep within the marked area. There's a large bathhouse with restrooms, changing rooms, and showers; there's also a good snack bar with outdoor picnic tables. On Mondays in July and August from 7:00 to 9:00 P.M. there are free bandstand concerts at the gazebo. Everything from folk to rock 'n' roll can be heard. Children like to dance down front, and couples can walk the beach and still hear the music.

Pirate Adventures (all ages)

Town Cove, Orleans; (508) 255–8811; www.pirateadventurescapecod.com. Open mid-June through the Sunday of Labor Day weekend. Price: $17 per child.

Pirate Adventures sets sail in Town Cove in Orleans, and if your kids like pirate adventures a la Peter Pan complete with painted faces, sailor sashes, sailor odes, and swashbuckling yarns, then matey, all aboard! Follow the secret treasure map to claim your booty! Reservations a must!

Skaket Beach (all ages)

Skaket Beach Road, Orleans; (508) 240–3775 or (508) 255–0572 (beach office); www .town.orleans.ma.us. Nonresident's fee: $10; you can park at both Nauset (see entry above) and Skaket Beaches for the same price and try two beaches in one day! Direc-

How to Eat **a Lobster**

For the uninitiated in the fine art of eating a lobster, we offer this primer.

1. Assemble your tools: a nutcracker, a lobster pick or fork, and a lobster bib (eating lobster can be a very messy undertaking).

2. Twist off the claws, crack them open with the nutcracker, remove the meat, and dip in drawn butter.

3. Separate the tail from the body (bend it until it breaks away), then split the tail down the middle to get to the meat. You may see a green or red line in the center of the tail meat. This is the liver or tomalley and is a treat to some lobster connoisseurs. *WARNING:* Eat the liver only if it is green.

4. Open the main body of the lobster and hunt down the lobster meat in the small pockets. Other sources of meat are the small claws (break them off the body) and the flippers of the tail.

tions: Take exit 12; turn right off the exit and take the first left onto West Road. Follow West Road until the end (facing Skaket Beach Road). Take a left onto Skaket Beach Road for Skaket Beach.

Skaket Beach, Orleans's bay beach, is popular with families who enjoy playing in tidal flats. Facilities include restrooms, lifeguards, two beach chairs for the handicapped, changing rooms, and a snack bar.

Cape **Sports Teams**

- **Cape Cod Baseball League.** Looking for something to fill your family's summer vacation evenings? Between mid-June and mid-August, the Cape Cod Baseball League is just the thing. Ten towns on the Cape field teams made up of the country's top college baseball players, who play before enthusiastic small crowds and, more often than not, big-league scouts. Past players have included Carlton Fisk, Chuck KnobLauch, Darian Erstad, Charles Nagy, Mo Vaughn, Nomar Garciaparra, Jeff Bagwell, Frank Thomas, Will Clark, and Eric Hinske. The league conducts weekly clinics for kids. For more information, contact the Cape Cod Baseball League at Box 266, Harwichport 02646; (508) 432–6909; www.capecodbaseball.org.

- **Cape Crusaders Soccer Team.** The only professional sports team on the Cape since 1993, the Cape Crusaders are part of the PDL (the Player Development League), the league that develops and showcases the top college players. The Cape Crusaders are owned and operated by Massachusetts Premier Soccer, who also own the Boston Renegades. (Massachusetts Premier Soccer can be proud of their record; the Crusaders were the 2002 PDL national champions, and the Renegades were the W1 national champions for 2002!) Preseason games are held in April; the season runs from May to August. Former Crusader players include Kevin Wiley, Casey Schmidt, and Francis O'Karoh. Games are played at Dennis/Yarmouth High School's Alan Carlson Field (tickets are $8.00 for adults, $5.00 for children 14 and under). The team also runs a summer soccer day camp for ages 4 to 8 and ages 9 to 14 (Jr. Crusader/Jr. Renegades; sign up information can be found at www.mpsbr.com). For more information, contact the Cape Crusaders at 112 State Road, Sagamore Beach 02562, (508) 888–0865; www.capecodcrusaders.com.

Other Things to See and Do

French Cable Station Museum, corner of Cove Road and Route 28,Orleans; (508) 240–1735. Open June and September, Friday through Sunday 1:00 to 4:00 P.M.; July through August, Monday through Saturday 1:00 to 4:00 P.M. Rare collection of undersea telegraph cables, instruments, and memorabilia.

Goose Hummock Kayak, Route 6A (off the Route 6 rotary) on town cove, Orleans; (508) 255–2620 or (508) 255–0455; www .goose.com. Canoe and kayak rental. *NOTE:* This is a challenging area to paddle.

Kid's Kaboodle, 115 Route 6A, Orleans; (508) 240–0460. Unique clothing for infants and young children.

The Playhouse, 120 Main Street, Orleans (on the way to Nauset Beach); (508) 255–1963; www.apa1.org. Musical dramas, comedies, and original works. A new show every month. Children's theater series on Saturday mornings in the summer and select shows during the year.

Pleasant Bay Kayak Adventures, 16 Cross Road, South Orleans; (508) 255–2349; www.pleasantbaykayak.com. Family tours and eco-tours.

Where to Eat

Hot Chocolate Sparrow, 5 Old Colony Way, Route 6A, Orleans 02653; (508) 240–2230; www.hotchocolatesparrow.com. Coffee and chocolate bar (specializing in drinks, desserts, and ice cream). $

Joe's Bar and Grill at the Barley Neck Inn, 5 Coach Road, East Orleans; (508) 224–0212; www.barleyneck.com. Casual, comfy, and kicked-back with a creative, highly acclaimed kitchen. $–$$$

Land Ho!, corner of Route 6A and Cove Road, Orleans; (508) 255–5165; www.land-ho.com. The kale soup is a specialty here, but everything's good (from deli to fish and chips). Kids' menu. Open daily year-round. $$

Where to Stay

Barley Neck Inn and Lodge, 5 Beach Road, East Orleans; (508) 255–8484 or (800) 281–7505; www.barleyneck.com. An annual favorite of *Yankee Magazine,* 1 mile from Nauset Beach across from a saltwater marina. Seventeen rooms, American traditional in decor with two interesting restaurants: the dining room and Joe's Beach Road Bar and Grille. **Free** continental breakfast and freshwater pool. $–$$$

Kadee's Gray Elephant Guest Studio's, 216 Main Street, East Orleans; (508) 255–7608. Charming rooms with queen-size beds, kitchenette facilities, and private baths. Not for large families. Breakfast basket included in rate on first night of stay. $$

Eastham

Eastham is where Myles Standish and his band first met native tribes in 1620, after the Pilgrims' landing in Provincetown and before their settlement of Plymouth. The meeting spot is commemorated by a bronze marker at the top of the dunes of First Encounter Beach. Today most visitors go to Eastham to enter the Cape Cod National Seashore, which covers nearly 27,000 acres of the outer Cape. It is administered by the National Park Service (see listing below). The **Eastham Chamber of Commerce** can be contacted at P.O. Box 1329, Eastham 02642; (508) 255–3444 or (508) 240–7211; www.easthamchamber.com for visitor information.

First Encounter Beach (all ages)

Samoset Road, Eastham; (508) 255–3444 or (508) 240–7211. Directions: From Route 6 North, turn left on Samoset Road. Parking is $10 a day June through Labor Day, Free the rest of the year.

First Encounter Beach is named for the site where the members of the *Mayflower* company and the Nauset tribe first encountered one another. The Pilgrims determined that the soil was too sandy to support farming. Look for the bronze plaque erected to commemorate the event. Restrooms and calm waters add to your family's comfort and safety (particularly the bay side of the beach). This is the largest Eastham Bay Beach.

Cape Cod National Seashore (all ages)

Off Route 6 on Nauset Road, Eastham; (508) 255–3421; www.nps.gov/caco. Parking at Little Creek parking lot is $10 and includes a free bus shuttle to Coast Guard Beach. The National Park Service also provides tours of the original brick lighthouses during the summer; ask for a schedule at the Salt Pond Visitors Center information desk (open 9:00 A.M. to 5:00 P.M.). A Cape Cod National Seashore Seasonal Pass is $30.

Be sure to visit the Salt Pond Visitors Center in Eastham, where helpful guides offer complete information on the seashore and walking trails (the Nauset Marsh Trail is especially scenic), as well as orientation talks and guided field trips. Respect the rules set forth by the Park Service; they are designed to protect this unique and fragile area. Two major points of interest are Coast Guard Beach and the Nauset Lighthouse.

Coast Guard Beach is one of the best beaches along the National Seashore and can be reached by shuttle bus. The bathhouse is one of the Cape's best. To reach Coast Guard Beach from the Salt Pond Visitors Center, continue on to Doane Road or take the 1.6-mile Nauset Trail bicycle path (a spur off the Cape Cod Rail Trail). Little Creek Road will be on the left; park and take the shuttle.

Nauset Light, the red-striped lighthouse, has a complicated history. In 1923 the brick building was moved from Chatham, where it was one of two lights. Because of soil erosion, the building was moved again to its current location in 1997. The site it now occupies was also the site of the first of the three lighthouses that sat in a row on the cliffs of Nauset from 1838 until 1911. The original "Three Sisters" were moved to Cable Road at Cape Cod National Seashore, not far from the Salt Pond Visitors Center. Nauset Light's single red stripe helped mariners to distinguish it from other Cape Cod lighthouses during the day. The round ball at the top of the tower is called a ventilator ball; it allows air to circulate and cool the lantern room, where the light-house's beam rotates. Nauset Light Beach is lifeguarded, and there can be heavy surf at times.

Other Things to See and Do

Eastham Windmill (Oldest Windmill on the Cape), Corner of Samoset and Route 6, Eastham. Original gristmill built circa 1680.

Little Capistrano Bike Shop, 341 Salt Pond Road, Eastham; (508) 255–6515; www.littlecapistranobike.com. Bike rentals.

Where to Eat

Lobster Pool, 4380 Route 6, North East-ham; (508) 255–9706. Rustic setting with great food; the seafood is especially fresh. Children's menu. $$–$$$

Where to Stay

Captain's Quarters, Route 6, Eastham; (508) 255–5686 or (800) 327– 7769; www.captains-quarters.com. Complimen-tary bicycles and continental breakfast, seventy-five rooms, heated outdoor pool, tennis courts. Along the Cape Cod Bike Trail. $–$$

Wellfleet

The focus in Wellfleet falls equally on the arts and the natural world. Many of the year-rounders and summerhouse owners who live in or near Wellfleet's tiny, pictur-esque harbor are artists, writers, actors, and other arts-oriented people; under their influence several arts day camps are run each summer for children and families. Well over half of Wellfleet's area is conservation land. Much of it is in the care of the Cape Cod National Seashore; the rest is part of the 1,000-acre Wellfleet Bay Wildlife Sanctu-ary. Write or call the **Wellfleet Chamber** for a vacation guide at P.O. Box 571, Well-fleet 02667; (508) 349–2510; www.wellfleetchamber.com.

Wellfleet **Ocean Beaches**

- **Cahoon Hollow Beach**—town beach with restrooms. Parking: $15.

- **Marconi Beach**—part of the Cape Cod National Seashore. Great bath-house. Parking: $7.

- **White Crest Beach**—town beach, broader than Cahoon Hollow; rest-rooms. Parking: $15.

Wellfleet Bay Wildlife Sanctuary (all ages)

West side of Route 6, South Wellfleet; (508) 349–2615; www.wellfleetbay.org. Visitor center open daily from May through October, 8:30 A.M. to 5:00 P.M.; November through April, Tuesday to Sunday, 8:30 A.M. to 5:00 P.M. Trails are open from dawn to dusk year-round. Admission: $5.00 for adults, and $3.00 for children. Excursion costs vary, usually $25.00 to $35.00 per day per program. If you've been a member of the Audubon Society for at least a year, you and your family can camp here.

Massachusetts Audubon Society's Wellfleet Bay Wildlife Sanctuary offers a myriad of nature-oriented activities for families: bird and bat watches; trips through salt marshes; guided trail walks at all hours of the day and night; and several excellent self-guided walking trails, where you'll see a variety of birds and coastal animals (watch for turtles). Write to P.O. Box 236, South Wellfleet 02663, for schedules and reservation information.

The Wellfleet Drive-In (all ages)

On Route 6 just north of the Eastham-Wellfleet line, Wellfleet; (508) 349–7176; www.wellfleetcinemas.com.

The Wellfleet Drive-In wears two hats: From 8:00 A.M. to 4:00 P.M. on Wednesday, Thursday, weekends, and Monday holidays, April through fall, it's a flea market; in the evenings it's a 700-car first-run drive-in movie theater with dairy bar, minigolf, play-ground, and snack bar. An indoor cinema theater with four screens and an outdoor minigolf course ensure that the whole crowd is pleased no matter what the weather.

Other Things to See and Do

Marconi Wireless Site, Marconi Beach, South Wellfleet. Site of first transatlantic communication.

Where to Eat

Finely JP's, Route 6, South Wellfleet; (508) 349–7500. Intimate restaurant serving excellent food, very popular with the local residents. Menu runs the gamut from fish to pasta to beef and chicken. $$

The Lighthouse, 317 Main Street, Wellfleet; (508) 349–3681; www.mainstreet lighthouse.com. Hearty breakfasts are particularly good. $–$$$

Moby Dick's, Route 6A across from Gull Pond Road, Wellfleet; (508) 349–9795; www.mobydicksrestaurant.com. Seafood in the rough. Sit inside at picnic tables with interesting nautical artifacts scattered about. Overlooks marshland. $–$$

VanRensselaer's, 1019 Route 6, South Wellfleet; (508) 349–2127; www.van rensselaers.com. Opposite Marconi wireless site. Bright and airy, family-oriented restaurant serving breakfast and dinner only, with a breakfast buffet on the weekends. Something for all tastes. $–$$$

Where to Stay

Wellfleet is a cottage colony mecca. One of the best is:

Surfside Colony, Ocean View Drive, along the Cape Cod National Seashore, South Wellfleet; (508) 349–3959; www .surfsidevacation.com. One-, two-, and three-bedroom cottages are available (200 steps from the beach), all with kitchens, fireplaces, and screened-in porches; some have roof decks as well. Write to P.O. Box 937, South Wellfleet 02663. $$–$$$

Truro

Truro is best known for its beaches and the plethora of summer houses and cottages that dot its high hills and dunes. For such a beautiful place (over half of the town is park or conservation land), it's remarkably untouristy. To reach the town center, as it were, of Truro, take the Pamet Road exit off Route 6. The **Truro Chamber of Commerce** is on Route 6A, Truro; (508) 487–1288.

Corn Hill Beach (all ages)

Castle Road, Truro. Take Castle Road from the center of Truro (follow signs from Route 6), then follow it to Corn Hill Beach. Parking is $10 for the day.

Corn Hill Beach is the place where Myles Standish and his desperately hungry group "borrowed" their first corn from the natives. A marker on the cliff at the edge of the bay indicates the spot where the event took place. This is also a great place for shelling. *NOTE:* No lifeguards here.

Cape Cod Light/Highland Light and the Highland Museum (all ages) 🔆

Off Highland Road, Cape Cod National Seashore, Truro; www.capecod.net/ths. Interior tours of the lighthouse and the Highland Museum run by the Highland Museum and Lighthouse Inc. (508–487–3397 for the museum, 508–487–1121 for Lighthouse Inc.). The lighthouse is open May through October, the museum daily June through September from 10:00 A.M. to 4:30 P.M. Free for children under 12, $3.00 for adults.

The first light that sailors see when they make the trip from Europe to Boston is that of Cape Cod Light, the oldest lighthouse on the Cape. Because it was built on the highlands of Truro, it is also known as the Highland Light. The present buildings date from 1857, but the first lighthouse constructed on this spot went up in 1798. Highland Light's precarious position on eroded cliffs made it likely that it would tumble into the ocean, so the Truro Historical Society successfully spearheaded efforts to move it to its present site 450 feet back in 1996. Ownership of the Cape Cod Light was transferred from the Coast Guard to the Cape Cod National Seashore. At night children will enjoy looking for the light's bright white beam, which is visible during the drive on Route 6 from Truro to Provincetown. Highland is the highest (182 feet above sea level) as well as the tallest (66 feet) lighthouse on the Cape. The museum gives you a peek into the past and is operated by the Truro Historical Society. Of special interest are native Wampanoag artifacts, Pilgrim tools and furniture, and mariner history. There is a tremendous amount of shipwreck artifacts because there have been 100 shipwrecks in the last 100 years (the winds drive the ships into the shallows).

Head of the Meadow Beach (all ages)
Head of the Meadow Road (off Route 6), North Truro; www.nps.gov/caco. Parking is $10 for the day, $30 for the seasonal national seashore pass.

The part of the Head of the Meadow Beach that's maintained by the Cape Cod National Seashore (the town of Truro manages the remainder) has restrooms and outdoor showers. There are no lifeguards here, but on a calm day this beach is one of the best along the national seashore.

The Pilgrim Heights Area (all ages)
Off Route 6, North Truro; www.nps.gov/caco. Free.

The Pilgrim Heights area of the national seashore has a nice trail to the place where the Cape's first European visitors found freshwater. Take the Pilgrim Spring Walk from the interpretive shelter. The Small Swamp trail is a short, fairly flat loop.

For bicycle enthusiasts, there's a 2-mile path from Head of the Meadow Beach stopping near High Head Road.

Pilgrim Lake Sand Dunes (all ages)
Highhead Road off Route 6 at the south end of Pilgrim Lake. Park at the Highhead parking lot at the Cape Cod National Seashore, Truro; (508) 487–1256 (Province Lands Visitors Center, Provincetown); www.nps.gov/caco. Free.

The Pilgrim Lake area of the Cape Cod National Seashore is the only place along the National Seashore where visitors can legally walk over the enormous sand dunes that roll across this part of the Cape. Previous visitors have worn away much of the sand and, with it, the beach grass that covers and preserves the dunes; therefore, the National Park Service restricts foot traffic on the dunes to this area.

Where to Eat

Adrian's, 535 Route 6, North Truro; (508) 487–4360; www.adriansrestaurant.com. Casual dining, eat indoors or outdoors overlooking the bay. $–$$$

Montano's Restaurant, 481 Route 6, Truro; (508) 487–2026; www.montanos .com. Italian cuisine and New England seafare. Dinner only, early-bird specials. Kids' menu. $–$$

Whitman House, Route 6, Truro; (508) 487–1740; www.whitmanhouse.com. Traditional Cape Cod setting. Voted best dining spot on the outer cape by *Cape Cod Life,* 1995–1998. Early-bird four-course boiled lobster special with all the fixings is very reasonable. $$–$$$

Where to Stay

Kalmar Village, 674 Shore Road, North Truro; (508) 487–0585 or (617) 247–0211; www.kalmarvillage.com. Cottage colony on private Beach Point; swimming pool, grills, and picnic tables outside each room; across from the national seashore. A list of available baby-sitters is maintained. $–$$$$

Provincetown

At the fist end of the Cape, Provincetown is an eclectic collection of open-minded artists, fishermen, windworn buildings, and seaside moors. Go here for the beaches, the whale watching, and the people-watching, which is especially good in this, New England's most tolerant seaside community. The **Provincetown Chamber of Commerce** is located at 307 Commercial Street, Provincetown 02657; (508) 487–3424; www.ptownchamber.com.

Herring Cove Beach (all ages)

Herring Cove Beach is at the end of Route 6, Provincetown; (508) 349–3785; www.nps.gov/caco. Parking is a one-time day fee of $10 (accepted at all National Seashore beaches). A Cape Cod national seashore pass for the season is $30.

One of Provincetown's best beaches for families is Herring Cove Beach, which has gentler waves than Race Point (see entry below). A snack bar, showers, and restrooms are available here. To be sure of a parking place in the summer, arrive early. *CAUTION:* There has been nude bathing reported on the stretch of beach to the left of the bathhouse, even though it is prohibited. Families should seek the beach to the right of the bathhouse.

Long Point Lighthouse and Wood End Lighthouse
(ages 12 and up) 🏛

Commercial Street, Provincetown. Not appropriate for young children or for anyone without sturdy footwear and good balance; best walked at low tide.

When it was built in 1827, Long Point was the center of a busy fishing community on the tip of the Cape. Now isolated at the end of a long breakwater, Long Point Lighthouse (and its companion, Wood End) can best be viewed from the rotary at the end of Commercial Street (while you're here, look for the plaque that commemorates the first landing place of the Pilgrims). If your family is up for a long walk along a rocky breakwater, park the car at the rotary and walk along the breakwater for about a half hour to reach Long Point. Another half-hour walk, to the end of the breakwater, will lead to Wood End Lighthouse. The unusual tower is square; most lighthouses are circular. Wood End was built in 1873. It flashes a red light every fifteen seconds, whereas Long Point flashes a green light; together they mark Provincetown Harbor's entrance. *CAUTION:* It's a long walk—bring something to drink and watch the tides.

Whale-Watching Tours
The best of the many whale-watch cruises are:

- **Dolphin Fleet,** McMillan Pier, Provincetown; (508) 349–1900 or (800) 826–9300; www.whalewatch.com. The ticket office is located in the Chamber of Commerce building on Commercial Street. The *Dolphin* operates from April through October. Rates, depending on the season, are $24 for adults, $20 for children 5 to 12, **free** for children under 5. There is a $2.00 discount given to seniors and AAA members, as well as a discount coupon that can be found on their Web site.

  Originators of whale watching on the East Coast, scientists and naturalists from the Center for Coastal Study guide every cruise and are available to answer questions.

- **Portuguese Princess**, MacMillan Wharf, Provincetown; (508) 487–2651 or (800) 442–3188; www.princesswhalewatch.com. The ticketing center is located at 70 Shank Painter Road. The *Princess* operates from April through October. Rates, depending on season, are $24 for adults, $20 for children 5 to 12; **free** for children under 5. Discounts include a AAA discount, early-bird special rates, and a discount coupon on their Web site.

  The *Portuguese Princess* is associated with WhaleNet, a data collection consortium of research and educational groups. A naturalist is on board with running commentary to help enhance the experience.

A Whale of a Trip

You'll find whale-watching trips advertised everywhere along the Cape (and in Boston and on the North Shore, too, for that matter), but the best place from which to take one is Provincetown. Why? Because it's closest to Stellwagen Bank, the whales' feeding ground, which is only 6 miles from Provincetown; other trips take much longer to reach the same spot. Most of the whale-watching expeditions from Provincetown are about three and a half hours long, but some last all day. Regardless of the weather on shore, be sure to bring a warm sweater and long pants for everyone in your party—even at the height of the summer, the wind on the open ocean can be downright cold.

Provincetown Heritage Museum (all ages)
460 Commercial Street and corner of Center Street, Provincetown; (508) 487–7098.

Art collection and model of the vessel *Rose Dorothea*. The museum has been extensively renovated.

The Provincetown Museum and Pilgrim Monument Tower
(all ages)
High Pole Hill, Provincetown; (508) 487–1310; www.pilgrim-monument.org. Open daily, April 1 through November 30, 9:00 A.M. to 5:00 P.M.; until 7:00 P.M. in July and August. The last admission is forty-five minutes before closing. Admission: $7.00 for adults, $3.50 for children 4 to 14, free for children under 4.

The Provincetown Museum and Pilgrim Monument is worth a visit for the view from the 252-foot-high tower that was modeled after the Campanile, or bell tower, in Siena, Italy. The tower was built to commemorate the landing of the Pilgrims. On a clear day the view of the curving Cape is breathtaking. The museum focuses on maritime history, Provincetown's diverse history, and the whaling industry.

National Seashore Visitor Center

While you're in the Province Lands area, stop at the **Province Lands Visitors Center** (508–487–1256). The center is open from 9:00 A.M. to 5:00 P.M. May through October.

Race Point Beach (all ages)

End of Race Point Road, off Route 6, Provincetown; (508) 349–3785; www.nps.gov/caco. Parking is a one-time day fee of $10 or $30 for a seasonal sticker (accepted at all National Seashore beaches).

Race Point has large sand dunes and smaller crowds, making it a great family beach. Race Point Beach is sheltered since it's the middle ground between the bay and the ocean. The waves are a little bigger, and the water is a little colder than Herring Cove Beach. Public showers and restrooms are available. Arrive early to get a parking spot.

Race Point Lighthouse (all ages)

Race Point Beach, Provincetown; (508) 487–9930; www.nps.gov/caco.

The 2-mile walk to reach Race Point Lighthouse is along Race Point Beach (bring refreshments, especially drinks; the long sandy walk back to the car can be tough for kids). Race Point Lighthouse was erected in 1816 to help ships navigate around the treacherous "knuckles" of the Cape to Provincetown. Between 1816 and 1946 more than a hundred shipwrecks were recorded in this area. Race Point Lighthouse has a white light and a foghorn that warns ships of low-visibility conditions. Race Point Lighthouse is managed by the Coast Guard although it's on National Seashore grounds. If your family doesn't have the energy to take the long walk to Race Point, the best view is from the Province Lands Visitors Center's observation deck. Race Point Lighthouse is also visible from Herring Cove Beach.

Other Things to See and Do

Art's Dune Tours, 9 Wash Avenue (corner of Standish and Commercial Streets in the center of Provincetown), Provincetown; (508) 487–1950 or (800) 894–1951; www.artsdunetours.com. Price changes seasonally, but it's approximately $15.00 per adult and $8.00 per child ages 6 to 11 for the one-hour tour. By reservation only. Go to the heart of the Cape Cod National Seashore. The dune tour traverses the sand, the shore, and the Atlantic. Each truck holds seven to eight passengers.

Expedition Whydah Sea Lab, MacMillan Wharf, Provincetown; (508) 487–8899; www.whydah.com. Authentic pirate treasure discovered from sunken ships.

Norma Glamp's Rubber Stamps, 357 Commercial Street, Provincetown; (508) 487–1870. Wide variety of stamps and colorful ink pads.

Where to Eat

Cafe Blasé, 328 Commercial Street, Provincetown; (508) 487–9465. Outdoor dining in a fun setting. $–$$

Lewis Brothers Ice Cream, 310 Commercial Street, Provincetown; (508) 487–1436. $

Michael Shay's, 350 Bradford Street, Provincetown; (508) 487–3368. Seventeen-foot salad bar, specializing in ribs and seafood; cozy decor with a wood-burning stove. Kid's menu. $$

Where to Stay

Provincetown Inn, 1 Commercial Street, Provincetown; (508) 487–9500 or (800) WHALEVU; www.provincetowninn.com. Private beach and outdoor pool. Rates include continental breakfast. Kids under 12 eat and stay for **free** from late June to mid-September. $–$$$$

Race Point Lighthouse Keepers House, Race Point Beach, Provincetown; (508) 487–9930. The property consists of a three-bedroom house with a kitchen, living room, and bathroom. Bring your own food and water (the running water isn't drinkable) and gas lanterns. Open April to November. $$

Martha's Vineyard

Martha's Vineyard provides more spectacular beaches and seaside atmosphere with less stress and fewer visitors than you'll see on the Cape. Only 7 miles from Falmouth at its closest point, the island is more populous and cosmopolitan than neighboring Nantucket. The Vineyard boasts large expanses of deep forest and acres of rolling farmland. The colorful cottages and Flying Horses Carousel in Oak Bluffs are beloved to the lucky children who live on the island as well as those who visit. Annual visitors treat their island vacations as sacred family rituals, booking their reservations as far as six or eight months ahead. Try to make your family's ferry and accommodations plans as early as possible.

The **Martha's Vineyard Chamber of Commerce** has a sophisticated telephone messaging system for ordering visitor information. The chamber can be reached at (508) 693–0085; www.mvy.com.

Destination Insider has a reservoir of rooms and represents most hotels and inns. Contact them at (508) 696–3900 or (866) 696–3900; www.vineyard.destination insider.com.

Trust **the Trustees**

Trust the trustees to do things right! The Trustees of Reservations offer tours that focus on Martha's Vineyard's fragile wildlife as well as natural history tours of Martha's Vineyard. If you are in the mood for more adventurous, active touring, the trustees have canoeing, fishing, and kayaking guided tours. You can reach them at (508) 693–7662 or (508) 627–3599.

The **Black Dog**

You will see Black Dog T-shirts everywhere. Children will probably enjoy reading *The Story of the Little Black Dog* by J. B. Spooner and Terre Lamb Seeley to help explain the popularity of the Black Dog!

Tisbury (aka Vineyard Haven)

Tisbury has great restaurants and shopping in a more relaxed setting than some of the other Vineyard towns. Vineyard Haven Harbor is a more romantic setting than bustling Oak Bluffs.

Nip N'Tuck Farm (all ages)
Vineyard Haven; (508) 693–1449. Open late spring through September.

Tours feature old farm buildings and farm animals. Buggy and hayrides are a treat for all ages. Seasonal farm stand sells farm-grown vegetables.

Other Things to See and Do

Black Dog General Store, two locations: Water Street and State Road, Vineyard Haven; (508) 696–8182 or (800) 884–9707 (customer service and mail order); www.theblackdog.com. Here's where you can buy those Black Dog T-shirts, sweatshirts, and hats that everyone seems to be wearing.

Island Cove Mini Golf, 369 State Road, Vineyard Haven; (508) 693–2611. Minigolf, rock climbing wall, grill, and ice cream.

Martha's Vineyard Bike Rentals, 4 Lagoon Pond Road (at Five Corners), Vineyard Haven; (866) 306–5351; www.marthas vineyardbikes.com. Children's mountain and hybrid bikes. For families with small children they have baby seats, joggers, and Burley trailers. Will deliver to any location.

Vineyard Playhouse, 24 Church Street, Vineyard Haven; (508) 693–6450 or (508) 696–6300; www.vineyardplayhouse.org. Family classics, recent hits, and holiday shows.

Winds Up, 199 Beach Road, Vineyard Haven; (508) 693–4252; www.windsupmv .com. Rent kayaks, sailboats, canoes, and other water-based equipment. Lessons can be arranged.

Where to Eat

Black Dog Bakery and Cafe, two locations: Water Street and State Road, Vineyard Haven; (508) 693–8190 or (508) 693–4786; www.theblackdog.com. Delectable desserts and baked goods all day, with sandwiches served at lunchtime. $

Black Dog Tavern, Beach Street Extension, Vineyard Haven Harbor, Vineyard Haven; (508) 693–9223; www .theblackdog.com. Full menu serving breakfast, lunch, and dinner. Fun and salty atmosphere. $$$

Zephrus at Mansion House, 9 Main Street, Vineyard Haven; (508) 693–3416; www.zephrus.com. Serving lunch and dinner, indoor dining or outdoor-protected patio; kids pasta of the day! $–$$$$

Where to Stay

Mansion House, 9 Main Street, Vineyard Haven; (508) 693–2200 or (800) 332–4112; www.mvmansionhouse.com. Rooms have different amenities ranging from soaking tubs, fireplaces, and ocean views to suites that have galley kitchens. At the health club and spa there is a chlorine-free, 75-foot pool with lifeguard (swimming classes in season). Full breakfast comes with the room. $$–$$$$

Martha's Vineyard Family Campground, 569 Edgartown Road, Vineyard Haven; (508) 693–3772; www.campmvfc .com. One mile from the Vineyard Haven ferry; only campground on Martha's Vineyard. A limited number of one- and two-room cabins are available. Tent sites (maximum of four people per site) and RV sites are also available, complete with campfire area. The main building has showers, restrooms, a laundry room, a rec hall, and a grocery store. $–$$

Oak Bluffs

The colorful gingerbread cottages of the Wesleyan Grove Campground were built here during the late nineteenth century to replace the tents used by Methodist parishioners who camped and worshiped here every summer. Observe the no-bicycles rule and quiet time, which begins at dusk and ends at sunrise.

Flying Horses Carousel (all ages)

Bottom of Circuit Avenue, Oak Bluffs; (508) 693–9481; www.mvpreservation.org /carousel.htm. Open daily 10:00 A.M. to 10:00 P.M. June to Labor Day, weekends in April and May, 11:00 A.M. to 4:30 P.M. September through October. Price: $1.00 per person, $8.00 for a ten-ride pass.

An old wooden building houses the Flying Horses Carousel, a national historic landmark that's wonderfully alive with merry-go-round lovers of all ages. It's the oldest operating carousel in the country; the horses were carved in 1876. There's even a brass ring.

Cycle Around . . .

A 10-mile flat bike path shuttles cyclists between Edgartown and Oak Bluffs. The far end of the Edgartown part of the path leads to Katama and South Beach.

Do You Know **the Score?**

Community sings are held weekly at 8:00 P.M. Wednesdays during July and August at the Tabernacle, Oak Bluffs, Cottage Colony Campground. Hymns, folk songs, rounds, spirituals, and patriotic songs are the standard. Donations accepted.

Hy-Line Cruises (all ages)

Information line is (508) 778–2600 or (800) 492–8082; www.hy-linecruises.com. Price: $28.00 round-trip or $14.00 one-way for adults, half-price for children 5 to 12, free for children 4 and under. Bikes are $10.00 round-trip, $5.00 for one-way.

Hy-Line Cruises has the only interisland ferry service between Oak Bluffs in Martha's Vineyard and Straight Wharf in Nantucket. The two-hour-and-fifteen-minute cruise has a snack bar and plenty of restrooms on board. Departures are three times a day, and reservations are not necessary (the ferry always has space).

Other Things to See and Do

Take it Easy, Baby, 35 Circuit Avenue, Oak Bluffs; (508) 693-2864. Specializing in vintage and new clothing for adults and kids.

Where to Eat

Giordano's, 107 Circuit Avenue, Oak Bluffs; (508) 693-0184; www.giosmv.com. Open for lunch and dinner, May to mid-September. Serves up enormous portions of spaghetti, fried clams, fried chicken, and the like. $–$$$

Jimmy Seas Pan Pasta Restaurant, 32 Kennebec Avenue, Oak Bluffs; (508) 696-8550. Food served in the pan it was cooked in—brought sizzling to your table. Casual atmosphere, huge portions, open only for dinner. $$–$$$$

Where to Stay

Oak Bluffs Inn, 64 Circuit Avenue, Oak Bluffs; (508) 693-7171 or (800) 955-6235; www.oakbluffsinn.com. Open April to end of October. Rates include breakfast. A cupola-topped, three-story pink building; nine comfortable rooms, including three in the carriage house. $$–$$$$

Cottage Museum (all ages)

Oak Bluffs; (508) 693-7784. Open Monday through Saturday during the summer. Price: $1.50 for adults, 50 cents for ages 3 to 12, under 3 is free. View a typical cottage house complete with period furnishings and vintage photographs that explain the history of the Martha's Vineyard Camp Meeting established by the Methodists.

I Scream, **You Scream**

Mad Martha's is a Martha's Vineyard institution serving twenty-three great homemade ice-cream flavors and seven kinds of nonfat yogurt. My favorite is the red, white, and blue apple pie ice cream. Try one of their unique to-die-for chocolate lovers dream sundaes, such as the Sinful Chocolate Sundae or the twelve-scoop Pig Sundae (ordered by saying "oink"). There are several locations on the island:

- 23 Lake Street, Oak Bluffs; (508) 693–2262 (ice-cream and coffee shop)
- 20 Union Street, Vineyard Haven; (508) 693–5883
- 7 North Water Street, Edgartown; (508) 627–8761

Edgartown

Stately homes line the narrow streets of this seaport village. A great yachting center, Edgartown attracts seafarers today. Walk to Edgartown Lighthouse from North Water Street. In 1828 the lighthouse was built on what was then an island in Edgartown Harbor; after a storm in the early twentieth century, a sandbar emerged from the water and attached the smaller island to the Vineyard. The **Chappaquiddick Passenger and Vehicle Ferry,** (508) 627–9427, operates year-round (from 7:00 A.M. to midnight in season). Catch it at Dock Street in Edgartown for a short five-minute crossing.

Felix Neck Wildlife Sanctuary (all ages)

Off Edgartown–Vineyard Haven Road to Felix Neck Drive, Edgartown; (508) 627–4850; www.massaudubon.org (click on sanctuary). Open year-round. Trails open daily from dawn to dusk. The visitor center is open daily from June to October, and Tuesday through Sunday from October to May from 8:00 A.M. to 4:00 P.M. Admission: $4.00 for adults, $3.00 for seniors and children 3 to 12, free for children under 3.

A preserve that's affiliated with the Massachusetts Audubon Society, Felix Neck Wildlife Sanctuary comprises 350 acres of forests, salt marshes, and fields, as well as beaches and an excellent interpretive center that conducts guided nature walks year-round. There are several pleasant 1½-mile hiking trails that leave from the sanctuary's exhibit building. A magnet for bird-watchers; sightings have included ospreys and swallows.

Children's **Favorites**

Delightful children's books with Island settings are:

- *Morning Beach* by Leslie Baker. Set in Martha's Vineyard.
- *Nat, Nat the Nantucket Cat* by Peter W. Barnes, illustrated by Susan Arciero. Set in Nantucket.

South Beach (older children and strong swimmers)
Off Katama Road, south of Edgartown. Restrooms and changing rooms in season only. Free.

Also known as Katama Beach, South Beach is the most popular beach on the island. Lifeguards patrol about three-quarters of the beach. There are no public facilities off-season. South Beach is not appropriate for younger children or weak swimmers, since the undertow can be treacherous. It's accessible by shuttle bus from Edgartown.

Joseph Sylvia State Beach (all ages)
Beach Road, Edgartown to Oak Bluffs. Open year-round. Free.

This 2-mile-long beach is owned by the state and maintained by the county. The section of Joseph Sylvia State Beach known as Bend-in-the-Road Beach in Edgartown is a nice spot for kids; there are no facilities, although there are lifeguards in-season.

My Toi and East Beach (all ages)
Dike Road, Chappaquiddick; (508) 627–7689. Directions: From the Edgartown/Chappaquiddick Ferry, take Chappaquiddick Road for 2½ miles to Dike Road (a dirt road on the left at the curve).

The property comprises a Japanese-style garden with ornamental bridges arching over ponds (one of which leads to a serene island). Farther down the road is East Beach ($3.00 per adult, children **free**), part of Cape Poque Wildlife Refuge and Wasque Reservation (www.thetrustees.org).

Vineyard Museum (all ages)
59 School Street (corner of Cooke Street), Edgartown; (508) 627–4441; www.marthas vineyardhistory.org. Open mid-June through the end of October, Tuesday through Saturday 10:00 A.M. to 5:00 P.M.; from November to mid-June, Wednesday through Friday 1:00 to 4:00 P.M., Saturday 10:00 A.M. to 5:00 P.M. Winter pricing: $6.00 for adults, $4.00 for kids. Summer pricing: $7.00 for adults, $4.00 for kids 6 to 15, under 6 free.

The Vineyard Museum is a campus of five buildings: the Cooke House, the Carriage Shed, the Pease House, the Foster Maritime Gallery, and the Fresnel Lens Tower. Everything on display relates to the history of Martha's Vineyard.

The Cooke House is a colonial home built in 1765 with eleven rooms of exhibits relating to the life and history of Martha's Vineyard and its residents. In the attached Tool Shed various tools and equipment are on display.

The Carriage Shed displays seagoing vessels and land vehicles, including a boat used during whaling days, pieces of shipwreck found off the coast, a hearse, a nineteenth-century fire engine, and a wagon.

The Pease House is a nineteenth-century home with five gallery spaces: a permanent exhibit, a Native American exhibit, and an ever-changing exhibit done by local students. Two exhibits currently on display are oral histories of island residents and artwork from whaler's logbooks. A museum shop is located in this building.

The Foster Maritime Gallery is a research library that has maritime exhibits.

The Fresnel Lens Tower with the original Fresnel lens from the Gay Head Lighthouse is the last structure on the campus. The lens, a series of more than 1,000 prisms, was replaced by an electric light. The lens is lighted up for a few hours every evening.

Other Things to See and Do

Edgartown Harbor Tours, bottom of Main Street, Edgartown; (508) 939–9282; www.edgartownharbortours.com. Departs hourly noon to 6:00 P.M. Price is $18.00 per adult and $8.00 for kids.

World of Reptiles and Birds at Felix Neck, off Edgartown–Vineyard Haven Road, Edgartown; (508) 627–5634. Educational programs featuring these creatures are held on the weekends.

Where to Eat

Among the Flowers, 17 Mayhew Lane off North Water Street, Edgartown; (508) 627–3233. Open May through June and September through October for breakfast and lunch; July and August for breakfast, lunch, and dinner. Cafe serving PBJ and other regular fare. $–$$

Atria, 137 Main Street, Edgartown; (508) 627–5850; www.atriamv.com. Open for dinner April through January. A very "in" place in Edgartown, great food. $$$–$$$$

The Seafood Shanty, 31 Dock Street, Edgartown; (508) 627–8622; www.the seafoodshanty.com. On the harbor, next to Memorial Wharf. Great family restaurant, serving lunch and dinner, specializing in local seafood. $–$$$$

The Wharf, 3 Lower Main Street, Edgartown; (508) 627–9966. Open year-round for lunch and dinner. Great family-style restaurant. $–$$$

Lighthouse Tours

The lighthouses of Edgartown, Aquinnah/Gay Head (508–645–2211), and East Chop are maintained by the Martha's Vineyard Historical Society (508–627–4441). The society opens the lighthouses on a limited basis from late June to September (for tours and views) usually one and a half hours prior to and a half hour after sunset on weekends (the East Chop Lighthouse is open on Friday only) from mid-June to early October. The price is $3.00 per person for this gorgeous view.

Where to Stay

Edgartown Commons, 1 Pease Point Way, Edgartown; (508) 627–4671 or (800) 439–4671; www.edgartowncommons .com. Playground, outdoor swimming pool, grills, and kitchen facilities in the rooms. Close to town and a public transportation stop. $$–$$$$

Shiretown Inn, 44 North Water Street, Edgartown; (508) 627–3353 or (800) 541–0090; www.shiretowninn.com. Open year-round. Old whaling captain's home with outlying carriage house and cottage. Lovely gardens; close to the harbor. On the National Register of Historic Places. $$–$$$$

Summer House, 96 South Summer Street, Edgartown; (508) 627–4857; www.summerhousemv.com. Open mid-May to mid-October. A comfortable home in a quiet part of Edgartown. It's run by a schoolteacher who's one of the friendliest Vineyarders we've met. Children over age 10 only, please. $$$

Victorian Inn, 24 South Water Street; Edgartown; (508) 627–4784; www.thevic .com. Rates include breakfast, tea and cookies in the afternoon (in the garden!). Open Valentine's Day to New Year's. Located a block away from the harbor and in the center of the shopping district. Each charming room has its own personality (some with four-posters and harbor views). Children 8 and older. $$–$$$$

West Tisbury

West Tisbury is a typical New England village, with its prerequisite white church, general store, and fine clapboard homes.

Cedar Tree Neck Wildlife Sanctuary (all ages)
Indian Hill Road, West Tisbury; www.mvy.com/conservation.html.

Three hundred acres with trails through forests, dunes, and beach. Scenic trails and hilltop views. No picnicking or swimming allowed. Owned and managed by Sheriff's Meadow, a Martha's Vineyard land trust.

Amazing
Vineyard Facts

Martha's Vineyard bike paths cover about 22 miles past picturesque villages and scenic views.

Manuel Correllus State Forest (all ages)

Off Edgartown–West Tisbury Road and Barnes Road; (508) 693–2540; www.state
.ma.us/dem/parks/corr.htm. Open year-round dawn to dusk. **Free.**

The 5,140 acres of Manuel Correllus State Forest are crisscrossed with bike, eques-
trian, and hiking trails. Park near the Barnes Road entrance to the park.

Martha's Vineyard Fair (all ages)

35 Panhandle Road, West Tisbury; (508) 693–4343 or (508) 693–9549. Held in late
August; admission charged (last year it was $20 per adult).

This old-fashioned fair is a bit more upscale than other state fairs, having dressage
and jumper demonstrations, a dog show, and gymnastic events. The midway features
rides, games, and fried food.

Oldies but Goodies

The Silverscreen Society (508–696–9369; www.mvfilmsociety.com) sponsors "Movies under the Stars" at the **Featherstone Center for the Arts** in
Oak Bluffs (Barnes Road ½ mile north of the Vineyard Haven/Edgartown
road blinker) on Wednesday nights during July (rain date Thursday
nights). Movies start at 8:00 P.M., and admission is $6.00 per adult, $4.00
per child under 12, or $15.00 a carload (no sneaking anyone into the
trunk!). Introduce silver screen classics to your kids that you haven't
seen since you were their age! Movies from the thirties to the sixties are
shown Thursday nights at the **Grange Hall,** State Road in West Tisbury.
Showtime is at 8:00 P.M. with a short introduction prior to the film. Tickets are $6.00 for adults and $4.00 for those under 18. To round out this
old-fashioned down-home evening, lemonade and popcorn can be
purchased!

Swan Lake

Our youngest daughter's trip to the Vineyard isn't complete without a stop to feed the swans and ducks in the lovely pond next to the West Tisbury Police Station.

Polly Hill Arboretum (all ages)

809 State Road, West Tisbury; (508) 693–9426; www.pollyhillarboretum.org. The arboretum is open year-round (except Wednesday) Memorial Day to Columbus Day from 7:00 A.M. to 7:00 P.M.; dusk to dawn the rest of the year. The visitor center is open from 9:00 A.M. to 4:00 P.M. Thursday through Tuesday Memorial Day to the end of September and then weekends through Columbus Day. In July and August tours are offered at 10:00 A.M. and 2:00 P.M. Suggested donation: $5.00 for adults, 12 and under are free.

Initially a sheep farm, the Butcher family (Polly's parents) purchased forty acres of the farm in 1926. Polly eventually inherited the property, and she acquired twenty more acres, increasing the size of the piece to its present sixty acres. Polly planted seeds and nurtured plants that weren't native to the Vineyard, and through natural selection and crossbreeding, she got a hardier stock that was able to survive the harsh conditions of Vineyard soil and climate. Your family is free to roam and discover the famous North Tisbury azaleas, the Tunnel of Love, and the Dogwood Allee. No pets please.

Other Things to See and Do

Alley's General Store, State Road, West Tisbury; (508) 693–0088. Old-fashioned country store.

Crow Hollow Farm, Tiah's Cove Road, West Tisbury; (508) 696–4554; www.crow hollowfarm.com. Trail rides on the farm and neighboring conservation lands. Lessons given.

Kayaks of Martha's Vineyard, Lamberts Cove Road, West Tisbury; (508) 693–3885; www.kayakmv.com. Rentals, guided trips, and lessons.

Long Point Wildlife Refuge, Edgartown–West Tisbury Road, West Tisbury; (508) 693–3678; www.thetrustees.org. Price: $9.00 per car, plus $3.00 per adult. Six hundred and thirty-two acres, 2 miles of trail, and a beach. Boating and swimming activities, tours at 8:30 A.M. and 1:00 P.M. (Call 508–693–7392 for tour reservations.) The beach here is considered by many to be the best on the Vineyard.

Menemsha Hills Reservation, North Road, Chilmark; (508) 693–3678; www .thetrustees.org. Free. Two hundred and eleven acres, 3 miles of trails.

Troubled Shores Comedy Lab, State Road, Grange Hall, West Tisbury; (508) 939–9368; www.troubledshores.com. Original sketch comedy show at 8:30 P.M. every other Monday in July and August.

Warbird Flight, Martha's Vineyard Airport, West Tisbury; (508) 221–0741; www .warbirdflight.com. Scenic flight over Martha's Vineyard and its lighthouses.

Wimp Improv at the Grange Hall, State Road, West Tisbury; (508) 939–9368 or (508) 696–8475; www.wimprov.com. Performances Wednesdays June through October at 8:00 P.M. July and August has an additional Tuesday night show. The new feature is Imp, improv for kids with shows every other Monday at 7:00 P.M. in July and August. All proceeds are donated to local charities.

Where to Stay

Cove Apartments, 22 Runner Road, West Tisbury; (508) 693–9199. One-bedroom apartments with kitchens, sleeping up to four people. Pond canoeing and beaches nearby. $$

Hosteling International, West Tisbury Road, 1 Edgartown Road, West Tisbury; (508) 693–2665 or (888) 901–2087; www.capecodhostels.org. Five dorms, open April 1 to mid-October. Children are welcome. Credit cards accepted. $

Aquinnah (formerly known as Gay Head) and Menemsha

Aquinnah, or Gay Head, is known for its breathtaking cliffs and views of the ocean. It's a more remote, sparsely populated area of Martha's Vineyard. The Aquinnah Cultural Center opened its first phase, a traditional longhouse, in summer 2000. Eventually a museum, gallery, and visitor center will complete the campus. If you've seen the film *Jaws,* you may recognize Menemsha and Dutcher's Dock, which served as a backdrop in many of the film's harbor shots.

Aquinnah/Gay Head Beach (all ages)
State Road near Aquinnah Circle, Aquinnah; (508) 645–2300. Parking is $15.

Below the colorful clay cliffs, Aquinnah/Gay Head Beach is very popular during the summer. Because parking is limited and the beach extends south for several miles, it's rarely crowded. *NOTE:* There are no lifeguards here, and the closest restrooms (50 cent charge—bring change) are on the center of the circle. You'll probably see people climbing up the cliffs. Resist the temptation; if caught, you will be fined. The worst of the cliffs' erosion is a direct result of foot traffic. Moreover, the cliffs are the private property of the Wampanoag tribe, who run the town of Aquinnah/Gay Head. *CAUTION:* Nude bathing on some stretches of beach.

Gay Head Lighthouse (all ages)
Aquinnah/Gay Head; (508) 645–2211. Open mid-June to mid-September for tours. Opening one and a half hours prior to sunset and closing a half hour after sunset. Price: $3.00 per person.

The redbrick Gay Head Lighthouse is a spectacular setting. On Friday, Saturday, and Sunday evenings during the summer, you can go up to the lighthouse's observation deck to watch the sun setting over the Sound.

Where to Eat

Aquinnah, on the cliffs, Gay Head; (508) 645–3867. Open late May through the summer, seven days a week; Friday and Saturday off-season. Serving breakfast, lunch, and dinner in season. Beautiful views and bountiful food. Fresh seafood and pasta specialties; children's menu. *TIP:* As the sun sets, the local, friendly, and curious skunks make their way to the outside deck. Moral: Go early! $–$$$$

Home Port, 512 North Road, Menemsha; (508) 645–2679. Open mid-May to mid-October for dinner. Casual seafood restaurant just steps from the water. Reservations required. $$$$

Where to Stay

Duck Inn Pigout, 10 Duck Pond, off State Road, Gay Head; (508) 645–9018. Open year-round. Comfortable, health-oriented bed-and-breakfast. The kids will enjoy Annie the Dalmatian, Franklin the Scaredy Cat, Webster the Manx Cat, and Van Gogh and Daisy the pigs, the inn mascots; parents will love the hot tub and massages. Children are welcome and one room is available to guests with pets. (One night **free** with a week's stay.) $$–$$$

Nantucket

Nantucket's unique character has much to do with its distance from the mainland—it's a good 30 miles out to sea. Unlike cosmopolitan Martha's Vineyard, Nantucket (which means "faraway island" in the Wampanoag language) is more traditional and less crowded, even during the summer. Moors cover a large percentage of the island, and its bike paths and long beaches make for wonderful family vacations. The stocky Brant Point Lighthouse is one of New England's shortest beacons (it's just 31 feet high); it's also one of Massachusetts's most photographed spots. When you leave the island by ferry, you'll see lots of visitors throwing pennies overboard as the ship rounds Brant Point. This tradition supposedly ensures that they will return to the island.

For a visitor information packet, contact the **Nantucket Island Chamber of Commerce,** 48 Main Street, Nantucket 02554 (508–228–1700; www.nantucket chamber.org). Also helpful is the **Nantucket Visitor Service Center,** 25 Federal Street, Nantucket 02554; (508–228–0925; www.nantucket-ma.gov), open daily in season 9:00 A.M. to 6:00 P.M. For information on hotels, B&Bs, and condos, call Martha's Vineyard and Nantucket Reservations at (800) 649–5671 or (508) 693–7200; www .mvreservation.com. For information on the ferry service to Nantucket from the Cape area, see the Hyannis Ferries sidebar or the Freedom Cruise Line in Harwichport in this chapter. For interisland ferry service provided by Hy-Line Cruises, see the Martha's Vineyard section in this chapter.

Fun **Facts**

Nantucket is 14 miles long by 3½ miles wide—and nearly 40 percent is protected conservation land.

Actors Theatre of Nantucket (all ages)

2 Centre Street (at the Methodist Church), Nantucket; (508) 228–6325; www. nantuckettheatre.com. Box office open 4:00 P.M. to 9:00 P.M.

The Actors Theatre in Nantucket has been a tradition in Nantucket since 1985. The summer season repertoire can range from the dramatic to the comedic play; from readings to a short-play festival; from an improv comedy group to a family matinee!

Children's Beach (all ages)

Off South Beach Street on Harbor View Way, Nantucket; (508) 228–7213. Free.

Children's Beach on Nantucket Harbor is appropriately named because it's perfect for very young children. There is no surf. It's very scenic, and your kids can watch the harbor activity and wave at the steamship passengers as they go to and fro from the island. It offers a wheelchair-accessible restroom, lifeguards, an excellent snack bar, a playground, a grassy play area, picnic tables, and organized activities for kids. Thursday and Sunday evening band concerts are held in July and August; Friday evenings there are movies. Children's Beach is well located and is a short 2 blocks from town.

Dionis Beach (all ages)

Dionis Road, off Eel Point Road, Nantucket; (508) 228–7213. Free.

Beach swimming is safe for children because there is no surf. Lifeguard on duty in-season; wheelchair-accessible restrooms. Limited parking.

Light Up My Life

Three memorable Nantucket Lighthouses are:

- **Brant Point Lighthouse** (Nantucket Harbor entrance, second oldest lighthouse in the nation)
- **Great Point Lighthouse** (northern tip)
- **Sankaty Head Lighthouse** (eastern tip)

Marcia's Favorite Nantucket Island
Biking Paths

The Nantucket Visitor Service Center has all the bike paths consolidated onto one easy-to-use map.

- **Madaket Bike Path.** The prize at the end of the path (approximately 5 miles) is Madaket Beach, great for sunsets but dangerous swimming for kids. The path can have some inclines and sharp curves. A 1-mile extension off this bike path goes on to Dionis Beach.

- **Polpis Bike Path.** This is the longest bike path (8 miles), with some gradual hills and curving corners.

- **'Sconset Beach Bike Path.** Families enjoy biking to 'Sconset Beach via the 7-mile 'Sconset Bike Path, which parallels Milestone Road. There are some mild hills. It's approximately one hour to 'Sconset.

- **The Surfside Bike Path.** A 3-mile-long, flat trail that leads from the town of Nantucket to its best beach. Take Main Street to Pleasant Street; turn right on Atlantic Avenue and proceed to Surfside. The path can be crowded.

Francis Street Beach (all ages)
Washington Street Extension, Nantucket; (508) 228–7213.

Francis Street Beach is a small beach located on Nantucket Harbor, so it's a mild beach for children to play around the water with a public restroom, kayak rental, and calm water. Four blocks from the center of town.

First Congregational Church and Tower (all ages)
62 Centre Street, Nantucket; (508) 228–0950; www.nantucketfcc.org. **Open mid-June to mid-October, Monday through Saturday 10:00 A.M. to 4:00 P.M. Suggested donation: Adults $2.50 and children 3 to 12 50 cents.**

The tower offers magnificent views of Nantucket on a clear day (Nantucket is only 14 miles long, and the tower is located near the midpoint of the island).

Jetties Beach (all ages)
Bathing Beach Road, Nantucket; (508) 228–7213. **Free. Ample parking.**

Lots of facilities—tennis courts, wheelchair-accessible restrooms, showers, a snack bar, a volleyball net, kayak and windsurfing rentals, beach-accessible wheelchair, tennis and swimming lessons by the week, boardwalk onto the beach, and a playground—

plus rental chairs and lifeguards make this Nantucket's best beach for families. Since Jetties Beach is approximately ¾ of a mile from town, the NRTA (Nantucket Regional Transit Authority) shuttle is recommended over walking and dragging the children and assorted paraphernalia (pick it up downtown). Jetties Beach is where the annual Sand-castle and Sculpture Day contest is held in mid-August.

Madaket Beach (all ages)
Madaket Road, Nantucket; (508) 228–7213. Free.

Madaket Beach on the south shore is one of the most beautiful beaches on the islands. Sunsets are to be savored here. The surf can be rolling and heavy at times, so it's best to keep a firm grip on children. Restrooms and lifeguards. Occasional erosion due to weather and surf. There is limited parking, and Madaket is quite far from town (relatively speaking), so take the NRTA shuttle from town.

Maria Mitchell Association (all ages)
The Maria Mitchell Association is headquartered at 3 Vestal Street; (508) 228–9198; (www.mmo.org). Properties include the Aquarium, the Hinchman House, the Maria Mitchell Birthplace, the Loines Observatory, the Marcia Mitchell Observatory, and the Science Library. The properties are at various locations just beyond Main Street in Nantucket. The observatories and Science Library are open year-round; other properties are open seasonally Tuesday through Saturday from 10:00 A.M. to 4:00 P.M. A visitor pass including all association properties is $10.00 for adults, $7.00 for children 6 to 14, under 6 free. This is the most cost-effective way to buy tickets for the museum because individual locations charge $4.00 for adults and $3.00 for kids.

Maria Mitchell was the first professional woman astronomer to discover a comet (the Maria Mitchell Comet), and she did it on Nantucket, from the roof of the Pacific Bank located downtown. Her father constructed an observatory on top of his bank building on Main Street. The **Maria Mitchell Observatory** (3 Vestal Street; 508–228–9273) is a research facility but conducts daytime tours for daytime observation of the sun and sunspots. There are also permanent exhibits on display. The tours are at 11:00 A.M. Tuesday through Saturday during the summer season and at 11:00 A.M. on Saturday during the off-season. Later, the **Loines Observatory** was constructed (59 Milk Street Extension; 508–228–9273); it is known for its nighttime tours held on Monday, Wednesday, and Friday at 9:00 P.M. mid-June through mid-September, and Friday evenings only September through mid-June. The visitor pass doesn't include the nighttime tour, which charges $10.00 per adult and $6.00 per child ages 6 to 14 (under 6 is free). Maria Mitchell was the librarian at the Nantucket Athenaeum for twenty years before becoming an astronomy professor at Vassar College. The library of the **Maria Mitchell Center** (2 Vestal Street; 508–228–9219) has a section for kids, as well as a fascinating collection of Maria's nineteenth-century science books and papers. Next door is **Maria's birthplace** (1 Vestal Street; 508–228–2896), which has the telescope she was using when she discovered "her" comet. The **Aquarium** (28

Washington Street; 508–228–5387) gives visitors an insider's look at the marine life of the island through its many displays and sponsors field trips. The **Hinchman House** (7 Milk Street; 508–228–0898) is a natural-history museum focusing on Nantucket's natural habitats; popular Nantucket ecology and birding trips are offered.

Nantucket Community School's Children's Summer Theatre and Camp (ages 8 to 18)

Nantucket High School Auditorium, 10 Surfside Road, Nantucket; (508) 228–8513. Children's theater program from end of June through mid-August.

Children perform in adaptations of popular and widely known plays and musicals. Plays are mounted with professional sets and costuming. This children's summer theater (since 1996) is by children and for children. One-week sessions make it doable for visitors.

Nantucket Life Saving Museum (all ages)

158 Polpis Road, Nantucket; (508) 228–1885; www.nantucketlifesaving.org. Open June 15 through Columbus Day, 9:30 A.M. to 4:00 P.M. Admission: $5.00 for adults, $2.00 for children 6 to 12, free for children under 6.

The museum is a reproduction of an original lifesaving station on Nantucket. Memorabilia includes lifesaving equipment (a rare surfboat and an authentic beach cart), original photographs, artifacts from sunken ships (the *Andrea Doria,* a luxury cruise ship with registry from Italy, went down in Nantucket waters in the 1950s), and remains from Island lighthouses (the Great Point Lighthouse lens was recently installed in the Lantern Room).

Cisco Beach (ages 7 and up)

End of Hummock Pond Road, Nantucket; (508) 228–7213. Free.

Heavy-surf beach on the south side of Nantucket, beautiful raw views of the untamed sea. Lifeguarded, but recommended for children and adults that know how to swim. Limited parking.

Marcia's
TopAnnualEvents
on Cape Cod, Martha's Vineyard, and Nantucket

- **Daffodil Festival,** April, Nantucket; (508) 228–1700; www.nantucket chamber.org

- **Spring Fling,** end of April, Heritage Museums & Gardens, Sandwich; (508) 888–3300; www.heritagemuseumsandgardens.org

- **Brewster in Bloom,** end of April, Brewster; (508) 896–3500; www .brewstercapecod.org

- **Maritime Week,** Cape Lighthouses open to the public, May; (508) 362–3828; www.capecodcommission.org

- **Rhododendron Week,** mid-May to mid-June, Heritage Museums & Gardens, Sandwich; (508) 888–3300; www.heritagemuseumsand gardens.org

- **Figawi Race Weekend,** late May, Hyannis to Nantucket and back, Hyannis; (508) 778–6100; www.figawi.com

- **Nantucket Film Festival,** mid-June, Nantucket; (508) 325–6274; www.nantucketfilmfestival.org

- **Kid's Day,** mid-June, Heritage Museums & Gardens, Sandwich; (508) 888–3300; www.heritagemuseumsandgardens.org

- **Portuguese Festival and Blessing of the Fleet,** Macmillian Wharf, late June, Provincetown; (508) 487–3420; www.provincetown.com

- **Oak Bluff's Harbor Festival,** June, Oak Bluffs; (508) 693–3392

- **West Tisbury's Farmer's Market,** June through September, West Tisbury, Martha's Vineyard; www.mvy.com

- **Fourth of July Fireworks,** July 4, Hyannis, Falmouth Heights, Provincetown, Chatham, and Edgartown

- **Illumination Boat Parade,** July 4, Shawme Pond, Sandwich; (508) 888–4361

- **Mashpee Pow-Wow,** July, Tribal Grounds, 483 Great Neck Road South, Mashpee; (508) 477–0208

- **Daylily Days and Sale,** mid-July, Heritage Museums & Gardens, Sandwich; (508) 888–3300; www.heritagemuseumsandgardens.org

- **Barnstable County Fair,** July, Barnstable County Fairgrounds, East Falmouth; (508) 563–3200; www.barnstablecountyfair.org
- **Edgartown Regatta,** mid-July, Edgartown, Martha's Vineyard; (508) 627–4361; www.mvy.com
- **Falmouth Road Race,** August, Falmouth to Woods Hole; (508) 540–7000; www.falmouthroadrace.com
- **Peter Rabbit's Annual Fair,** August, Thornton Burgess Museum, Water Street, Sandwich; (508) 888–6870; www.thorntonburgess.com
- **Moshur Pageant,** August, Aquinnah; (508) 645–9265; www.wampanoagtribe.net
- **Cape Cod Air Show,** early August, Otis Air Force Base, Bourne; (508) 968–4003; www.capecodairshow.org
- **Carnival Week Parade,** mid-August, Provincetown; (508) 487–2313 or (800) 637–8696; www.provincetown.com
- **Oak Bluffs' Fireworks,** mid-August, Oak Bluffs Harbor, Martha's Vineyard; (508) 693–0085; www.mvy.com
- **Illumination Night,** mid-August, Oak Bluffs, Martha's Vineyard; (508) 693–0085; www.mvy.com
- **Sandcastle and Sculpture Contest,** mid-August, Jetties Beach, Nantucket; (508) 228–1700; www.nantucketchamber.com
- **Scallop Festival,** September, Buzzards Bay Park, Bourne; (508) 759–6000; www.capecodcanalchamber.org
- **Cape Cod Stampede Professional Rodeo,** early September, Barnstable County Fairgrounds; (508) 563–3200; www.capecodstampede.org
- **Harwich Cranberry Festival,** mid-September, Harwich; (508) 430–2811; www.harwichcc.com
- **Striped Bass and Bluefish Derby,** mid-September through mid-October, Martha's Vineyard; (508) 693–0085; www.mvy.com
- **Oktoberfest,** early October, Mashpee Commons, Mashpee; (508) 539–1400, extension 519; www.mashpeechamber.com
- **Pilgrim Monument & Lighting,** November, Provincetown; (508) 487–1310; www.pilgrim-monument.org
- **Christmas Stroll,** first Saturday in December, downtown Nantucket; (508) 228–1700; www.nantucketchamber.org

The Black **Heritage Trail**

The African Meeting House, 29 York Street, is the second oldest structure in the United States built by and for free Africans. It was used as a church, a school, and a meeting place. This historic building is now owned by the Museum of African American History, Boston. For a self-guided tour brochure of important African American sites on Nantucket, call (508) 228–9833. Open Tuesday through Saturday 11:00 A.M. to 3:00 P.M. year-round. Fees: $3.00 for adults, $1.00 for ages 12 and under.

Miacomet Beach (ages 7 and up)
End of Miacomet Road (paved road turns to dirt, go about a half mile to the end for Miacomet Beach. *WARNING:* **Do not take any of the branch turns, or you may end up at a nude beach—not a family oriented outing for most people!), Nantucket; (508) 228–7213. Free.**

Even though this is a south-side beach with heavy surf, there is a freshwater pond that is great for swimming, especially for beginners. Lifeguards on duty and a parking lot are your only amenities.

'Sconset Beach (all ages)
Siasconset Road to the end of Gulley Road, Nantucket; (508) 228–7213. Free.

'Sconset Beach, a long, remote, narrow stretch, can be a bit seaweedy, but your family may overlook the inconvenience if you enjoy having lots of room to yourselves (artists and rich folks hang out in this part of the island). There's a swingset here, too. There are no restrooms or snack facilities here, but the beach is lifeguarded in season and restrooms are nearby. Occasional erosion due to weather. In fact, more homes have been lost to the sea here in the last ten years than on the entire east coast! Luckily, the erosion has stopped in the last year and a half.

Surfside Beach (ages 7 and up)
Surfside Road, Nantucket; (508) 228–7213. Free.

Surfside's heavy surf, typical of the south side of the island, makes it inappropriate for families with younger children, but strong swimmers who love bodysurfing will enjoy it. This beach can be crowded with college kids and surf casters, but Surfside is long enough to accommodate everyone. Facilities include a large parking lot, accessible restrooms, showers, rental chairs and umbrellas, and a snack bar. Lifeguards are on duty. This beach is available via the Nantucket Regional Transit Authority, which can be boarded in downtown Nantucket.

Whaling Museum (all ages)

Broad Street, Nantucket; (508) 228–1736 or (508) 228–1894; www.nha.org. Open year-round. Admission: $10.00 for adults, $8.00 for children. An inclusive pass available for an extra fee allows entry to all historical sites operated by the Nantucket Historical Association, the museum, and walking tour. The History Ticket is $15.00 for adults and $10.00 for kids under 18, and it's good for a year if you don't wish to see all the sights at once. Also there is a discounted family ticket for $35.00.

Nantucket in its heyday was the whaling capital of the world. Visit the Whaling Museum to see a vivid explanation of the phrase "Nantucket sleigh ride." That's what happens when your harpoon gets stuck in a whale's back, and the whale decides to take you and your companions for a ride through the waves. Start your visit with one of the three daily lectures before touring the whaling museum. The historical properties consist of:

- **Hadwen House,** 96 Main Street—Built in 1845, symbol of the wealth accumulated during Nantucket's era as the "Whaling Capital of the World." Set aside a half hour for the guided tour.

- **Jethro Coffin House,** Sunset Hill Road—Oldest surviving home in Nantucket (1686). Allow thirty minutes for the guided tour.

- **Old Mill,** Prospect Street—Oldest operating mill in the country. Guided tour lasts for half an hour.

- **Old Gaol,** 15 R Vestal Street—Set aside fifteen minutes for the self-guided, text-paneled tour and a good twenty minutes to find it (you are now being challenged to do it in less time!). Defunct jail built in 1805. Last resident prisoner in 1933.

- **Quaker Meetinghouse,** 7 Fair Street—This is the first museum acquired by the Nantucket Historical Association. Early Quaker meeting house built in 1838. Brochure on site will be your guide (budget twenty minutes).

- **Fire Hose Cart House,** 8 Gardner Street—Rare firefighting equipment on display. Self-guided tour (taking about fifteen minutes) of the last firehouse on Nantucket Island dating back to the mid-1800s.

All properties are open in season Monday through Saturday 10:00 A.M. to 5:00 P.M. and Sunday noon to 5:00 P.M. Call for the schedule for other times of the year.

A Great Read for Kids

A great read for kids is *Where Does the Trail Lead* by Burton Albert and Brian Pinkney.

Readers' Choice

The Nantucket Athenaeum on Lower India Street (508–228–1110) is one of the oldest continually operating libraries in the United States. It contains many artifacts, including scrimshaw, paintings, sculpture, and ship models. There's a children's wing, as well as an adjoining park with a play area for kids. The first librarian was the first woman to discover a comet, Maria Mitchell.

Other Things to See and Do

Adventure Tours of Nantucket, Lower Main and Easy Streets, Nantucket; (508) 228–1686; www.nantucket.net/tours /adventure. One-and-a-half-hour tour of Nantucket with commentary.

Brant Point Beach and Lighthouse, end of Easton Street, Nantucket. Great spot for viewing the ferries rounding the bend into Nantucket Harbor. *WARNING:* Strong undertow and big drop-off.

Coskata Coatue Wildlife Refuge, Wauwinet Road, Nantucket; (508) 228–5646; www.thetrustees.org. **Free.** Trustees of Reservations property. *WARNING:* Dangerous swimming but scenic trails.

Nantucket Babysitters' Service, 5C Windy Way, Nantucket; (508) 228–4970; www.nantucketbabysitters.com.

Nantucket Bike Shop and Car Rental, 4 Broad Street, Steamboat and Straight Wharfs, Nantucket; (508) 228–1999; www.nantucketbikeshop.com. It's all in the name. **Free** delivery on multiple-day bike rentals; rent 4x4s and Geo Trackers.

Nantucket Kayak Rentals, Commercial Wharf, Nantucket; (508) 325–6900. Lessons are available as well as the equipment.

Rosewater Carriage Company, 8 Winn Lane, Nantucket; (508) 228–9252. Romantic horse and buggy rides through Nantucket town.

Sesachacha Heathlands, Polpis Road to Barnard Valley Road, Nantucket; www .massaudubon.org. Price: $3.00 adults, $2.00 for kids. Audubon Wildlife Sanctuary on 862 acres; trails open dawn to dusk.

Shearwater Excursions, Children's Beach Public Pier or Walter Barret Public Pier, Nantucket; (508) 228–7037; www .explore nantucket.com. Seal, whale watch, and ecotours. Private charters for fishing and other sea adventures by reservation only.

Sky's the Limit, 5 the Courtyard, Nantucket; (508) 228–4633. Great place to buy a unique kite to fly at a Nantucket beach.

Where to Eat

Atlantic Cafe, 15 South Water Street; Nantucket; (508) 228–0570; www.atlantic cafe.com. Open year-round for lunch and dinner. A relaxing, reasonably priced restaurant that serves excellent chowder; children's menu. $–$$$

Even Keel Cafe, 40 Main Street, Nantucket; (508) 228–1979; www.evenkeel cafe.com. Open year-round for breakfast, lunch, and dinner. Downtown location, garden patio, and indoor cafe. Full menu. Rich desserts and coffees make for a great family break from touring. $–$$$

The Rope Walk, 1 Straight Wharf, Nantucket; (508) 228–8886; www.theropewalk .com. Charming restaurant at the end of Straight Wharf overlooking the sea and the harbor. Food matches the panoramic view. $$–$$$

Sweet Inspirations/Nantucket Clipper Chocolates, 26 Centre Street, Nantucket; (888) 225–4843 or (508) 228–5814, www.nantucketclipper.com. Chocolate lovers don't need inspiration, just the address. $–$$

Where to Stay

The Beachside, 30 North Beach Street, Nantucket; (508) 228–2241 or (800) 322–4433; www.thebeachside.com. Open mid-April to the end of October, and late November through early December. Double-decker motel near Jetties Beach; three two-room suites are available. Children under 16 stay **free** in their parents' room. Complimentary breakfast. $$–$$$$

Harbor House, South Beach Street, Nantucket; (508) 228–1500 or (866) 325–9300; www.harborhousevillage.com. The 104-room Harbor House prides itself on its Happy Harbor Club Kids Program, offered seven days a week, 9:00 A.M. to 4:00 P.M., **free** to guests' children ages 3 to 13. An activity staff supervises the kids, and various themed programs are offered. An outdoor swimming pool is open Memorial Day to Labor Day. Breakfast included in-season. $$–$$$$

The Ivy Lodge, 2 Chester Street, Nantucket; (508) 228–7755; www.nantucket .net/lodging/ivy. Very cozy and a great value. Nice proprietors. $$–$$$

Nesbitt Inn, 21 Broad Street (P.O. Box 1019), Nantucket 02554; (508) 228–0156 or (508) 228–2446. Open March to December. Pleasant inn that welcomes families who don't mind sharing bathrooms with other guests. There's a swingset in the backyard, a deck overlooking the garden, and games in the living room; families are welcome to use the grill in the backyard. Continental breakfast is provided. $$

The Cottages/Boat Basin, New Whale Street, Nantucket; (508) 325–1499 or (866) 838–9253; www.thecottagesnantucket .com. Waterfront cottages with decks overlooking the wharf area. $$$$

Index

About the Author

Marcia Glassman-Jaffe received a B.A. in psychology from the University of Massachusetts in Amherst and a masters in education and human development with a concentration in travel and tourism administration and policy from George Washington University in Washington, D.C. Marcia got her start in the travel industry as a travel agent and eventually worked as part of a management team. She later did tourism research for the Boston Organizing Committee on the viability of Boston as a host city for the Summer Olympics. Marcia also served as a research associate for an adventure travel book before authoring *Fun with the Family Massachusetts*. Marcia lives on the North Shore of Massachusetts with her husband, Mark, and their three daughters: Marisa, Mallory, and Morgan.